Software Security

Software Security: Concepts & Practices is designed as a textbook and explores fundamental security theories that govern common software security technical issues. It focuses on the practical programming materials that will teach readers how to implement security solutions using the most popular software packages. It's not limited to any specific cybersecurity subtopics, and the chapters touch upon a wide range of cybersecurity domains, ranging from malware to biometrics and more.

Features

- The book presents the implementation of a unique socio-technical solution for real-time cybersecurity awareness.
- It provides comprehensible knowledge about security, risk, protection, estimation, knowledge, and governance.
- Various emerging standards, models, metrics, continuous updates, and tools are described to understand security principals and mitigation mechanisms for higher security.
- The book also explores common vulnerabilities plaguing today's web applications.

The book is aimed primarily at advanced undergraduates and graduates studying computer science, artificial intelligence and information technology. Researchers and professionals will also find this book useful.

Software Security
Concepts & Practices

Suhel Ahmad Khan
Rajeev Kumar
Raees Ahmad Khan

CRC Press
Taylor & Francis Group
Boca Raton London New York

CRC Press is an imprint of the
Taylor & Francis Group, an **informa** business

A CHAPMAN & HALL BOOK

First edition published 2023
by CRC Press
6000 Broken Sound Parkway NW, Suite 300, Boca Raton, FL 33487-2742

and by CRC Press
4 Park Square, Milton Park, Abingdon, Oxon, OX14 4RN

CRC Press is an imprint of Taylor & Francis Group, LLC

Library of Congress Cataloging-in-Publication Data
Names: Khan, Suhel Ahmad, author. | Kumar, Rajeev, author. | Khan, R. A.
(Raees Ahmad), author.
Title: Software security : concepts & practices / Suhel Ahmad Khan, Rajeev
Kumar, Raees Ahmad Khan.
Description: First edition. | Boca Raton, FL : Chapman & Hall/CRC Press,
2023. | Includes bibliographical references and indexIdentifiers: LCCN 2022037986 (print) | LCCN 2022037987
(ebook) | ISBN 9781032356310 (hardback) | ISBN 9781032361598 (paperback) | ISBN
9781003330516 (ebook)
Subjects: LCSH: Application software--Development. | Software architecture.
| Computer software--Security measures. | Data protection. | Computer security.
Classification: LCC QA76.76.D47 K527 2023 (print) | LCC QA76.76.D47
(ebook) | DDC 005.1--dc23/eng/20221024
LC record available at https://lccn.loc.gov/2022037986
LC ebook record available at https://lccn.loc.gov/2022037987

ISBN: 978-1-032-35631-0 (hbk)
ISBN: 978-1-032-36159-8 (pbk)
ISBN: 978-1-003-33051-6 (ebk)

DOI: 10.1201/9781003330516

Typeset in Palatino
by SPi Technologies India Pvt Ltd (Straive)

In the Memory of My Father, Brother & My Beloved Daughter
Late Nazir Ahmad Khan
Late Naseem Ahmad
Late Areeba Suhel

Contents

Preface

The book *Software Security: Concepts and Practices* aims to build software security principles and techniques that will assist developers in detecting and measuring security early in the software development life cycle, resulting in secure software. It is clear that security issues arise as a result of a lack of built-in security features. Early and suitable efforts for security estimation must be made in order to build appropriate software. Early in the software development life cycle, it has become obvious that removing vulnerabilities, correcting defects, and eliminating unwanted/unwanted complexities leads to secure software development. Software security has become a big concern in recent years, and it is likely to worsen in the years ahead. For security issues, there is no simple solution available. As a result, integrating security into software development has grown difficult. Attempts to integrate security at the end of the software development process add complexity, cost, and time to the process.

Early detection of security and associated hazards, on the other hand, may aid in lowering development costs and increasing end-user confidence. Changes performed during the design phase are less expensive because the phase provides the software's blue print. As a result, the research has chosen the challenge of improving software security throughout the design phase. Security issues developed during the design process have a negative impact on the software life cycle. According to Gary McGraw, nearly half of all security concerns are discovered at the design stage. The irony is that the design phase receives very little attention throughout the development life cycle. Furthermore, because design flaws may go undetected during the phase, maintenance costs may be up to 90% higher than the total cost of the software development life cycle. Measuring security throughout the design process is a critical step in enhancing security during the development of object-oriented software. The object-oriented design's security can be assessed using appropriate evaluation methodologies and metrics. Given the importance of addressing security throughout the design phase, a security measure, such as a software security meter, must be developed. There is a need to establish a framework in the form of a book in the absence of an acceptable framework for software security metric development at this stage.

The book will help practitioners solve future difficulties by assisting in the development and validation of software security during the development life cycle. Furthermore, security is described as a system of laws, regulations, and procedures that govern an organization's administration, protection, and transfer of sensitive information. Confidentiality, integrity, authenticity, availability, and non-repudiation are some of the terms used. By focusing on software security during development, you can safeguard it from unauthorized use, access, disclosure, and modification. The attackers are not just at fault for the incidents recounted; software designers and developers are also to blame. Attackers do not build security gaps on their own; instead, they take advantage of software flaws. Vulnerabilities are flaws in software that are introduced during development. Even the presence of a single vulnerability can result in irreversible financial and reputational damage to a business. Despite the fact that there have been numerous life-threatening security incidents, it is still viewed as an afterthought while designing software. Frequently, security measures are sprayed on fully created software. Ironically, security professionals can never be certain that they have discovered and patched all security flaws. As a result, security has become a significant challenge. In order to thrive in today's competitive world, software developers must consider not only their consumers but also their competitors. Software security refers to the process of addressing security at each stage of the software development life cycle. It's the concept of creating software that can perform needed functions even if it's under assault. As a result, it's all about producing safe software, which means designing secure software and teaching software practitioners, architects, and users how to do so.

The goal of this book is to describe software and security principles early in the software development life cycle so that security assurance efforts can be optimized at all stages. The purpose of the book is to provide a means of identifying security issues, risks, and threats during the design phase of software development. Organizations can utilize the measurements to gain insight into the security of software under development. Security metrics, architecture, and estimate models are examples of software security aspects that govern the objectives defined by developers and organizations. Furthermore, the proposed book's goal is to produce security knowledge connected to management and governance for higher education, which can be utilized to identify problems at various stages and address them there to save money, time, and effort. Other contributions include a systematic phase-by-phase approach for software development, such as the development and testing processes.

Key Features

This book, focusing on software security and its assurance in practice, has been planned to suit the needs of its audience. Key features that distinguish it from other books, includes the following:

- Broad Audience: Unlike other software security books that are commonly designed by keeping software security practitioners in mind, this book is prepared for a larger audience, including academicians and practitioners.
- Security Assurance Embedding: Concept of software security assurance has been modeled as a phase-embedded activity rather than treating them as separate and post development activity.
- Leaning by Objectives: Each chapter of this book starts with a set of objectives, to which a prospective should be targeted to achieve rather than leaving the student directionless.
- Review Questions: Each chapter ends with three types of review questions, including objective type, short-answer type, and descriptive through provoking questions.
- Key Terms: Each chapter ends with the list of key terms, as these terms generally refer to certain abstract concepts, may be used for better and crisp communication.
- Bibliography: Each chapter ends with the list of key references for the concepts in the chapter to enable the users to find in-depth information related to the content of the chapter.
- Useful Links: Lists of useful website address have been appended to each of the chapters for quick references on needed topics.

Organization of the Book

Chapter 1 – Software and Security Concepts: An overview security: software perspective, security components, security characteristics, security types, security myths, security planning, software security assurance, software security models, software security measurements and metrics.

Chapter 2 – Software Security Problems: Major causes to software security, connectivity, extensibility, complexity, sustainable factors for software security, risk management, point of interaction, acquaintance, Cigital's risk management framework, stage-1: understanding, stage-2: identification, stage-3: synthesize, stage-4: mitigation, stage-5: validation, security engineering: an inclusive approach.

*Chapter 3 – Threats To Security:*Physical threat, nonphysical threat, information security, common threat, security threats, security vulnerability, security risk, secure development, Microsoft secure development life cycle, OWASP software assurance maturity model, security threat classification, errors, fraud and theft, threat to personal privacy, threat impact analysis, protection and mitigation strategies, software update and upgrade daily, privacy and privileges security of accounts, security training in employees, hunt for network loopholes frequently, implementation of multi-factor authentication.

*Chapter 4 – Software Security Metrics:*Software security metrics, defining good security metrics, security metrics collection, security metrics development process, security metrics development framework, premises, generic guidelines, conceptualization, planning, development, theoretical validation, empirical validation, packaging.

*Chapter 5 – Software Security Estimation:*Security estimation, software security estimation, security risk estimation, vulnerability assessment, vulnerability assessment framework, security profiling, environmental profiling, strategic profiling, technical profiling, operational profiling, operation ability, security measurement process, measures and metrics, and indicators, technical metrics.

*Chapter 6 – Secure Software Architecture:*Software architecture, security architecture andmodels, security architecture process, components of security architecture process, security model, software security best practices.

*Chapter 7 – Software Security Assurance:*Software security assurance, goals, responsibilities, establishing software security assurance program, recognition, review, categorization, estimation, training and adaptation, information security assurance framework, risk management, resource management, incident management, training and awareness program, technology integration, performance management, cyber security assurance framework.

*Chapter 8 – Secure Software Development Process:*Secure development, the secure development framework, securing requirement phase, securing design phase, securing coding phase, securing testing phase, securing deployment phase, secure maintenance.

*Chapter 9 – Software Security Testing:*Software testing, security testing, software security testing process, an integrated approach, security test strategy and plan, design security test cases, execute security test cases, capture security test result, capture security test metrics, qualitative assessment, security test closure report, software security testing tools.

*Chapter 10 – Implementing Security Testing: A Case Study:*Planning for Security Testing, Security Test Case Optimization Framework, Test Case Evaluation, Optimization of Security Test Cases, Contextual Interpretation, Automated Security Testing, Impacts and Importance

*Chapter 11 – Implementing Security: A Case Study:*The Concept, Implementations Perspective, An Integrated Approach, CIA Perspective, Vulnerability Perspective, Analyzability: A Case Study, Assessment Reflection, Experiences and Societal Impacts

*Chapter 12 – Knowledge, Management and Governance for Higher Security:*Secure knowledge management, security concerns for knowledge management system, importance of security knowledge andexpertise, security governance, effective security governance and management, effective versus ineffective security governance, enterprise software security framework, secure project management, scope of the project, reflection of project plan, tools, knowledge and expertise, estimating the nature and duration of required resources, project and product risks, measuring software security, process measures for secure development, product measures for secure development, maturity of practice, protecting information, audit's role, operational resilience and convergence, a legal view, a software engineering view, e-governance framework in India: e-kranti : national e-governance plan (NEGP) 2.0, vision and objectives, the objectives of e-kranti, principles of e-kranti.

*Chapter 13 – Research Trends in Software Security Estimation:*A multidimensional approach, research trends in security estimation, and future prospects in security estimation.

Acknowledgments

Everything that man did not know was taught to him by the Almighty. Acquiring knowledge is a never-ending process. Man acquires knowledge throughout his life, from the cradle to the grave. The purpose of life is to explore that fertile path of knowledge that comes into our lives as a blessing for learning after confronting many complex secrets and consequences. The Almighty has imbued man's existence with hope and rational thoughts, enabling him to differentiate between right and wrong through his materialism and describe himself as the most remarkable creation of his universe. This book is very insignificant contribution in the vast ocean of knowledge whose care taker is Almighty.

I am thankful to Professor Ram Shringar Rao, NSUT, New Delhi, for providing moral support, encouragement and consultations. I am also thankful to Dr. Alka, DIT, BBAU, Lucknow for providing moral support, encouragement during the drafting of book content. I am also thankful to all my friends and colleagues for providing moral support. I express my sincere thanks and grateful to all the experts from India and abroad for honouring me with their valuable observations during the Expert-Review process.

Last but not the least; I cannot afford to forget to express my indebtedness to my mother, my wife, my children, brothers and sisters. I have neglected some of the duties towards them and appreciate their tolerance even in the worst circumstances. On the contrary, they have been a source of inspiration and consolation for me.

Thank you to everyone who contributed to the book's chapter reviews and editorial team members also. The authors also express gratitude to the acquiring editor, Mr. Gauravjeet Singh Reen who thoroughly reviewed numerous sources during the process of finalising the book proposal.

Suhel Ahmad Khan

Authors

Suhel Ahmad Khan is an Assistant Professor in the Department of Computer Science, Indira Gandhi National Tribal University (A Central University), Amarkantak, Madhya Pradesh, India. He has 13 years of teaching and research experience. His areas of interest are Software Engineering, Software Security, Security Testing, Data Mining, and Network Security. He has completed one major research project with PI, funded by UGC, New Delhi. He has published numerous papers in conferences and reputed journals including IEEE, Elsevier, IGI Global and Springer, etc. Dr. Khan is an active member of various professional bodies IAENG, ISOC-USA, IACSIT, and UACEE. He was awarded a National Fellowship in 2012 for a PhD program funded by UGC, New Delhi.

Rajeev Kumar is an Assistant Professor in the Administrative Staff College of India, Hyderabad, India. He earned his PhD in Information Technology from Babasaheb Bhimrao Ambedkar University, Lucknow, India. Since he began his research in 2012, he has done both theoretical and practical work on durability engineering and has used the concept of durability in several fields. He has 8 years of research and teaching experience. He has published more than 50 research publications in reputed international journals and conferences, including IEEE, Elsevier, IGI Global, Springer, etc. His areas of interest include Durability Engineering, Security Engineering, and Computational Techniques.

Raees Ahmad Khan (Member, IEEE, ACM, CSI etc.) is a Professor in Babasaheb Bhimrao Ambedkar University, (A Central University), Lucknow, India. He has more than 20 years of teaching and research experience. He has published more than 300 research publications in conferences and reputed journals including IEEE, Springer, Elsevier, Hindawi, and IGI Global, etc., with good impact factors. He has published several monographs and edited volumes, not only in English, but also in Chinese. His research interests are in the different areas of Software Engineering.

1

Software and Security Concepts

> When you can measure what you are speaking about, and express it in numbers, you know something about it; but when you cannot measure it, when you cannot express It is numbers, your knowledge is of a meager and unsatisfactory kind: It may be the beginning of knowledge, but you have scarcely, in your thoughts, advanced to a stage of science.
>
> William Thompson, a.k.a. Lord Kelvin (Thomson, 1894)

Security has multifaceted qualities. Controlling the digital retrieval of important attributes is the fundamental security premise. The phrase 'Software Security' refers to the study of software-induced security threats as well as the techniques for managing them. Good software security practices take advantage of best practices developed using software engineering principles and incorporate security into the development life cycle in the early stage to learn and understand common problems, including security design. These particles also analyse all-purpose software analysis with a complete risk analysis and testing objective. More relevant questions are required to discuss in the preview of security goals as to what we will secure and from whom? How can attach harm to us? What are the direct and indirect ways an attacker can adopt to breach us? What security measures should be taken for identification and prevention? How much security is enough security? It is highly required to know 'how much is the impact' and explore the possibilities for measurement. A famous quote by Lard Kelvin, 'If we can't measure, we can't control', deploys an idea for security estimation and impact analysis. Security evaluation is an essential component of the risk- management process. Recent tragedies and chaos caused by unsecured software allow attackers to compromise security by identifying application weaknesses that can lead to high costs. An example of smart phone security is very fruitful to understand how application weaknesses lead to violating the intended functionality with the help of malicious activities. This rapidly growing industry is enforcing numerous actions, including policies for password protection, multiple methods for device locking, remote wipe, and hardware encryption, to prevent malicious applications on devices [1, 2].

On March 1, 2011, a larceny containing a Trojan called DroidDream was reported by the third-party application on 'Google's official Android Market'. In March 2020, a Trojan called Dridex was reported again and entered into the top ten malware list, which can be responsible for downloading ransomware like 'BitPaymer' and 'DoppelPaymer'. Availability of such cases in our application is becoming a principal concern for software development industries. Identification, mitigation, and software improvement are the primary concerns associated with the software security engineering discipline [3, 4].

Applying security estimation techniques using various parameters on software may profoundly influence the security of the final product. It is highly considered that security analysis can identify the strength and weaknesses of software and provide a concrete

DOI: 10.1201/9781003330516-1

foundation for improved cost–benefit analysis. The existence of security vulnerabilities within the application is an integrated part of software development and may cause the violation of security requirements. This may lead to unauthorized disclosure of information, destruction, or modification of data with the software application. It is evident from literature reviews related to software security that attackers produce more than 90% of security-related issues for the software through familiar software flaws. Disruptions resulting from security breaches can endanger lives and the environment, severely damage industrial and social infrastructure, compromise privacy, or damage the viability of the entire business sector. Therefore, it is essential to develop high-quality and secure software applications to gain a competitive advantage in today's market. Detecting security vulnerabilities earlier in application development makes excellent business sense and reduces the overall security exposures of the applications and their data [5].

Due to the robustness of the standardization of the functionality of program activities, security issues are emerging most for researchers, security professionals, industry trends, and digital technologies. Software design security is urgently needed to maintain the model's effectiveness in terms of financial feasibility and user-friendliness by managing design complexity that should not exceed acceptable standards. Therefore, complexity can be observed as one of the most critical factors of design security with a negative impact. Software security can be examined by using the concept of estimation theory while developing software through appropriate observation of design activities, measurement of security features, and the respective impacts on software [6, 7].

Quantitative methods are more advanced strategies than conceptual approaches to developing and presenting existing and newly developed products with reliable mechanisms that can assess the practical impact of security measures. It is necessary to evaluate the performance and the level of protection. Undesirable threats are responsible for software vulnerabilities. It can affect privacy, availability, integrity, and other areas of application security such as authentication, authorization, and denial of services. Nothing can be predicted without quantification. Therefore, safety measurements have become urgent to estimate application immunity and resilience.

1.1 Objectives

This chapter aims to:

- Understand and describe security in general.
- Appreciate the need, importance, and significance of security evaluation.
- Define and understand security, its properties, components, and types.
- Realize the facts related to various myths with regard to software security processes.
- Enumerate and realize numerous software security issues.
- Visualize the different perspectives of software security.
- Identify the software security factors.
- Realize the importance and significance of software security models and metrics.

1.2 Security: An Overview

The enactment of the Computer Security Act of 1987 (145), which later became Public Law No. 100-235, expanded the explanation of computer security protection and increased awareness of problematic computer security. In the late 1990s, the joint venture of NSA & NIST focused on new computer security criteria for the procurement of computers by federal agencies. This joint venture also considered the requirements of the 'Information Technology Security Evaluation Criteria (ITSEC)' of the European Community, which are under consideration as an international security standard. The outcome of this alliance is acknowledged as the Common Criteria, and it is the base of computer protection documents today. Underfunding by DARPA, the National Research Council published a report entitled 'Computers at Risk' that expressed concern regarding computer security status in the United States and made recommendations about the requirement for additional corresponding security structure. The committee's report also recommended the publication of a comprehensive set that clearly defines essential qualities and security requirements, generally accepted as the 'General System Security Principles (GASSP)' [2, 5, 6].

As a worldwide inventiveness, contribution and endorsement have been acquired from various reputed groups such as the 'International Information Systems Security Certification Consortium (ISC)²', 'International Standards Organization (ISO)', 'Institute of Internal Auditors (IIA)', and 'International Common Criteria Effort'. The 'Information Systems Security Association (ISSA)' decided with the coinciding adherence of the IISF to acquire the direction required to confirm and endorse such significant organization for work as the 'Generally Accepted Information Security Principles (GAISP)'. GAISP has an extensive regulatory hierarchy that provides a reliable and reasonable framework for global information security. The final GAISP will provide three levels of assistance to guide security professionals at all technical and management levels. These overacting values involve general principles, general functional principles, and detailed principles of responsibility. 'International Consortium for Information Systems Security Certification or (ISC)²' covers the following ten areas within the general knowledge structure:

1. Management of information security system
2. Methodologies for access control systems
3. Cryptographic techniques
4. Physical security
5. Security architecture for enterprises
6. Application security
7. Networks and telecommunications
8. Security laws, investigations, and ethics
9. Business continuity planning
10. Operational security

According to the security expert, Guru Gary McGraw,

Software security is about understanding software-induced security risks and how to manage them. Good software security practice leverages good software engineering practice. It involves thinking about security early in the software life-cycle, knowing and understanding common problems (including language-based flaws and pitfalls), designing for security, and subjecting all software artifacts to thorough, objective risk analyses and testing.

The experts recommended software security as a knowledge-intensive field [5, 6].

1.3 Security: Software Perspective

The primary security principle is the management of those who have the right to use physical or intellectual property. Our society is increasingly dependent on information technology, and one indication of this is the increasing use of portable devices. A report on mobile application threat and vulnerability states that over 205 billion times mobile apps are downloaded on devices. A study taken by Juniper Research quotes that around 40% of the world's adult population uses the mobile baking application, approaching two billion in numbers. These vast numbers contain vulnerabilities around 38% in IOS mobile applications and around 43% in android applications. Most of the security issues are related to insecure data storage. The vulnerabilities in services directly related to insecure data storage are password protection, personal data privacy, and financial credentials protection. Hackers exploit approximately 89% of vulnerabilities to access Smartphone's for stealing data with the help of malware. This report provides a significant figure to understand the cause of weakness in security mechanisms:

- Availabilities of 60% of client-side vulnerabilities
- The exploitation of 89% of vulnerabilities that can be possible without any physical access
- The exploitation of 56% of vulnerabilities that is possible without administrator rights

The US Department of Homeland Security released a roll call on identified threats to mobile devices running the Android operating system (OS) on Jul 23, 2013. It stated that approximately 44% of Android users were accessing version 2.3.3 through 2.3.7, known as 'Gingerbread'. It was first released in 2011 and had a significant number of security vulnerabilities available in the previous versions. Few identified security threats to the mobile OS such as 'SMS (text message) Trojans', 'rootkits', and 'fake google play domains'. Smartphone users always try to update their mobile OSs constantly. Always 'Mac OS X' and 'iPhone OS' require users to be able to enter a password or PIN to sign in to their computer, iPhone, or iPod Touch. The most famous mobile OS, Android, holds a higher proportion of market share with open-source architecture that classifies the primary target for malware attacks [8, 9].

Business and governments have increased their efficiency and production by establishing new partnerships relying on software over the last 20 years. The conclusion drawn from the above observations is that security assessment has turned into a crucial component for all phases of SDLC. This is because different types of viruses, spyware, hacking, and internet deception came into existence in the routine limelight. From the customer's perspective, securing computers and distinctive information against threats is essential. The software's maximum-security measures ensure safe entry and exit to the (www) world wide web. Security estimation is a crucial element of the risk-management process. Prevalent failures and defalcation reason due to insecure software leads to the elevated expenditure and available vulnerabilities of applications that permit intruders to violate security breaches.

Industry based on smart phones is rising at rapid rates, and involved companies are imposing 'strong password policies, device locking, remote wipe, and hardware encryption' to avoid malicious applications in devices. However, various vulnerabilities that are part of the design can lead to the breach of security requirements in the system and result in unauthorized disclosure, destruction, or modification of data. Security guru Gary McGraw identified risk management, software security touch points, and knowledge as the essential support for software security. The absence of these three fundamental pillars in any software system confirms incomplete security. Knowledge that fits some unique personality in any field cannot outclass the similar in a further generation. This is why people inhibit understanding the immense knowledge of famed people who are not yet alive.

Information gathered from various sources should be disseminated to generate profits for individuals and organizations. This knowledge will increase productivity when used with an integrated approach. The security literature shows that principles, strategy, policy, various vulnerabilities, exploits, attack patterns, and historical risk evaluations are the inherited components of software security knowledge. These knowledge components provide significant support for security software. It is highly required to train thoroughly software security professionals about security knowledge for extensive and detailed coverage to deal with security issues and complications. It will provide a platform for higher management to develop security policies in a very systematic, cohesive, and sensible manner, concerning three pillars of software security [10, 11].

An editorial taken from Steven Lavenhar of Cigital imparts the observation from learning that cost–benefit analysis is considered an effective means for improvements throughout the SDLC by decreasing software defects (including security flaws) in applications. A review conducted and analyzed by 'Software Engineering Institute (SEI)' states that around 60% of organizations suffer from inadequate quality assurance. The cost of correcting defects during the development life cycle phases is directly proportional to development time and cost. If the weaknesses persist for a longer time, they will be responsible for uncontrolled complexity and more expensive to correct as depicted in Figure 1.1. With so many flaws, including security flaws, vulnerabilities, and bugs, security engineers spend more time in fixing them at the initial stage of development.

Project managers can achieve the shortest probable schedule by addressing security throughout the SDLC. This can be done successfully, especially in the early stages, to increase the probability that the software will become more secure the first time. Connectivity, complexity, and extensibility are the three major responsible factors for most security problems. A study published by Barry Boehm states that 20% of software modules are typically responsible for 80% of errors. Another study on different IBM projects found that 57% of the errors occurred in only 7% of the modules. Fragile modules are more complex and less structured. The sooner vulnerabilities are detected and an attempt is made to address them, the easier it will be to fix the problem [11].

Nothing can be guaranteed to be secure. Therefore, security should be reflected as a relative phenomenon. Security goals are always a concern to what we will secure and from

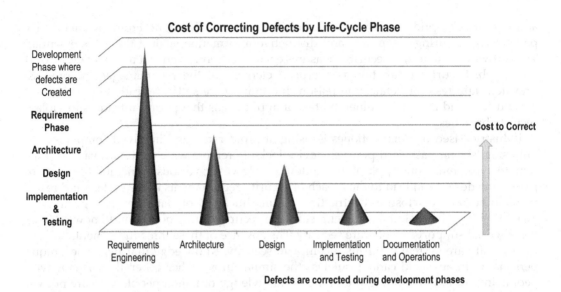

FIGURE 1.1
Cost of correcting defects by life cycle phase.

whom? How can we get rid of the attackers? What techniques or methodologies should we adopt to secure our software?

The preceding discussion emphasizes an essential insight for determining what will be the procedure for impact analysis and whether it can be measured? A renowned scientist named Lord Kelvin states that 'we can't control if we can't measure'. This mind-blowing idea provides subsequent steps for prevention as per the most famous quote: 'prevention is better than cure'. It is indispensable to take initiatives or preventive measures before the expected consequences faced by developers. The growth and proliferation of internet facilities will work two-fold for both developers and intruders to provide opportunities and easiness concerning access services. They try to find out the vulnerable area or entry point to breach applications. Once they succeed in their motive, the malicious code spreads very quickly to get control over the system. As the applications are not performing as expected or have exceeded its average intensity, security issues become the highly prioritized agenda for researchers and security professionals. Incorporating security mechanisms into the development life cycle for building secure products or applications is the most highlighted trend reported based on increased security incidents for the various applications, including trading, online sales, purchase, billing, and banking [12–15].

1.3.1 Security Components

Software security is a comprehensive property that can be appropriately managed only by different quality attributes. The idea of software security wraps both conventional and classical dependability attributes. The key components of software security include authentication, authorization, auditing, confidentiality, integrity, availability, privacy, and non-repudiation. Due to the multidimensional nature of security attributes, identifying security values at a single step is not a feasible solution for the long-term sustainability of products or services. It measures all the parametric values and attributes used in that application or software package during the whole development process. For example, confidentiality, integrity, and availability (CIA) are widely used to evaluate information security systems. Further justification of these securities attributes and their involvement in the development of software applicability is being discussed in Section 1.3.1 [12, 14, 16–20]:

a) **Confidentiality**: Confidentiality refers to unauthorized disclosure of information. It also limits access to information in the right direction and prevents disclosure of information to unauthorized users. Confidentiality works as a security policy that ensures that no one can access the data or information outside of this system which furthermore ensures that a protection technique is also implemented here. Confidentiality is a broader concept of privacy that limits access to an individual's personal information. It requires a trusted binding mechanism of design and its total supporting services and related components. It ensures that there is no chance of leakage of information. It strengthens the mechanism that data is preserved and intruders can't violate data's sanctity.

b) **Integrity**: Integrity is the concept of credibility of information resources. It allows the possible authorized changes to ensure that appropriateness of design or information must be ensured at the origin level or source level during alteration of information. It refers to the trustworthiness and guaranteed veracity of information. Researchers also identified that the decomposition, abstraction, behavior of components, maximum depth of hierarchy, and coupling affect the integrity of the design. In information security, integrity means that data cannot be modified undetectably. System and data integrity refer to the requirement that information is protected from improper modification. Integrity is lost if unauthorized charges are made to the data or system by either intentional or accidental acts. If the loss of system or data integrity is not corrected, continued use of the infected system or corrupted data could result in inaccuracy, fraud, or erroneous decisions. Also, integrity violation may be the first step in a successful attack against system availability or confidentiality. For all these reasons, loss of integrity reduces the assurance of a system. Integrity expresses the nature of a quantity, property, or function that remains unchanged when a given transformation is applied to it.

c) **Availability**: Availability is the readiness for correct services, which can also be defined as the degree to which a system or component is operational when required for use. For any information system to serve its purpose, the information must be available when it is needed. This means that the computing system units used to store and process the information, security control units used to protect it, and the communication channels used to access it must be functioning correctly. Suppose a mission-critical system is unavailable to its end. In that case, system functionality and operational effectiveness, for example, may result in loss of productive time, thus impeding the end provides an excellent structuring mechanism at the class level. It decomposes the whole structure into a well-designed unit for better reusability and security. It reduces the design complexity by decomposing its functional privileges between services and requests into the class hierarchy. It strengthens the mechanism that data is secure from intruders.

d) **Authentication**: Authentication refers to validating the user credentials like user id, password, access code, and transaction id for accessing the web or window-based software applications. The different kinds of needs and motives are covered through software applications. The mechanism to validate authentic users is framed accordingly by creating separate or combined login applications for individual users or multiple users with generated valid tokens for corresponding IDs. Whenever an unauthenticated user attempts to access the application and violates the authentic procedure, the following request is rejected to interrupt intruders. The continuous attempt of fake login redirects users to the previous or blocks stage. This works as a litmus test to identify between valid users and intruders.

The behavior of components always binds the authenticity of OO design. Behavior expresses itself as net functional efforts which work as entry or exit criteria to control or execute the direction of applied methods in classes. An authentication mechanism, a trusted identification mechanism, is always used to provide proof of user identification. The user must be identified as a person, a program, a process, or an entity that directly or indirectly correlates with the authentic specification. For security concerns in OO design, class entities always follow a trusted binding mechanism for the execution environment by confirming the identification process through sharing methods or attributes.

e) **Authorization**: Authorization confirms that activity may initialize to operate by an authenticated set. The source of an authenticated unit may be an essential user, computer system, network-enabled device, or any remote sources with legitimate linking. Such a mechanism enables a sense of protection to its respective users and prevents malevolent budge. Some useful techniques are available for authorization estimation that control data tampering and information disclosure threats. The idea is to confine the design applications based on the user's business context specifying the highly impacted applications. The.NET environment first checks the approved claims against retrieving sensitive columns of the database.

f) **Non-repudiation**: Failure to override the data transfer requires that the senders of the data or the recipients cannot deny their further involvement in the process. In the case of non-refusal, data transfer treatment is a special case of data transfer in which receiving the data transfer involves making and saving the requested changes in the data set. To verify a denial, it is necessary to examine the net impact on the denial-related monitoring data. The requirements for every data transmission subject to non-repudiation are as trusted authorization is always used for the sender, receiver, and the scope of any data changed or transmitted. Note that this requirement includes trusted data transmission, trusted authentication of users, and trusted authorization of users and processes for the specific data scope. Trusted binding is used to bind the sender to the data sent and to bind the receiver to data received. The authorization, binding, and data transmission are handled as a single atomic operation within the boundary of the secure authorized process.

A trusted mechanism is always used to provide traceability and audit. This trusted mechanism ensures data persistence of the audit data so that it cannot later refute the means of authentication and data transmission. Every data transmission is preceded by an absolute definition of the data and identification that binds the data to the sender. Every data receipt is preceded by an absolute definition of the data and identification that binds the data to the recipient. No other mechanism outside the trusted mechanisms sets the value of any control data that indicates whether each of the trusted mechanisms is executed correctly or the value of any of the control data is generated by the trusted mechanisms. If any of the above requirements or mechanisms fails, non-repudiation fails.

g) **Privacy**: As per the understanding of the privacy mechanism, it offers how his or her information should be disclosed. It is better to examine the net effects on privacy requirements for endorsing the privacy mechanism. It will always behave like a trusted confidentiality mechanism to access a user's personal information. The secure requirement includes reliable data transfer, strong user and process authentication, strong non-denial for processes, and access to a user's personal information for a given data field. Accessing users' personal information using any existing privacy and confidentiality mechanism for data control confirms the defined scope of access for all users. A reliable non-repulsion method is applied for all amendments to the organized data that portray each user's scope of utilization. It is noticeable that such a requirement encompasses the demand for consistent data transmission and trustworthy authentication for users, data, and processes. Apart from the reliable mechanism, no other mechanism defines any monitoring data that each trusted mechanism is functioning correctly or the value of any data determined by the trusted mechanism.

1.3.2 Security Characteristics

Due to increasing complexity, connectivity and expansion, the software is becoming more vulnerable to attacks. The security of the software is endangered at various positions during its life cycle, together with unintentional and deliberate choices and actions by insiders and outsiders who have no connection with the organization. A subsequent amount of efforts are being made by researchers and practitioners to develop secure software focusing on research into 'high-integrity software'. Despite all the efforts made, there are very few software developed with a high degree of security. Regardless of where security is a factual requirement and where the security design is accessible as an integral part of the implementation squad, there is no guarantee that the complete impact will convene the security objectives of the secure software development cycle. It involves complex processes that affect the preliminary contribution of business users, project managers and software developers, and information security professionals to develop functional and secure products. But to understand the importance and realize the need for security, it is compulsory to recognize and explore prominent features. These characteristics are described in the following sections [16–20].

1.3.2.1 Ability to Trust

The fundamental property of trust establishes a set of balances between trust or and trustee. It will act like physiological beliefs among all participants. Trust always tries to build a strong relationship with its participants through symmetric and asymmetric communication. Vulnerabilities may lead to a lower proportion of belief between the stakeholders. Trust is a journey, not a destination. Physical and logical components of security, reputation, and human cognition have a mutual impact on trust. Transparency is the preferable building block for trust. The impact of trust can be evaluated in terms of a quantitative or qualitative manner for better understanding and higher security.

1.3.2.2 Defects Ramifications for Security

Defects in software are capable of compromising security. Defects may introduce security vulnerabilities that may exploit the intended functionalities of software applications.

These security flaws can violate the security policies and damage the expected operations. Intruders can exploit the defects to gain unauthorized access to the computer system.

1.3.2.3 Pervasive Approach

The term 'security' should be explored in the broader sense. The pervasiveness of security is an inclusion of the multidimensional nature of security, and it must be explored in every dimension to know about the actual impact of security attributes.

1.3.2.4 Failure-Free Operations

Security is the property that is capable of running the applications under malicious conditions. It guarantees that operations under execution are failure free. Security measures are responsible for minimizing the impact of failures.

1.3.2.5 Attack Resilience

Another important property of security is building the mechanism for attack resilience. The different security factors, including authentication and authorization, enable protective mechanisms for application and system development. It is an activity to test your system operations to determine how much it is resilient under predetermined threats and whether it can locate the organizational gap against a targeted threat.

1.3.2.6 Conformance: Acting According to Specific Accepted Standards

The first step for software developers is to identify pre-existing and non-functional requirements for software development. The basic functional requirements provided by the system are called functional requirements, and non-functional requirements are additional requirements such as time, performance, availability, scalability, and reliability constraints. The degree of compliance of the software with its functional requirements is consistent with the requirements of the software.

1.3.2.7 Robustness of Operational Defense

The definition of robustness in computer science states how a computer system deals with errors during execution. In this situation, proper management with erroneous input is highly desirable. Latest trends, including robust programming, robust machine learning, and robust network security, are available in computer science, exploring a new research dimension. Robustness can also be validated with the help of fault injection techniques.

1.3.2.8 Trustworthiness

The trustworthiness of secure software is that it performs for a specific purpose, when necessary, with new changes made in recent times, and without unwanted side effects, behaviors, or exploitative weaknesses. The definition of trustworthiness demonstrates dependency, including availability, reliability, maintainability, accountability, and survivability. The term operational flexibility that strengthens the trustworthiness of security is a set of procedures that permit people, processes, and information systems to become accustomed to changing patterns. The term directly indicates the stability that affects the security life span of the software. Quantitative definitions suggest that trustworthiness is also related to availability, reliability, accountability, and survival.

1.3.2.9 Damage Control

A regress approach is required to find out the applications' unidentified weaknesses that come under the realm of damage control. In this case, the possible ways of damages must be identified and acted accordingly upon to mitigate them. After detecting and recovering the cause of damages, the system will return to the error-free stage. Several mechanisms are available for the identification and mitigation for damage control.

1.3.2.10 Defect Removal

It is evident from the literature that around 60–90% of existing computer defect is because of software faults. Generally, software faults are because the design faults occur when a designer either misunderstands a specification or makes a mistake. In order to tolerate the defects in a system, its effects must be identified. Using several defect identification mechanisms is highly required to determine the error state within the application design. The manifestation of the fault will generate errors somewhere in the system.

1.3.3 Security Types

Security is essential to have peace of mind. The Institute for 'Security and Open Methodologies (ISECOM)' in the OSSTMM 3 defines security as a form of protection in which a distinction is made between an asset and a threat. Computer security is one of the essential branches of information technology that deals with data protection over distributed or a stand-alone system. Security technology requires constant improvement as every organization depends on computers. The different types of computer security shown in Figure 1.2 are given below.

1) **Network Security:** It is one of the leading fields of computer science whose specialization deals with computer networking and security of its infrastructural setup. Network administrators or system administrators are the two key position holders. They are responsible for implementing security policies, resource allocation required in the form of hardware and software, and building mechanisms to protect network resources from unauthorized access and adequate services to authenticated users. A network security system usually relies on layers of security and incorporates several components, including networking monitoring and security software and hardware and equipment. All components work collectively to enhance the overall security of computer networks.

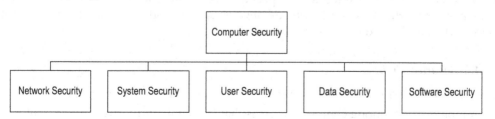

FIGURE 1.2
Classification of computer security.

2) **System Security**: An (operating) system is accountable for controlling ingress to system resources that will contain sensitive data. Therefore, the system must include a certain amount of protection for such data and must control access to those parts of the system that administer this protection. System security is concerned with all aspects of these arrangements.

3) **User Security**: User security refers to how the components of a site policy and a user's policy configure the user's environment to provide security for their programs and data.

4) **Data Security**: This course of study is responsible for data protection through any means, whether it may be accidental or intentional. Various mechanisms are being used to safeguard our data or limit the accessibility of unauthorized modification, destruction, or disclosure through physical security, administrative controls, and logical controls.

5) **Software Security**: This course of action will explore an idea to protect software against malicious attacks. It will continue functioning correctly under potential risks developed through various software vulnerabilities and attacks that exploit them, including buffer overflows, SQL injection, session hijacking, etc. It is an initiative for developing and implementing software having an appropriate protective environment for data and resources managed by the software.

1.3.4 Security Myths

Naturally, myths proliferate in a discipline as tangled and murky as software security. Various myths about software security, its applicability to software applications, usage, and features have been discussed in the last several years. Few of them have been identified and discussed, and their facts have been presented.

1.3.4.1 Security Myth: 1

1.3.4.1.1 No Need to Worry About Security; I Have Exerted Enough Recitation to Control It

Enough security is always better. But it doesn't mean that you are safe. Nobody can compromise the sensitive, critical, and confidential information of users. No one can get 100% security on any ground. You have to pay for this in the bandwidth between philological and technical acceptability of human behavior.

Fact: The opinions of different security experts are entirely different; the more security, the better. Bruce Schneider, a security expert and author of several books, including the most recent *Liars and Outliers*, explains why the often-discussed concept of security, i.e. 'you can't get enough', is irrelevant. Schneider explains, more security isn't necessarily better. You can get maximum but at a specific price. Sometimes additional security costs more than it's worth. Autocratic software development includes a trade-off between optimal security and limited cost and resources.

1.3.4.2 Security Myth: 2

1.3.4.2.1 Good News! I Have Installed Anti-Virus Software, and I Am Now Free from Viruses

A common opinion among computer users is that installing anti-virus software will make them safe from viruses. Nowadays, deploying a solution to secure our confidential and critical information is mandatory. An anti-virus plays a vital role in this protection field up to a specific limit. Installing an anti-virus on your computer is like getting the vaccine for a particular disease.

Fact: Be aware! Installing anti-virus without proper updates is like taking expiry pills for a disease. It is advisable to be mindful that anti-virus will not help at all in case of abuse by trusted insiders. To maintain the sanctity of your computer, you have to timely update the anti-virus and sweep your system regularly to remove unreliable attachments.

1.3.4.3 Security Myth: 3

1.3.4.3.1 Installing a Software Patch Will Fix All Security Holes

Numerous software industry opinions are available to deploy security patches after software development for fixing security issues. The software patch is a step to deal with security, but this is not a complete and mandatory methodology.

Fact: It's always a good plan to install patches as soon as they become available; however, patches can create as many issues as they solve. To be at their most effective, patches need to be combined with general good habits and safe computing.

1.3.4.4 Security Myth: 4

1.3.4.4.1 Software Security Is Always a Cryptographic Problem

By default, software developers understand that security is an attribute or function and that cryptography is the most common security in the minds of developers. The idea is that you can generously dust your schedule with the magic crypto fairy, and it will be safe.

Fact: Firstly, security is defined as a system property, not something that will make it safe after adding one or more features. Secondly, cryptography is complex to precise. Not only is the math complex, but functional cryptography is also complete with enormous ambiguity results that are easy to misunderstand. Cryptography can be used to access the standard security features with various substitutions, including identity management, robust authentication, and Payment Card Industry (PCI) compliant.

1.3.4.5 Security Myth: 5

1.3.4.5.1 Software Security Is a Tool to Find out Bugs in Lines of Codes

Every time bugs matter for software security. Half of the security issue at the implementation level is attributed to bugs.

Fact: It is true that half of the bugs are identified at the implementation level. The other half loads different types of errors at the design level. Not only have you had to fix the bugs but more to educate your developers to know the top ten design flaws and prerequisite knowledge to avoid them.

1.3.4.6 Security Myth: 6

1.3.4.6.1 Secure Only High-Risk Software Applications

Organizations developing high-risk application software require complete attention to avoid vulnerabilities during development.

Fact: Another security myth is highly prevalent and requires prompt attention for active disruption. Considering risk analysis only for prioritized or high-risk projects will not be fruitful. Even applying the same strategies for other projects, that level of effort will never be zero. Provide an alternative mechanism to minimize the cost analysis ratio for low-risk projects.

1.3.4.7 Security Myth: 7

1.3.4.7.1 We Don't Have a Software Security Problem

A report published in IBM's 2014 'Cyber Security Intelligence Index' states that human error is accountable for 95% of all security breaches. It is highly required to train employees to know their role in dealing with security compliance and the consequences of non-compliance.

Fact: This myth or false impression is sufficient for any organizational downfall. Such organizations that have such justification presently are not dealing with web-based application development under international compliance standards for application development or have not faced any attacks on their application. Such negligence will lead to an inimitable lesion of faith and confidence in customers.

1.3.5 Security Planning

Major security concerns include the developers' fraternity lacking awareness, sensitivity, education, training, and attention, growing threats, versatility, complexity, rapidly increasing code size, openness, and connectivity. Overriding all these so-called stubborn attitudes is complacency toward security per se. Security is still considered a post-development activity and is an after-thought once bitten or severely risked for damages. Though such attitudes appear unaffordable, at least from now on, we need to live with its vast amounts of legacy software for a safer future. We do only whatever feasible, such as patching in a piecemeal approach.

Software Security Assurance (SSA) may be referred to as the process of ensuring software is designed and developed to operate conveniently at a desired level of security. It must be consistently performed without any potential harm resulting from 'loss, inaccuracy, alteration, non-availability or misuse' of assets, controls, and protection. Moreover it is imperative to implement systematic processes to build security resilience in the software, primarily as a product and as far as possible without threats after that in the life cycle. It is necessary to protect against intentional subversion or forced failure by preserving the three compelling properties: confidentiality, integrity, and availability.

There appears to be a need for the paradigm shift! Better processes can lead to a better product. The software has to be developed for a high potential malicious environment and not a security-conducive one. Security cannot be an after-thought – except due to infeasibility but requiring reverse-engineering. By adopting a 'prevent-only' policy as a prime approach, security can be assured by highly formalized security-sensitive SDLC phases. Standards need to be established in practice. And that it may be in place by proactive practices on securely-functional, CIA-sensitive and formally modeled requirements led the design of high immunity 'software components' irrespective of the criticality, usage, and scope [21–23].

1.4 Software Security Assurance

Software Security Assurance is a practice that assists design and implements tools that protect information and resources designed by that software. Software is a resource in itself, and thus it should be given proper security. The basis for gaining rational assurance is that the software will consistently demonstrate all the properties compulsory to make certain that the software in operation will persist to function consistently despite the occurrence of sponsored (intentional) defects. Protecting these documents with the most sensitive properties includes quality, reliability, usability, interoperability, security, and tolerance. Obviously, this type of software needs to withstand most attacks and resist most attacks that it cannot withstand. It needs to identify damage and restore regular operations as soon as possible after an attack that it cannot withstand or be patient. Security assurance is a software feature known as Software Security Assurance (or just software assurance). There are two main types of SSA actions.

- To ensure that processed information by the system has an appropriate sensitivity category and security requirements are being developed as per the expected norms of the system.
- Another focus must be on tools and data for software maintenance and management and security software.

Some of the most comprehensible key trending security elements, in the first instance, include secure developments, vulnerability remediation, disclosure practices, and independent security verifications and validations. SSA initiatives beyond these are based on several secondary means: threat modeling, refactoring components, cryptography, vulnerability/weakness databases and enumeration, static/dynamic analyzers, sandboxing, quality control strategies, etc. However, all these means are neither meeting the ends nor promising both in effectiveness and efficiency [1, 2, 13, 21, 23].

1.5 Software Security Models

A simple approach to software security calls for treating security as an additional characteristic of software quality. The problem is that conventional quality assurance is designed to validate a set of features against a specification. Software security, however, needs additional diligence than well-implemented security features. The reality is that a specific procedure to achieve a high-quality outcome concerning established quality issues does not promise good results concerning safety issues. Ultimate security is not a derivative of higher quality; it needs elevated consideration toward security improvement. The software security assessment technique helps software professionals and researchers working in the area of security evaluate their policies and procedures and confer a process to establish the present state of their security programs relative to accessible policies and to accomplish goals for improvement.

Various security studies are available for the initiative taken for security improvement and catering resources with improved optimization, including 'The Building Security in

Maturity Model: pronounced BSIMM'. BSIMM developer team is responsible for working on already acquired software security initiatives and provides support to others who want to develop their software security initiatives. The BSIMM is suitable if business objectives for software security consist of informed risk-management assessment – clarity on what is 'the accurate inclusion to accomplish' for everyone concerned in software security, cost reduction through standard, repeatable processes, and enhanced code quality [5–7].

In the 1980s, security analysis turned into systems analysis and architecture. In 1988, 'Frederic Copigno and Sylvain Martin' published a methodology for evaluating and validating software security. Wang and Wulf proposed a Security Measurement (SM) framework for measuring the reliability of a system. It was founded on framework theory and formal measurement methods. The framework includes four aspects: the definition of software security, the selection of units and scales, the evaluation method's description, and the matrix's validation. This study highlights the need to develop guidelines to determine the safety and analyze quantification results [24].

Bharat B. Madan worked on modeling and measuring security attributes of software systems. The *'Semi-markov model'* was developed for an intrusion-resistant system such as the *'SITAR system'* to model and measure security attributes. This model is used to determine the steady-state probabilities leading to the availability of a computing system. This allows multiple intrusion resistance strategies to be used to protect intrusion resistance with various effects such as privacy, compromise, data integrity, and denial of service attacks. The proposed study evaluates the possibility of a security breach due to the violation of various security functions [12].

Michael Yanguo Liu shared a pioneering idea for measuring the security architecture of service-oriented software systems. In his research, Liu recognized internal security attributes and certain features based on standard service-oriented software models. In addition, a structure for the classification and formal evaluation of subsequent safety indicators has been proposed. Liu developed a measurement abstraction paradigm called the 'System Interaction Impact Model (USIE)' that can be used to uncover and analyze security issues associated with service-oriented software architecture [25].

David Gilliam et al. provided a comprehensive mechanism to identify software weaknesses in the applications. Integrating a model-based approach with feature-based testing using temporal logic features provides reliable validation at all life cycle stages. Anders Bond proposed another study on security measurement, and Niels Paulson discussed the framework for measuring the security of components in distributed information systems. This framework discloses the purpose, strengths, and weaknesses of component security. The proposed study proposes a methodology for combining various features that affect security components, such as the environment in which they operate with specific functions [26].

1.6 Software Security Measurement and Metrics

For the measurement of software security, security metrics are being used to quantify. Software metrics are an endeavor to quantify several attributes of software developed during software product development. It provides an improved procedure for checking the status of security controls for specific entries. The estimation technique is directly related to the safety parameters and all the consistent components of the security system. Necessary means to ensure security is security for assets, operational stability, and support for civil security. Strategic corporations and outcome-focused schemes are known for developing more secure software and reducing threats and vulnerabilities. In the late 1990s, a separate discipline from the computer and network security, known as Software Security, began to flourish. Researchers began to put additional emphasis on learning the skills regarding tactical programming and studying the behavior a programmer can contribute to or unintentionally destabilize the security of a computer system. What types of bugs and flaws lead to security problems? How can we identify problems systematically? [28–29]

The ultimate reliance on technology to protect information resources from malicious risk or damage has increased accountability levels. Ineffective software security evaluation is responsible for economic failure and reputation damage in the software security industry. Security has now turned into the leading front for software industries. Security monitoring and improvement is a critical issue in software security engineering. Safety measurements and re-analysis of grafting strategies will make identifying program strengths and weaknesses easier and offer a source for risk, cost, and benefit analysis. Such work as a total, with a direct contribution to the realm of knowledge, may be directly or indirectly crucial for the following:

- To develop a cohesive understanding of roles and responsibilities to eradicate the deficiency of enterprise-wide software security goals and vision.
- To design and develop specific guidelines that remove the guesswork from the developer's intelligence and resolve the issue of consistency between security analysts.
- Establish a universal risk framework as a component of government efforts to calculate risk impact at project management or portfolio level consistently.
- The security objective rationale exhibits that the declared objectives are perceptible to all assumptions, threats, and organizational policies.
- It may help to estimate software security and provide cost estimation of a software project, which may be helpful to evaluate and plan new activities.
- It may help to decide the effect of various software development technologies, especially reuse technology for impact analysis through quantitative evaluation of several inherent qualities, including productivity, quality, lead-time, maintainability, etc.
- The security requirements rationale reveals that requirements for the product or system or the environment must be traceable and meet the expected objectives.

Measurement can be challenging, especially in software, due to its abstract nature. There are different techniques to measure these abstract concepts and create real-world metrics. It can be used as an integral part of the design process to support software developers in improving their product quality. Based on certain predefined conditions, it may be highly required to recognize positive and negative elements of system design. The impact analysis of these identified components will support developers in controlling the perceived complexity of system design. Another big challenge is using such measures to improve the security design process. To solve this purpose, we highly require the various metrics based on software development phases and software security [23, 27].

1.7 Conclusion

Software is under severe threat, much more than ever before! If so, what are the reasons? Careful consideration by Gary McGraw draws attention to the terms such as 'software in everything', 'unification of feeds', etc. Undoubtedly, the current era is emerging as the software-intensive systems. There is fast convergence of technologies, ably led by computing and communications to facilitate the same. Software is inevitably integrated or embedded to meet the ever-expanding desirable functionalities. Such a scenario makes the evolution of 'dependable software components' a highly justified ground to look at software security afresh and in a revolutionary than an evolutionary manner.

Key Terms

Software, Security, Software Security, Software Security Characteristics, Security Components, Security Types, Software Security Assurance, Software Security Models, Software Security Measurement and Metrics, Security Myths

Points to Remember

1. Quantitative analysis of software security at an early stage enables the basis for assessing security technologies.
2. Quantifying security will help address the trade-off between security objectives and costs.
3. Researchers and practitioners have strongly assumed that the results of the qualitative analysis can no longer be used and that changes made in the later stages of the software development life are more expensive than changes made in the early stages of software development.
4. The software security assessment is considered an essential constituent to improve software security.
5. Software security assessments are valid for developing and implementing security products, reducing the likelihood of security vulnerabilities being clarified and exposed by malicious customers or users.
6. The ultimate goal of incorporating security is to verify strength and prevent vulnerabilities from entering the program.
7. It has developed into a critical approach for ensuring software security and trustworthiness.

Objective-Type Questions

1 Security is a _____.

2 Security estimation is an integral part of _____.

3. _____ includes principles, guidelines, rules, vulnerabilities, exploits, attack pattern, and historical risk evaluation.

4. _____ is responsible for data protection through any mean whether it may be accidental or intentional.

5. _____ will explore an idea to protect software against malicious attack.

6. Security estimation is an essential component of _____ process.
   (a) Risk estimation
   (b) Software development
   (c) Software design
   (d) SRS design

7. Safety-relevant faults are:
   (a) stochastic
   (b) intentional
   (c) Both
   (d) None

8. A firewall is used in a system connected to a wide area network to
   (a) Avoid spreading of fire in the network
   (b) Stop unauthorized access by hackers
   (c) Scanning for viruses in various files
   (d) Fire spreading via network through cables

9. Security in the design of information system is used for
   (a) Inspection of system to know it was constructed as given specification
   (b) Protection of data and programs from accidental or intentional loss
   (c) Ensuring system processes data and reliability of results
   (d) Ensuring privacy preservation

10. By information system testing, we mean
   (a) To test an information system correctly
   (b) To determine system performance as per specifications
   (c) To determine system is performing optimally
   (d) To ensure proper functioning of a system

Short-Answer Type Questions

1. What do you mean by software security? Why it is not possible to ignore security at any level of development phase?

2. What is the role of software measurement in software development process?

3. Describe the importance of early estimation of security for secure development process.

4. List out various security components.

5. Write down the five security myths with facts not listed in this chapter.

6. Describe the concept of software security with risk perspective.

7. Briefly explain the different security characteristics with suitable examples.

8. Software Security Assurance is a key term for secure software process. Justify this with appropriate activities.

9. What are the roles of software security metrics in measurement? List out at least five security metrics used in this purpose.

10. How security models work to establish a theoretical background for research in a particular area? Put your own view on this.

Descriptive Questions

1. It is not possible to ignore security at the beginning of software development. Provide relevant research article to justify your answer with your own opinion.

2. Research the literature on software security and write a paper on software security estimation. Be sure to take a case study.

3. Review the literature available on software security attributes. Collect the different set of security attributes with proper justification.

4. Prepare a comparative study on software security estimation models.

5. Write a research review paper on 'software security assessment'. How to bridge the gap between academic & industry issues?

6. How can we measure security? Propose a security metric that can be used to measure the security of software.

7. Write a critical review on available security estimation frameworks for different levels of software development phases.

8. Describe the security assessment process and discuss how the findings of an assessment support initiatives within the organization?

9. Why do we emphasize that security development is an integrated approach? What are the benefits of this core idea?

10. What is the intended use of the security covered by the Software Security Assurance planning?

References

1. R. Lehtinen, *Computer Security Basics*. O'Reilly Publication, June 2006, ISBN:13-978-0-59-600669-3.

2. M. Bishop, *Computer Security: Art and Science*. Addison Wesley, 2002, ISBN: 0-201-44099-7.

3. [Online], Available at: http://www.msnbc.msn.com/id/38790670/ns/technology_and_science-Security/?gt1=43001 (accessed December 20, 2020).

4. I. Mkpong-Ruffin, "Quantitative Risk Assessment Model for Software Security in the Design Phase of Software Development", Ph. D. Thesis submitted to Graduate Faculty of Auburn University, Alabama, May 09, 2009.

5. G. McGraw, *Software Security: Building Security In*.Addison Wesley Professional, 2006, ISBN: 978-0-321-35670-3.

6. G. McGraw, "From the Ground Up: The DIMACS Software Security Workshop", *IEEE Security & Privacy*, 1, March–April 2003, pp. 59–66.

7. G. McGraw, "Software Security", *IEEE Security & Privacy*, April 2004, pp. 80–83.

8. C. J. Berg, *High Assurance Design: Architecting Secure and Reliable Enterprise Applications*, Addison Wesley Professional, October 13, 2005, ISBN: 0-321-37577-7.

9. J. Viega, *The Myths of Security: What the Computer Security Industry Doesn't Want You to Know*.O'Reilly Media, Inc., 2009, ISBN: 978-0-596-52302-2.

10. J. H. Allen, S. Bamum, R. J. Ellison, G. McGraw and N. R. Mead, *Software Security Engineering: A Guide for Project Managers*. Addison Wesley Professional, May 01, 2008, ISBN: 13: 978-0-321-55968-5.

11. J. Viega and G. McGraw, *Building Secure Software*. Addition Wesley, 2005.

12. B. B. Madan, K. Gŏseva-Popstojanova, K. Vaidyanathan and K. S. Trivedi, "Modeling and Quantification of Security Attributes of Software Systems", *Proceedings of the International Conference on Dependable Systems and Networks (DSN'02)*, IEEE, 2002, pp. 505–514.

13. G. H. Walton, T. A. Longstaff and R. C. Linger, "Technology Foundations for Computational Evaluation of Software Security Attributes", Technical Report CMU/SEI-2006-TR-021, Esc-Tr-2006-021, December 2006.

14. A. Ben Aissa, R. K. Abercrombie and A. Mill, "Quantifying Security Threats and Their Impact", *CSIIRW*, 09, 2009, ACM-978-1-60558-518.

15. S. Lawrence Pfleeger and R. K. Cunningham, "Why Measuring Security is Hard", *IEEE Computer and Reliability Societies*, 2010, 8, pp. 46–54. doi: 10.1109/MSP.2010.60

16. G. Booch, *Object-Oriented Analysis and Design with Applications*. Pearson Education, 2007, ISBN: 0-201-89551-X.

17. M. K. Reiter and S. G. Stubblebine, *Towards Acceptable Metrics for Authentication*. Murray Hill, NJ: AT & T Labs, Research, IEEE 1997, pp. 10–20, ISSN: 1081-6011/97.

18. K. Renaud, "Quantifying the Quality of Web Authentication Mechanism A Usability Perspective", *Journal of Web Engineering*, 2003, 3, 94–123.

19. C. Mallow, "Authentication Methods and Techniques", www.giac.org/cissp-papers/2.pdf.

20. M. Jakobsson, L. Yangand S. Wetzel, "Quantifying the Security of Performance-Based Authentication", *ACM*, 2008, pp. 61–69, ISSN: 978-1-60558-294-8/08. doi: 10.1145/1456424.1456435

21. L. Gong, 'Increasing Availability and Security of an Authentication Service', *IEEE Journal on Selected Areas in Communication*, 11 (5), June 1993, pp. 657–662.

22. Microsoft Certifications, Available at: http://msdn.microsoft.com/en-us/library/ee817656.aspx (accessed July 18, 2020).

23. Authorization, Available at: http://en.wikipedia.org/wiki/Authorization (accessed October 21, 2021).

24. C. Wang and W. A. Wulf, "Towards a Framework for Security Measurement", *Proceedings of National Information Systems Security Conference*, Baltimore, October 7–10, 1997, pp. 522–533.

25. M. Yanguo Liu, "Quantitative Security Analysis for Service-Oriented Software Architectures", Ph.D Thesis, Department of Electrical and Computer Engineering, University of Victoria, 2008.

26. D. P. Gilliam, T. L. Wolfe, J. S. Sherif and M. Bishop, "Software Security Checklist for the Software Life Cycle", *Proceedings of the Twelfth IEEE International Workshops on Enabling Technologies: Infrastructure for Collaborative Enterprises (WETICE'03)*, 1080-1383/03, IEEE, 2003.

27. I. Flechais, M. Sasse and S. M. V. Hailes, "Bringing Security Home: A Process for Developing Secure and Usable Systems", *NSPW'03*, ACM, August 2003, pp. 18–21.

28. D. Verdon and G. McGraw, "Risk Analysis in Software Design", *IEEE Security & Privacy*, 1540-7793/04, 2004, pp. 32–37.

29. Y. Deng, J. Wang and J. P. Tsai, "Formal Analysis of Software Security System Architectures", *IEEE*, 2001, pp. 426–434. doi: 10.1109/ISADS.2001.917448.

Useful Links

http://msdn.microsoft.com/en-us/library/ee817656.aspx

http://en.wikipedia.org/wiki/Authorization

https://techbeacon.com/security/secure-development-lifecycle-essential-guide-safe-software-pipelines

https://www.microsoft.com/en-us/securityengineering/sdl

https://www.synopsys.com/blogs/software-security/secure-sdlc/

https://www.sei.cmu.edu/about/divisions/cert/index.cfm

2

Software Security Problems

The changing nature of conflict calls for a new approach.

On Blog

The rapid growth of the internet and the integration of information and communication technology are recognized worldwide by our society [1]. Software is the key component of any computer system. The main cause of computer security breaches comes from the realm of unexpected behavior developed in an illogical manner. The information published in the *Wall Street Journal* states that 'more data has been lost due to poor configuration than anything else on the cloud' [2–3]. Vincent Liu, a partner at Bishop Fox, a computer security consulting firm, talks about a configuration error that users have set to allow access in relation to the visibility of their information in the cloud [4–6]. The defects can be easily exploited by malicious intruders. It is one of the ways that may lead to a successful rapid growth breach of security via targeting defects and vulnerabilities.

It is evident from literature on software and its security that two aspects are always working together, one is to build secure software with controlled operation ability and another one to manage software risk for application which is already deployed as discussed in Figure 2.1 [7–9]. These two phenomena sound similar but are quite different; what is the important thing between them is that first one is providing an opportunity to write your code, do some test and develop application as per the rule of SDCL and second one is providing space to manage the associated risk of the deployed applications [10–12]. This is the way to find out the security vulnerability of the application that may cause of major security issues, if they can't control or manage at early stage.

The best approach to ensure security is to protect the environment in which software are installed. Another mechanism for prevention is to control threats during development as well as operations [13–16]. The hackers or intrudes take advantages of such flaws in the software via installing spyware or different types of malware on user's system that can be executed after certain triggered mechanism as per their requirement and agenda. There are different sources available for software insecurity, and these related issues for security are as follows:

- Software, especially that is connected through networking and accessing web services, have bigger sources of insecurity
- Complexities of software
- Inadequate and incorrect assumptions taken by development team for executed input for projected external entities
- No premeditated relations between software components, including those provided by as third party
- Improper logical clarity for code behavior and appropriate use of modularity
- Inadequate input validation
- Error handling and exception handling

DOI: 10.1201/9781003330516-2

FIGURE 2.1
Component breakups for software application.

2.1 Objectives

On the successful reading of this chapter the learners shall be capable to accomplish the following:

- Understand and describe software security problems in general
- Define and understand sources of insecurity, its properties, components and types
- Enumerate and realize numerous software security weaknesses
- Realize the importance and significance of software security pillars
- Visualize the different perspectives of software security and risk estimation framework
- Realize the wider role of software security engineering

2.2 Major Causes to Software Security

Software developers face different challenges while strengthening security [17–20]. Numerous factors are available that cause software risk and a threat to software security. Literature reveals that in 1990, a single line buggy code is responsible for the failure of system which draws an attention to the idea of security engineering which states that software may continue its functionality under malicious attacks [21–23]. Nowadays a single line of codes is enough to develop perceived complexity and destabilize the entire system. T's 4ESS switch causes the system to drop by about 50% over long distances in nine hours, and at a loss of $60 million [24–25].

For modern enterprises and information system, software security plays a key role for business and their respective customer in terms of business profitability and sustainability [26–28]. It is reported to be one of the most important issues to ensure security access by designing highly dependable security systems.

Software is a domain that includes broader fields and factors that affect its security more effectively. Several internal factors can affect software security and cause vulnerability.

Further, in this same order, software design acts as a key function in software security [29–31]. Secure software design can provide the highest software security. Internal causes that can affect software security are factors which associate design-based qualities and properties along with flaw in software code or functionality like error code line, Wrong API call definition, issues in access management in various roles and many others same like these. All these are attributes that affect software security effectively through its internal functionality.

This type of effect creates dependability of software on these factors. Therefore, a slight change or flaw in these factors can lead the software into an exploitable situation [32–35]. There are various internal factors available that need more attention during software development for better security and fewer data breaches. Design issues like availability, integrity, confidentiality, durability, scalability, compatibility, and many other issues need more focus during the software development phase [36–38]. Various researchers are focusing on these factors and categorizing these attributes based on their effective importance toward secure software.

Moreover, it is always highly harmful to software to have internal flaws because mitigating them takes a complex remedy process and time. Further, to understand the concept more clearly let's take an example – There is bank software and the access management of software allows a cashier to access loan sanctioned related documents that are confidential property for a bank [39–41]. Additionally, the cashier needs to fetch financial document information related to client A then it is much easier for the cashier to extract information and use it for his benefit without proper authorization. This type of situation creates undoubtedly a data breach situation for banks.

According to security expert guru Gary McGraw, the indented functionality of software behaves properly under the malicious attack comes under the realm of software security which is a subset of engineering software [42–45]. There are three major components being discussed by security experts which are directly responsible in the form of totality to devastate logical phenomenon for expected outcome. These three influencing trends have a great impact on the growth and evaluation of software and its development process. Study reveals the significance of malicious codes availability with the rise of these factors in application development process. The trinity of problems is as follows:

- Connectivity
- Extensibility
- Complexity

2.2.1 Connectivity

In the age of internet, computer systems are connected to each other in the rapid manner to bring to light their daily needs like banking, reading, sales and purchase, gaming and to get connected with friends on social media. This is one of the ways which is responsible to increase the number of nodes via internet connectivity and more connectivity may lead to more error-prone environment [46–47]. This is the right place where hackers or intruders find out the applications weaknesses or loopholes in the connecting media to breach the information. There is a possibility in increment of attack vectors as the connectivity increases due to anonymous reasons like applications, channel, media and information or resource sharing, etc. It is a way to put your software at greater risk at user end and also server side. Another prospect of this opinion is that the connectivity between different computer systems is not limited. Internet is a medium which is helpful to provide the connectivity between a person using his home PC to enterprise networks which are workable for higher end uses or more sensitive information.

Connectivity is something that is directly connected to software structure and security. Connectivity is an attribute that gives a working ability to the software. Through the connectivity attribute of software, applications connect with their hosts and users then perform various types of operations like data extraction, storage, process, and alteration, etc. An issue in the connectivity of software creates a terrifying situation for software users and owners [48–49]. Mostly the connectivity issue is related to a network security problem that creates a door for various exploit situations. Weak network security produces issues in the connectivity of software, and additionally, this type of circumstance creates a plot for attackers to execute their harmful exploitations and attacks of software and steal or temper valuable data of software. Moreover, a connectivity issue led the software into a data availability-related problem. Data availability is a basic function of any software that ensures the presence of data for the authorized services to authentic user at the time they demand it. In a nutshell, we can say that connectivity somehow depends on network security of software and a flaw in the connectivity of software can lead the application into a serious cyber attack situation.

Every business will automate their self to cope with the business race and fast services. This is now the demand of time, but these types of demands generate more error-prone results [50]. A latest case has been logged on ransomware, which is the result of online fraud. People from an anonymous location demand for some ransom to breach the credentials of users. With the use of such connectivity mechanism through internet, malicious activity is being initiated to harm in socio-economic aspects. Different communication modes have been adopted for the transmission of information through networks such as email and web services, and luckily these systems are related to the internet, making them vulnerable to software attacks from remote sources. It has been reported that new ransomware 'Wanaa Cry' is spreading extensively, and few cases are being reported in India, and RBI recommendations to the banks says that 'Wanna Cry' encrypts files on infected windows systems and dispersion by exploiting vulnerabilities.

Attackers find out the loop holes over the software and with any physical involvement they can be ready to breach or exploit the vulnerability of software and its services. Another reason is recognized by Gary McGraw's statement regarding the unexpected linkage of legacy applications and the deployment of those services on demand. There are numerous reasons available to be a victim of insecurity by attackers that they are ready to enter through virtual door step:

- Not full support by old legacy systems to current standards
- No proper alignments for authentication and application-level protocols for old performing computer system and application software
- Exclusive dependence on host-to-host authentication with fragile passwords

2.2.2 Extensibility

The second component which makes an adverse effect on security and is an another cause to construct security problem is called extensibility. Extensibility can be explained as a power to extend itself on certain implementations considering future growth. It can be extensible if we add new features or further do any modification in functionality of the existing application. It is not mandatory for existing applications that they should easily accept the updates or extensions which are initiated according to recent time usage due to compatibility. One way to deal with such issues is to promote such types of applicability which can make an easier way to sustain extensibility through dynamic loadable device drivers and modules. The best examples are deployed in the case of web browsers which provide services support like emails clients, word processors and other different applicability via scripting and applets, etc.

Extensibility is software functionality that gives the ability to software for extending its properties and uses, and it also helps the software to measure how much effort and investment software wants to extend its functionality for future adaptation. Extensible software is one whose interior structure and information access controls are insignificantly or not prejudiced by the latest or altered usefulness. For illustration, recompiling or altering the first source code may be futile while varying software behaviour by the creator or developers. Software is a product that always develops with future advancement possibilities. Extensibility is a step or ability that refers to this quality of software, but on the other hand, it also causes some exploitation possibilities in software and reason for software security. Development is a process that is not 100% accurate and predictable circumstances are evolving and change every second, and this causes infrequency in software extensibility. Non-extensible software is not acceptable by the software industry.

Sometimes systems are not fully persuaded keeping extensibility approach in mind, and after deployment it becomes a technical challenge to bridge the gap between legacy systems and improved functionality in the current scenario. There are plenty of reasons available, why software professionals are not much interested to cope with extensible design and implementation. The following are as follows:

- It increases the complexity of software.
- Provides difficulty for development, testing, and deployment due to increased complexity.
- Due to improved complexity, extensible portion requires additional care, and implementation will take extra time that will be more time consuming and cost effective.
- Another big challenge for extensile systems is that it requires more time to understand the way about system extensibility, which will be required for implantation and future extension at a later stage.
- Sometimes, it degrades the performance of the system.

2.2.2.1 Classification of Extensibility Mechanisms

A researcher Matthias Zenger from EPFL, Switzerland, defined classification of extensibility mechanism in his work entitled 'Programming Language Abstractions for Extensible Software Components' in year 2004. The work reveals three different forms of extensibility. The types and definitions are adopted from research article as follows:

- White-box extensibility
- Gray-box extensibility
- Black-box extensibility

2.2.2.2 *White-Box Extensibility*

There is one major flexible and least restrictive form of extensibility which is responsible for the extension of software system by modifying or adding to source codes. It is known as white-box extensibility.

2.2.2.2.1 *Open-Box Extensibility*

Another form of extensibility which is invasive in nature and directly hacked into the original source code is known as open-box extensibility.

2.2.2.2.2 *Glass-Box Extensibility*

The third form of extensibility is known as glass-box extensibility. It allows modification into the separate extension starting from the veritable systems in a manner that does not influence the real one. Source code is visible in its original form but cannot be modified. If you want to extend, you can view and further modify the extended version separate from the original one without influencing the original.

2.2.2.3 *Gray-Boy Extensibility*

In this scenario, programmers get an option to extend system's specialization interfaces on the ground of further abstracted documentation. This interface registers all abstracts that are accessible for improvement and indicates how the extension relates with the parent system.

2.2.2.4 *Black-Box Extensibility*

Black-box extensibility consigns to the behavior in which a software system can be pervasive when no internal facts about a system's architecture and execution are accessible.

Black-box extensible systems are arranged and completed only through their interface specification.

2.2.3 Complexity

The rapid growth in modern information systems leads to major cause of security known as complexity. This complexity arises in software due to uncontrolled expansion in volume and enormous capacity of storage. Windows XP itself consists of at least 40 million lines of code, and nature of complexity automatically builds due to huge size. It is not easy to trace the defects within application due to developed complexity with increased lines of codes. Various reasons are available, including increased network connectivity, complexity of the code, sophistication of the attack, and easy access to the sound nature that largely transforms into systems where avoiding bugs in the application is a difficult task. This complexity is responsible for catastrophic and ever-increasing security breaches, which can cause serious damage to most software development organizations. Complexity is not the only factor that complicates the understanding of things, but with adequate complexity it can be complicated to appreciate everything. The complexity should not exceed assured limits. Software security needs to be a mandatory concern in favor of software development progress, but the complexity of applications or systems should never go beyond the standard acceptance level that models efficiency in terms of financial feasibility, and user

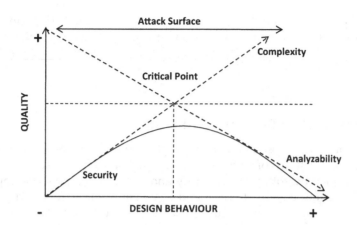

FIGURE 2.2
Security vs complexity.

friendliness and overall market value of the product may be lost. Therefore, complexity with negative effects can be considered as one of the major safety factors. The effect and consequences are illustrated in Figure 2.2.

Complexity is a term that incorporates numerous properties of a bit of programming, all of which influence interior cooperation. In software, as the quantity of elements builds, the number of collaborations between them would expand exponentially, and it would arrive at a point where it is difficult to know and see every one of them. This creates complexity in the design of the software. This type of complexity creates ambiguity for new developers to understand software functionality and workflow. Complexity issues create various security threats like data handling error, interoperability related issues, and many others. Software security is affected through the complexity of software and it inherits the functionality of software also. Software structure's multifaceted nature is hard to survey without utilizing intricacy measurements and measures. The complexity analysis is a long-term beneficial process for software development that gives some ideal advancement in software like quality enhancement of code, maintenance cost reduction, low compatibility issues, and many other functionality-based benefits. Moreover, it can be said that complex software is a headache for its owner as well as its user. There is a need in the industry to compress the complexity and increase the usefulness of the software.

The inherent nature of complexity summarizes that there are five characteristics that are frequent in all complex systems. Up to the lowest basic component level, complex systems are organized by subsystems that make up a complex hierarchy. The discovery of the nature of prehistoric components of a complex system, the selection of what components are in a system, etc., is comparatively subjective and fundamentally dependent on the conclusion of the supervisor of the system. Intra component association is usually stronger than inter component linkages. This information has the consequence of extrication on high-frequency dynamics of the components. It involves the internal organization of components from low-frequency dynamics linking interactions between components. Many complex systems are implemented with an economy of expression. This further stipulates that complex systems have common patterns. A simple, functional system is the foundation of complex system design from scratch and never exists and works. A simple system is a platform that starts from the beginning of the process. As the system evolves, objects that are considered complex turn into primitive objects from which complex systems are built, and these primitive objects could not be properly contrived. This should be used in accordance with the first and then developed by the actual behavior of the system.

2.3 Sustainable Factors for Software Security

Sustainable attributes are those that enhance and support software security and its maintenance during the run status of software. It is a significant job to ensure security and sustainability maintained by software frequently and daily. There are some approaches and attributes available that ensure effective and sustainable software security. The concept of sustainable factors for software security tries to present factors that are highly recommended for software developers and maintainers to use for applying security more efficiently and for a long time off period. To understand the scenario more clearly and easily, we categorize important factors and describe them in the following headings that give an idea and overview of sustainable factors for software security.

Using malicious code, the hacker takes advantage of faults to breach application software or systems. As software is ever expanding through the latest internet-enabled applications, with the increasing complexity and nature of prevalence, the most common software risks are adding fuel to the fire. Security can be improved by integrating software security best practices at an early stage of the software life cycle by understanding critical and common threats, designed for security, and releasing all software artifacts for comprehensive risk analysis and testing. Software security is a course of action for designing, developing, and testing software with security that classifies and exposes problems in the software itself. In such a direction, security professionals try to develop software that can tolerate constant attacks. Developers can develop a clear understanding of the best practices of applicable software security and can have a significant impact on software security issues. While all three issues, including the complexity, connectivity, and extensibility continue to negatively impact application security, we must begin to address these issues more accurately. The trinity of problem for software security may apply to risk management, software security touch points, and knowledge. A realistic, cost-effective software security plan can be resulted through proper applicability of these three pillars in gradual and evolutionary manner.

2.3.1 Risk Management

Risk management is a course of action to summarize and numerically analyze possible risks within the organization and software for better development and policy creation. A ceaseless risk in the executive's procedure is a fundamental piece of any way to deal with programming security. Programming security risk incorporates risks found in ancient rarities during affirmation exercises, risks presented by lacking procedure, and faculty related risks. A general risk is that the executive's structure can assist make with detecting programming security.

The risk broad structure is a fundamental way of thinking for moving toward ensuring security. The risk management process is a step that is developed associating the software development life cycle and enhances the importance of security during the development of software. For the motivations behind this depiction, consider risk as a way to deal with iterative risk examination that is profoundly incorporated throughout

FIGURE 2.3
Elements of risk management.

the product improvement life cycle. Figure 2.3 explores the elements of risk management.

Many major issues have been reported by software experts when improving security. Experts and industry researchers are always involved to find the right solution for secure software products. Risk is a problem that can disrupt a well-defined technique. Risk management is used not only to reduce the likelihood of emerging threats but also to improve performance through program delivery. A security risk management plan is a theoretical arrangement that scrutinizes the development of security programs for risk management. Security risk monitoring and management is a relevant process that is integrated into security design to develop secure applications. Risk management techniques support risk management activities throughout the software development process.

By executing a risk management plan and considering the different likely risks or occasions before they happen, an association can set aside cash and ensure their future. This is because the CEO's plan is a serious risk that allows an organization to develop a method for maintaining a strategic distance from the boundaries of an expected threat. An effective risk management process encompasses three steps in its risk identification, assessment and mitigation. It is a process that gives the ability to IT managers for identifying and remedying possible organizational risks.

Risk evaluation and the executives are worried about surveying the potential misfortunes that may result from assaults on the framework and adjusting these misfortunes against the expenses of security strategies that may decrease these misfortunes. A hierarchical security approach may encourage risk management among executives. Moreover, a risk management process in an organization is incorporated with the following steps described in Figure 2.4:

System Categorization: This step incorporates the categorization of hardware, software, system interfaces, information and data, people, etc. Additionally, the step provides information regarding system boundaries, the functionality of system, criticality, and situation of information and data.

FIGURE 2.4
Risk management process.

Threat Identification: In this step, examiner identifies previous cyber attack statistics of organization and their effect and resources, and then this step also examines various assets of the organization through various tools. After all these identification procedures, this step gives a threat statement in the end.

Vulnerability Identification: This step associates previous audit reports, comments during an audit, system security requirements, and test results. The step provides a potential vulnerability list in the end.

Control Analysis: In this step, the examiner analyzes the current control and access management configuration of the organization and also reviews the planned control strategy. This type of analysis gives a list of controls and planned controls that helps in managing risk. This analysis gave a list of controls and planned controls that help manage risk.

Likelihood Determination: This is a significant and most crucial step in risk management. In this step, the examiner evaluates the identified threats, vulnerabilities, and control strategies of the organization and then gives ratings to them for the next steps.

Impact Analysis: This step identifies the various risks that have impact on organizational assets like data integrity, data confidentiality, data availability, and many others like the same. This impact analysis is responsible for rating the evaluation of impacts by outcome examiners on different domains of the organization covering all potential threats, vulnerabilities, and control strategies.

Risk Determination: This step is a milestone where all the findings of the various identification processes get associated under one roof and examiner identifies possible likelihood risks as well as makes a decision for mitigation or ignorance of risk in organization specifically for every identified risk.

Control and Recommendation: During this step, the examiner recommends the control strategy for an organization that is more effective and constructive according to the security view.

Results Documentation: This is the last step for the risk management process, and this step provides a documented risk management process report for an organization that gives an ideal understanding to the organization about their security and requirements as well as the current situation.

Risk management processes are applied to the entire development process to differentiate and mitigate risk. The security risk management process by policy and direction has different focuses. Risk management is an important and challenging task for software developers and organization, but an effective risk management process can provide an effective security strategy for software development based on the relevant organization's risk assessment report.

2.3.2 Point of Interaction

Sustainable security is a term that is used to describe potential long-term security measures of software that gives durable and compatible security measures and characteristics to the software. Sustainable security is a term used to describe software's potential long-term security measures that give durable and compatible security measures and characteristics to the software. Sustainable security factors are a combination of two types of factors: first is security and second is sustainability. When both these factors combine with each other, then sustainable security factors generated for software security are shown in Figure 2.5.

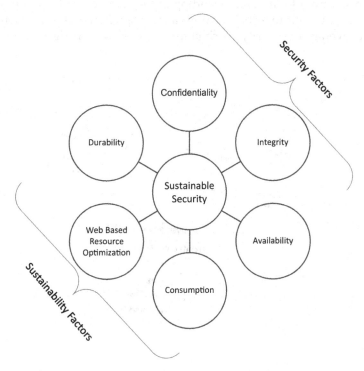

FIGURE 2.5
Sustainable security factors generation.

Additionally, to understand more effectively, take an example as in Figure 2.3.There are three security factors (confidentiality, integrity, and availability) that are described along with three sustainable security factors (consumption, web-based resource optimization, and Perdurability). When a developer focuses on these six factors as a combine and develops security measures in the design phase by focusing on these six factors, then we can say that the developed software is sustainable secure.

Moreover, this type of description and software development produces highly durable software security that can be used in different situations with different resources. This type of ability reduces the chances of a software crash when its resources and requirements get low or high. This type of software security development is important and highly recommended. Sustainable security development for software security is a new and effective approach that gives additional security ability to the software. This ability can help organizations and businesses invest fewer resources and get the same effective outcome from the software.

The best approach to ensuring security is to promote the most effective best practices or touch points with appropriate alignment through software development life cycles or to hone critical features to evolve security property into software. This is the most appropriate way for security experts to incorporate significant features of security into software. Security design should be considered from the beginning of development and security features should be tested and verified prior to the application being implemented. By setting up a system that follows disciplined processes, including security, costs can be more accurately identified and managed. Service and maintenance costs can be reduced, and repair time can be greatly reduced. It concludes that incorporation of security into the software development life cycle provides a significant result in terms of secure development with reduced cost and lower maintenance.

This mechanism provides an understanding of the common risks at both implementation and architectural levels to rectify the bugs and design flaws. The common observation and significant coverage of security touch points are as shown in Figure 2.6.

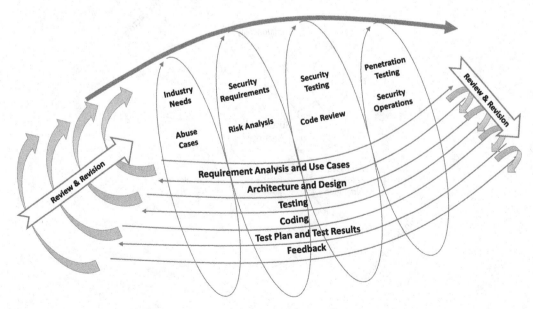

FIGURE 2.6
Softwaresecurity touch points.

2.3.3 Acquaintance

The software security fields are still in their infancy due to inexperienced security professionals and practitioners. It is an incredibly challenging issue for all. The already existing knowledge's best practices and training programs are working as a platform to support systems that are not addressing the issues at extreme level. The appropriate combination of these addressing moves can facilitate advanced understanding for both the design and architecture information of software systems, which in turn may allow the process of development and maintenance to be realized. This software will serve to develop some solid foundation for security practices.

Knowledge is a collection of facts. An excellent rationalization about knowledge and information is revealed in the book entitled *Building Security In*. It explains the difference between information and knowledge which are not the same thing. Knowledge is information in the context of work using processes and procedures. C and C ++ contain a checklist notice of potential security bugs. The similar information built into static analysis tools is knowledge. As per the security expert Gary McGraw, the software security knowledge is classified into seven knowledge catalogs which include:

- Principles
- Guidelines
- Rules
- Vulnerabilities
- Exploits
- Attack patterns
- Historical Risks

Further, those are in turn grouped into three knowledge categories, which are as follows and are depicted in Figure 2.7.

- Prescriptive knowledge
- Diagnostic knowledge
- Historical knowledge

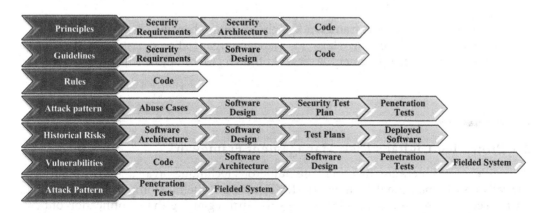

FIGURE 2.7
Mapping of knowledge catalogs to various software artifacts and software security best practices.

It can be implemented at any stage of the life cycle of application development. The best way to apply such knowledge is to educate or train them as per their skill domain. Various participants in software development, including software architects, developers, testers, and security analyzers, must be aware on critical software security issues. Exploration of knowledge will help those to be aware on critical reasons of security breaches and their optimized sensible solutions. It is an evolutionary practice regardless of your obtainable software development perspective.

2.4 Evolution of Risk Management Framework

The evolution of risk management emphasizes the significance of numerous organizational elements that impact the effectiveness of information security risk management at both the organizational and individual information system levels. The Risk Management Framework (RMF) is a collection of principles that regulate how the United States government's IT systems must be designed, secured, and monitored. In various subsidiary frameworks, NIST explicitly describes the risk management approach. NIST is the major building block to develop and nurture the information security risk management processes for secure development. The few recommendations are as follows:

- The most essential, titled 'NIST SP 800-37 Rev.1', describes the RMF as a 6-step process for architecting and engineering a data security process for new IT systems and recommends best practices and procedures followed by each federal agency while enabling a new system.
- The mechanism of risk assessment and risk mitigation throughout the system development life cycle is described in the supplementary document published by NIST SP 800-30 with the entitlement 'Guide for conducting risk assessment'.
- Another supportive document published by NIST SP 800-37 discussing the risk management formwork.
- At the end NIST SP 800-39 specifies the multi-tiered, organizational-wide risk management methodology required for RMF compliance in their technical report entitled 'Managing Information Security Risk'.
- NIST risk management framework include comprehensive, flexible, risk-based approach with following steps to manage organizational risk are: Prepare, Categorize, Select, Implement, Assess, Authorize, Monitor [51–55]

2.5 Protracted Cigital's Risk Management Framework

It is evident from literature that there are numerous techniques available to estimate risk. Cigital's Risk Management Framework (RMF) is one of the most important frameworks for the security professionals and beginners to learn regarding the identification of business and technical risk, risk ranking as per their severity impact, mitigation mechanism, and how to fix for more secure values. RMF is a framework to control risk in business

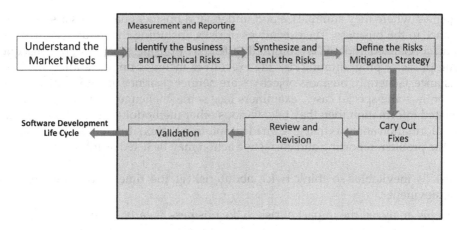

FIGURE 2.8
Protracted Cigital's Risk Management Framework.

context. It contains a multilevel loop fashion indicating that risk is a continuous process and all preventive measures should be properly aligned with identified risks factors at early stage [7]. During every stage of project, different factors of risk may influence the applicability directly or indirectly. Calculating once is not the ideal approach to control risk. The best way is to manage risk factors throughout the project over and over again. It should be categorized, ranked and mitigated using appropriate prevention techniques and should be maintained in log files for further learning and training program.

Protracted Cigital's RMF is fractal, which is mentioned in Figure 2.8. In other words, overall progress can be functional on many levels. The primary level is the project level. Each phase of the loop should obviously have some delineation during the entire project so that risk management can be effective. The six essential activities which are governed by RMF are as follows:

- First level is to recognize the business context.
- Second level is to categorize the business and technical risks.
- Third level is to synthesize and prioritize the risks, and construct a ranked set.
- Fourth level is to define the risk mitigation strategy.
- Fifth level is responsible for further review and revision based on observations.
- Sixth level is to carry out required fixes and validate for correctness.

The other additional stages, including the primary stage, are responsible for collecting all business needs which are most feasible. The validated information from last phase will be applied for further software development process which will produce more secure product. The discussion regarding respective phases of above-mentioned frameworks is as follows:

2.5.1 Stage 1: Understanding

This is the first stage for the RMF. Every assessment needs an understanding of where it is performed and which type of activity needs attention during the assessment. To understand these business-related information and data examiner conduct, the first stage of risk management where they summarize and understand business nature, its assets, and their importance to the business. The executives of risks, including the thoughts of risk abhorrence and specialized tradeoff, is profoundly affected by business inspiration. Consequently, the main phase of programming risk the executives includes understanding the business circumstance. Generally, business objectives are neither clear nor unequivocally expressed. Moreover, in some special cases, examiners face some challenges during extracting business-related information then they take various other methodologies like business finance related information analysis that give an ideal solution to this situation. The task performed during the problem reporting and corrective action may be listed as follows:

- Risk is inevitable, so think twice about risk at the time of development and deployment.
- Deeply analyzed the impact of risk to the business at early stage
- Clearly defined the goals of business
- Clear explanation needed as per the business goals for associated risks
- Set priorities of business in different circumstances as per the risk to evaluate the impact on business.

2.5.2 Stage 2: Identification

Business risks straightforwardly compromise at least one of a client's business objectives. The distinguishing proof of such risks assists with explaining and measure the likelihood that specific occasions will straightforwardly affect business objectives. Business risks have impacts that incorporate direct monetary misfortune, harm to brand or notoriety, infringement of client or administrative imperatives, introduction to obligation, and increment being developed expenses. The seriousness of a business risk ought to be communicated as far as money related or venture the board measurements. These incorporate, however, are not restricted to, piece of the pie (%), direct cost, level of profitability, and cost of the improvement.

Business risk distinguishing proof assists with characterizing and steer utilization of specific specialized techniques for extricating, estimating, and moderating programming risk given different programming curios. The recognizable proof of business risks gives a fundamental establishment that permits programming risk to be measured and portrayed in business terms.

The way to making risk the executives work for business lies in binds specialized risks to the business setting in a significant manner. The capacity to distinguish and profoundly comprehend risks is therefore basic. Revealing and perceiving specialized risks is a high-ability undertaking that typically requires long stretches of understanding. Moreover, during this stage examiners extract technical points of possible threats that can create risk for business in organizations and map them. Technical risk is a point that leads the organizational system into the possibility of exploitation and creates a dangerous situation for the organization. It is very important to mitigate technical risks in an organization for managing risk appropriately. This framework gives an approach and model to manage the business as well as a technical risk both at the same process with a proper system path.

- To recognize the risks challenged by the security targeted to business goals.
- Business risk impact analysis targeted to financial loss and other crucial issues of business.

- Need to express business risk severity in financial or project management terms.
- Mapping of technical risks with business goals.
- Provide a support for quantitative or qualitative assessment of business risk.
- Quantitative or qualitative assessment of business risk support for impact analysis and helpful for benchmarking.

2.5.3 Stage 3: Synthesize

Prioritizing risks may reveal new threats and bugs in security. There is always a possibility of risk with any working system, but the most important task is to first discover that risk and prioritize according to their severity and harmfulness. This leads to an appropriate response of proposed questions at the time of identification of associated risk for business goals. This phase is helpful to find out all types of risks and their likelihood. The appropriate impact analysis will help to prioritize and rank the risks as per their severity. Time to time different metrics are developed by researchers to find out the impact, likelihood, risk, severity according to their need, but that matrices must be validated theoretically and empirically over the time to mitigate the current scenario.

Identifying and understanding the risk is critical, but these procedures will not allow the company to mitigate or manage the risk. These steps are only initial steps that give a scenario idea to examiners. Synthesizing is an important step that is performed after proper understanding and identification. This step includes the prioritization of risks. Prioritizing and synthesizing risk can lead the management process into an outcome-based process. Prioritizing risk creates an idea related to risk's impact over organizational assets that gives an impact analysis benefits. Understanding the severity of risk is the most essential process of risk management because understanding risk from a business point of view is a significant job for examiners.

2.5.4 Stage 4: Mitigation

Whether is it worth full if you have a problem but you not have any idea how to control or fix it? Software security analysts have a great expertise to understand the technicalities within the application and respective knowledge of environment to trace anomalies, but the most challenging portion is to provide the immediate solution at lower cost that is highly required. Risk analysis is one of the easiest solutions to mitigate the problem. It should be tailored in such a manner that the organization can afford, integrate, and understand it. Proper validation techniques are highly required to mitigate risk.

After understanding the risk and their severity for organization or business, the following stage is to make a rational methodology for alleviating the risks in a financially savvy way. Any proposed relief exercises must consider cost, time to actualize, the probability of accomplishment, fulfillment, and effect over the whole corpus of risks. A risk-moderation procedure must be obliged by the business setting and ought to consider what the association can bear, incorporate, and comprehend. The system should likewise straightforwardly distinguish approval methods that can be utilized to exhibit that risks are appropriately relieved. Run of the mill measurements to consider in this stage are money related in nature and incorporate assessed cost takeout, rate of profitability, technique viability regarding dollar effect, and level of risk inclusion.

2.5.5 Stage 5: Validation

The motive of validation is very clear. It gives answer to the following question: *'Are all workforces in right direction'?'* At that time the mitigation strategy is executed. All artifacts are identified which may lead to problem, including architectural flaws in a design, requirements collisions, coding errors, or problems in testing.

Those portions and systems where issues have been recognized ought to be redressed. Risk alleviation is done by the methodology characterized in stage 2.4.4. Progress at this stage ought to be estimated as far as fulfillment against the risk alleviation procedure is concerned. Great measurements incorporate, yet are not constrained to, improvement against risks, open risk residuals, and any ancient rarity quality measurements recently recognized. This phase likewise includes the use of those approval methods recently distinguished. The endorsement phase provides some confidence that risks have been appropriately alleviated through antiquity improvement and that the risk relief technique is functioning. Testing can be utilized to exhibit and measure the adequacy of risk-moderation exercises. At this phase, the primary concern is to approve those product curios and procedures that do not offer unacceptable risks. This step should be defined and establish a repeatable, quantitative, visible evaluation procedure that can be executed regularly to ensure curio quality. Regular measurements utilized during this stage incorporate antique quality measurements just as levels of risk-moderation adequacy.

2.5.6 Stage 6: Review & Revision

The review and revision step is common in all stages, as one can enter into the review and revision step throughout their development life. This step is informal and essential, as review and revision make a framework more manageable. If required, assessment and modification are performed at all stages to develop more refined guidelines.

2.6 Security Engineering: An Inclusive Approach

In today's world, developers are under pressure from users to focus on better security design during application development. Violation of the security of the program can be a matter of life or death. A report says that there was a malware, Trojan, behind the fatal Spanish plane crash in 2008, killing 154 lives. The occurrence of these incidents was simply because of malware. In January 2010, more than 8,300 customers' ID cards were stolen from the National Bank of New York, USA, after they compromised and accessed an internet banking server. The presence of vulnerabilities is at the root of many software failures and can cause significant financial and reputational losses for both government and private organizations. The loss due to Code Red Worm has been estimated at $2.6 billion and due to Nachi Worm; operations at Air Canada and the CSX railroad were affected very badly. Due to the wide applicability of information systems, software security has become a crucial component of every software engineering process.

Software professional needs to highlight the reason of bad software, which leads to majority of security problems. Designers of modern systems must take security into account proactively. Defects are the major cause of the decline in security system. Security architectural designers must build a concrete mechanism to address design level flaws and implementation bugs at the time of development and deployment. The entire observation with its direct involvement in the field of knowledge may prove to be important, either directly or indirectly, in terms of the following:

- This software can help to better understand both the design and architecture of the system, which can understand the development and maintenance process.
- This can help identify and reduce existing vulnerabilities in software design in the early stages of software development, helping to achieve secure products.
- This helps to estimate the cost of the software project, which helps to predict the security of the program and to predict and plan new activities.

2.6.1 Software Security First: Societal Perspective

The pervasive nature of connectivity via internet and distribution of resources to everywhere constructs a complex computing infrastructure. It is everyone's job to provide maximum security to this computing infrastructure. The accessibility of software security in different forms of technology is mentioned in Figure 2.9.

- **Software security in the area of engineering and technology**

Information, no matter to which part of the globe it belongs to, is available in a click of the mouse. Intensive security oriented services ranging from internet banking, trading to online buying and selling, etc., are carried out unhesitatingly. These services require the privacy of the information and asset. When security intensive information floats everywhere, anyone having malicious intent can misuse this information. This may cause

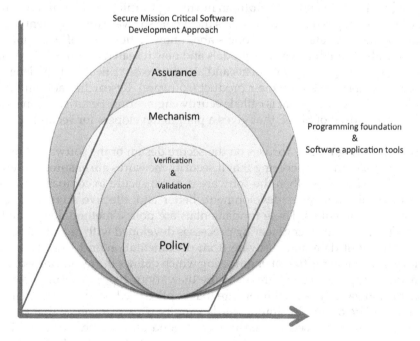

FIGURE 2.9
Accessibility of software security in different forms of technology.

harm to an organization or individuals. Moreover, the security breach of the software may be a matter of life and death of human being. A report says that there was a malware, Trojan, behind the fatal Spanish plane crash in 2008, killing 154 lives. It is evident from literature that software is now available in each area including civil engineering, auto mobile section, mechanical industry, embedded systems equipped with electronics and hardware components, missile technology, and many more. That's why software security will always remain the most influencing and important factor for critical assurance of safety.

- **Software security in business**

E-commerce and M-commerce are one of the revolutionary areas related to computer and software technology. By using latest techniques of artificial intelligence and data mining concepts, early investment of interest can easily be identified for all stakeholders of business processes with higher degree of security. Web-based software applications are primary tools to provide information for all stakeholders. Administrators are required to recognize the distributed environment of contemporary systems and take initiative to practice the principle of least privilege.

- **Software security in education and knowledge sharing**

Imparting any kind of knowledge and education is the most novel cause for human being. Advancement in technology is upgrading the standard of teaching and learning process. Higher accessibility of digital knowledge in limited time span is the biggest achievement of information technology. Software security techniques are enabled to protect digital information from intruders and hackers. The established mechanisms of privacy and safety are protecting digital data and are helpful in nurturing learning process among all.

Software engineering is a topic that covers the whole software development life cycle in it. Software engineering tells the developers about how to develop software and application systematically through its various models and new research findings [14]. Along with this, in recent years frequent cyber threats and attacks create critical and challenging tasks for software developers to secure their product (software). Researches add an extra point in SDLC for ensuring security that is called security engineering. Security engineering is an advanced new approach of SDLC that gives a path to developers for securely developing software.

Security engineering mainly focuses on the secure design of the software. It is strongly recommended in security engineering that if security measures are ensured by developers in the software design phase then the software is much secure in comparison of security measurement applications after development. Better and effective security engineering works on four fundamentals. These fundamentals are policy, methodology, validity, and reward. An effective security engineering process is developed with great policies that can ensure the security of data and software from documentation and legal view [14]. The methodology is the main portion of engineering which defines the technicality of approach and the methods applied in software to ensure the various types of security aspects. The third fundamental validity is used to ensure that applied methods for security in the software are appropriate or not. In simple words validity is used to verify that selected and implemented approach for security ensurance is good and effective or not. Finally, the reward is used to give a motive for employees and assets to work for a business that helps the organization to ensure software security.

2.7 Conclusion

Security is a greasy and multidimensional theory. No doubt, there are many different ways available to perceive security and risk associated with business goals. The major objective is to find out the appropriate issues related with software at early stage. The identified security problems may correlate with security measures for better estimation and prevention. The proposed pillars of security are helpful to rectify security problems in the frame of risk management, best practices, and knowledge. The RMF is helpful for the identification of security risk, synthesis, mitigation, and validation purpose through business context perspective. Security is a crucial issue, and it is everyone's job to learn more about security for optimal serviceability and support.

Software security is a topic that has received more attention in the current era in comparison to other fields. The reason behind this situation is the frequent and worldwide adoption of software for every work. 'The more acceptability, the more risk it has'; it is a statement that is sentenced by software engineering researchers. Currently, the statement is appropriate for software security. Previous 10 year's cyber attack statistics prove this statement and portray that software security is at high risk due to various advances and silent cyber attacks. Further, to secure software, it is important to apply security approaches to its design phase. The design phase is a point where every aspect of the software is open and available for developers to implement their security measures. This chapter gives an overview of the current software security scenario and its importance for security and cyber-attack-less industry. Risk management that is discussed briefly in this chapter tells us about measuring possible risks and threats related to software security. These potential risk factors have a key role in developing secure software from its origin (design phase). In a nutshell, the chapter tells that security engineering is the most significant and effective topic in the current era and needs extra attention as a pre-active approach in software development.

Key Terms

Software Security, Connectivity, Extensibility, Complexity, Risk Management Framework, Touch points, Knowledge.

Points to Ponder

- Security is a multidimensional attribute. To ensure a better process, a precisely specified and perspective framework, method, or roadmap is generally used and proves quite fruitful. It becomes evident through forgoing explanation that it is necessary to propose a security assessment technique or framework that is prescriptive in nature and can be easily used to measure design security and minimize vulnerability.
- Each type of security is an important consideration on every functional or nonfunctional movement of an organization which means 'business process security

is the key to the success of any enterprise'. Many of the hardware and software security tools are intended to offer security testing during an organization's online activities, but vigorous security systems are still needed to bear the risk and exposure to data transactions.

- Businesses in the current situation are concerned with developing customary security tools or resources that resist security pressures that are traditional and defend their business process against a nasty approach.

- Experts are trying to characterize risk factors in terms of vulnerability, threat, and consequences. However, the developers – the actual and direct user of all these contributions are unacquainted of the security-focused behavior and deliverables.

- To make all contributions made by experts to efficiently address security, there is need to ascertain a causal correlation between threat, attack, vulnerability, intrusion, error, failure, risk, asset damage, and vulnerability priority security indexing.

Objective-Type Questions

1. Accurate and complete data that enters the system for processing and remains accurate thereafter is said to have:
   a) Integrity
   b) Security
   c) Viruses
   d) Accidental deletion

2. Inaccurate data entry, worms and viruses, fraud and hardware malfunction are ways in which the following is included:
   a) Data Security
   b) Users
   c) Software
   d) Data Integrity

3. How are viruses spread?
   a) Through firewalls
   b) Downloading infected programs and files from internet
   c) Garbled information
   d) Install anti-virus

4. What are security controls?
   a) Controls that are intended to ensure that attacks are unsuccessful
   b) Controls that are intended to detect and repel attacks
   c) Controls that are intended to support recovery from problems
   d) All controls mentioned in points a–c

5. A system resource that has a value and has to be protected is known as
   a) Asset
   b) Control
   c) Vulnerability
   d) None of the mentioned

6. Circumstances that have potential to cause loss or harm are known as
   a)   Attack
   b)   Threat
   c)   Vulnerability
   d)   Control

7. An assessment of the worst possible damage that could result from a particular hazard is known as
   a)   Risk
   b)   Hazard probability
   c)   Hazard severity
   d)   Mishap

8. What threatens the quality and timeliness of the software to be produced?
   a)   Known risks
   b)   Business risks
   c)   Project risks
   d)   Technical risks

9. Which of the following is a systematic attempt to specify threats to the project plan?
   a)   Risk identification
   b)   Performance risk
   c)   Support risk
   d)   Risk projection

10. A weakness in a computer-based system that may be exploited to cause loss or harm is known as
   a)   Vulnerability
   b)   Attack
   c)   Threat
   d)   Exposure

Short-Answer Type Questions

1. What are the influential properties of secure Software?
2. Write down the differences between dependability and security.
3. Define size, complexity, traceability, and security.
4. Explore attack resistance, attack tolerance, and attack resilience.
5. How to influence the security properties of software?
6. How to assert and specify desired security properties?
7. Describe software security as a multidisciplinary effort.
8. Define general objectives of software architecture and design.
9. Define software security practices for architectural risk analysis.
10. What do you mean by software security touch point?

Descriptive Questions

1. Describe the framework for building an improvement program.
2. Explore the Cigital change program for maturity path sequence.
3. Provide the mechanism of steps to deploy software security best practices to build software.
4. Describe the latest security trends and issues.
5. Generate the mapping of software security knowledge catalogs to various software artifacts and software security best practices.
6. Explore a bird's-eye view of software security knowledge catalogs for academicians and researchers working in the area of software security.
7. Describe the concept of risk impact determination techniques.
8. Define the principles for software security in details.
9. Define security guidelines and attack scenario with suitable examples.
10. Justify your answer. The RMF is a multilevel loop.

References

1. Mad Mark's Blog. Available at: http://kohi10.wordpress.com/ (accessed on 06/06/2011).
2. Available at: http://www.msnbc.msn.com/id/38790670/ns/technology_and_science-Security/?gt1=43001
3. J. Viega and G. McGraw, *Building Secure Software*. Addition Wesley, 2005.
4. O. A. Alhazmi, Y. K. Malaiya and I. Ray, "Security Vulnerabilities in Software Systems: A Quantitative Perspective", *Data and Applications Security*, LNCS 3654, 2005, pp. 281–294, doi: 10.1007/11535706.
5. S. Ardi, D. Byres and N. Shahmehri, "Towards a Structured Unified Process for Software Security", *Proc. ACM, ICSE Workshop on Software Engineering for Secure Systems (SESS'06)*, ACM, 20–21 May 2006, pp. 3–9, doi: acm.org/10.1145/1137627.1137630.
6. S. T. Halkidis, A. Chatzigeorgiou and G. Stephanides, "A Qualitative Evaluation of Security Patterns", *ICICS*, LNCS 3269, 2004, pp. 132–144. Available at: http://arnetminer.org/viewpub.do?pid=314748.
7. G. McGraw, "Software Security", *IEEE Security & Privacy*, 2(2), 2004, pp. 80–83, doi:10.1109/MSECP.2004.1281254.
8. A. Alkussayer and W. H. Allen "A Scenario-Based Framework for the Security Evaluation of Software Architecture", *Proc. International Conf. Computer Science and Information Technology (ICCSIT'10)*, IEEE, 9–11 Jul 2010, pp. 687–695, doi: 10.1109/ICCSIT.2010.5564015.
9. I. Chowdhury and M. Zulkernine, "Using Complexity, Coupling and Cohesion Metrics as Early Indicators of Vulnerabilities", *Journal of System Architecture*, 57(3), Mar 2011, pp. 294–313, doi: 10.1016/j.sysarc.2010.06.003.
10. S. Heelan, "Vulnerability Detection Systems-Think Cyborg not Robot", *IEEE Security & Privacy*, IEEE, May–Jun 2011, pp. 74–77.
11. I. Chowdhury, B. Chan and M. Zulkernine, "Security Metrics for Source Code Structures", *Proc. Fourth International Workshop on Software Engineering for Secure Systems (SESS'08)*, ACM, May 2008, pp. 57–64, doi: 10.1145/1370905.1370913.
12. A. Ozment, "Improving Vulnerability Discovery Models", *Proc. ACM Workshop. Quality of Protection (QoP'07)*, ACM, 29 Oct 2007, pp. 6–11, doi:10.1145/1314257.1314261
13. J. Bansia and G. C. Davis "A Hierarchical Model for Object-Oriented Design Quality Assessment", *IEEE Transactions on Software Engineering*, 28(1), 2002, pp. 4–17.

14. A. Blyth and G. L. Kovacich, *Information Assurance Security in the Information Environment.* Springer, 2006.

15. M. Merkow and J. Breithaupt, *Information Security Principal and Practice.* Prentice Hall, 2006.

16. M. Bishop, *Computer Security: Art and Science.* Pearson, 2005.

17. D. Geer Jr., K. S. Hoo and A. Jaquith, "Information Security: Why the Future Belongs to the Quants", *IEEE Security & Privacy, IEEE,* 1(4), Jul–Aug 2003, pp. 24–32, doi: 10.1109/MSECP.2003.1219053

18. R. Marinescu and D. Raju, "Quantifying the Quality of Object-Oriented Design: The Factor-Strategy Model", *11th Working Conference on Reverse Engineering (WCRE 2004),* IEEE, 2004, pp. 192–201.

19. R. Savola and J. Holappa, "Self-Measurement of the Information Security Level in a Monitoring System Based on Mobile Ad Hoc Networks", *IMS 2005 – IEEE International Workshop on Measurement Systems for Homeland Security, Contraband Detection and Personal Safety Orlando,* FL, USA, 29–30 March 2005, pp. 42–49.

20. F. Copigneaux and Sylvain Martin, "Software Security Evaluation Based on a Top-down McCall-like Approach", *Aerospace Computer Security Applications Conference, 1988, Fourth,* IEEE, 1988, pp. 414–418.

21. Web reference. http://www.csoonline.com/read/070105/metrics.html

22. B. B. Madan, K. Gŏseva-Popstojanova, K. Vaidyanathan and K. S. Trivedi "Modeling and Quantification of Security Attributes of Software Systems", *Proceedings of the International Conference on Dependable Systems and Networks (DSN'02),* IEEE, 2002, pp. 505–514.

23. M. R. Stytz and James A. Whitaker, "Software Protection: Security's Last Stand", *IEEE Security and Privacy,* 1, 2003, pp. 95–98.

24. M. Sahinogly, "Security Meter: A Practical Decision-Tree Model to Quantify Risk' Infrastructure", *IEEE Security & Privacy,* 3, May/June 2005, pp. 18–24.

25. C. Perrin, "Design Simplicity Is an Important Element of Open Source Security", *IT Security,* 10 January 2011. http://www.techrepublic.com/blog/security/design-simplicity-is-an-important-element-of-open-source-security/4943?tag=mantle_skin;content

26. J. Allen," Measuring Software Security", *Extracted from the 2009 CERT® Research Annual Report,* Carnegie Mellon University, 2010, pp. 64–65. www.cert.org/archive/pdf/research-rpt-2009/allen-meas-soft-sec.pdf

27. B. Whyte and J. Harrison, "Secure Software Development-A White Paper, Software Security Failures: Who Should Correct them and How", Issue V1.0,June2008.

28. Available at www.techword.com/security.

29. G. Peterson, "Collaboration in a Secure Development Process, Part 1", *Information Security Bulletin,* 9, June 2004, pp. 165–172.

30. J. Du, Y. Yang and Q. Wang, "An Analysis for Understanding Software Security Requirement Methodologies", *2009 Third IEEE International Conference on Secure Software Integration and Reliability Improvement,* 2009, pp.141–149.

31. M. Paul, "The Ten Best Practices for Secure Software Development, (ISC)2".https://www.isc2.org/uploadedFiles/%28ISC%292_Public_Content/Certification_Programs/CSSLP/ISC2_WPIV.pdf

32. C. Wysopal,"Building Security into Your Software Development Lifecycle",30January2008,http://www.scmagazineus.com/building-security-into-your-software-development-lifecycle/article/104705/

33. How a Process Model Can Help Bring Security into Software Development, (ISC)2 Government Advisory Board Executive Writers Bureau, 4 March 2010.

34. K. M. Goertze, "Introduction to Software Security", 2009. https://buildsecurityin.us-cert.gov/bsi/547-BSI.html

35. M. Schumacher and U. Roedig, "Security Engineering with Patterns",*PLoP 2001 Conference,* 27 July 2001. http://www.uml.org.cn/sjms/pdf/PLoP2001_mschumacher0_1.pdf

36. R. T. Mercuri, "Analyzing Security Costs", *Communications of the ACM,* 46, 2003, pp. 15–18.

37. T. Neubauer, M. Klemen and S. Biffl, "Secure Business Process Management: A Roadmap", *Proceedings of the First International Conference on Availability, Reliability and Security (ARES'06),* IEEE, 2006. pp. 457–464.

38. M. S. Merkow and L. Raghavan, "Software Security for Developers", 27 September 2010.
39. Agile Software Development Doesn't Create Secure Software, View Point, 4 March 2011. http://agilescout.com/agile-software-development-doesnt-create-secure-software/
40. R. Sassoon, M. G. Jaatun and J. Jensen, "The Road to Hell Is Paved with Good Intentions: A Story of (in)secure Software Development", *Proc. International Conference on Availability, Reliability and Security (ARES'10)*, IEEE, 15–18 Feb 2010, pp. 501–506, doi:ieeecomputersociety.org/10.1109/ARES.2010.44.
41. J. McGovern and G. Peterson, "10 Quick, Dirty and Cheap Things to Improve Enterprise Security", *IEEE Security and Privacy, IEEE*, 8(2), Mar–Apr 2010, pp. 83–85, doi: 10.1109/MSP.2010.61.
42. G. McGraw, "From the Ground Up: The DIMACS Software Security Workshop", *IEEE Security & Privacy*, 1(2), Mar–Apr 2003, pp. 59–66, doi: 10.1109/MSECP.2003.1193213.
43. G. Hogland and G. McGraw, *Exploiting Software: How to Break Code*. Addison Wesley, 2004.
44. N. Moha, "Detection and Correction of Design Defects in Object Oriented Architectures", *Proc. Workshop. Object Oriented Reengineering(WOOR'03)*, 21 July 2003, pp. 949–950. http://www.etud.iro.umontreal.ca/~mohanaou/paper/ECOOP06/Moha06-DS_ECOOP.pdf
45. B. Alshammari, C. Fidge and D. Corney, "Security Metrics for Object-Oriented Design", *Proc. 21st Australian Software Engineering Conference*, IEEE Press, 6–9 Apr 2010, pp. 55–64, doi:10.1109/ASWEC.2010.34.
46. B. Alshammari, C. Fidge and D. Corney, "Security Metrics for Object-Oriented Class Design", *Proc. 9th International Conf. on Quality Software*, IEEE Press, 24–25Aug2009, pp. 11–20, doi:10.1109/QSIC.2009.11.
47. C. Wang and W. A. Wulf, "A Framework for Security Measurement", *Proc. National Information System Security Conference (NISSC'97)*, 1997, pp. 522–533. http://csrc.nist.gov/nissc/1997/proceedings/522.pdf
48. S. L. Pfleeger and R.K. Cunningham, "Why Measuring Security Is Hard", *IEEE Security and Privacy, IEEE*, Jul–Aug 2010, pp.46–54, doi: 10.1109/MSP.2010.60.
49. A. J. A. Wang, "Information Security Models and Metrics", *Proceeding of the 43rd ACM Southeast Conference, ACM*, 2005, pp. 178–184, doi: 10.1145/1167253.1167295.
50. D. Verdon and G. McGraw, "Risk Analysis in Software Design", *IEEE Security and Privacy, IEEE*, 2(4), Jul–Aug 2004, pp. 79–84, doi: 10.1109/MSP.2004.55.
51. https://www.sciencedirect.com/topics/computer-science/security-risk-management
52. https://csrc.nist.gov/projects/risk-management/about-rmf
53. https://nvlpubs.nist.gov/nistpubs/Legacy/SP/nistspecialpublication800-30r1.pdf
54. https://nvlpubs.nist.gov/nistpubs/Legacy/SP/nistspecialpublication800-39.pdf
55. https://nvlpubs.nist.gov/nistpubs/SpecialPublications/NIST.SP.800-37r1.pdf

Useful Links

https://www.wsj.com/articles/an-unexpected-security-problem-in-the-cloud-1505700061
http://indiatoday.intoday.in/story/atms-shut-down-india-wanna-cry-ransomware-attack/1/954284.html
Cigital. ITS4 http://www.cigital.com/its4/
D. Wheeler. Flawfinder http://www.dwheeler.com/flawfinder/
Secure Software. RATS http://www.securesoft.com/rats.php/.
http://www.studytechno.com/touchpoints-of-software-security.html
https://dinus.ac.id/repository/docs/ajar/Sommerville-Software-Engineering-10ed.pdf
https://www.cl.cam.ac.uk/~rja14/Papers/SEv2-c01.pdf
https://us-cert.cisa.gov/bsi/articles/best-practices/risk-management
https://www.sciencedirect.com/science/article/abs/pii/S1361372320300427

3

Threats to Security

One single vulnerability is all an attacker needs.

Window Snyder

Security is a topic that has the most significant concern in software, and its applicability is directly associated with real-world issues. Security is something that needs attention, novelty, and time to time update. It is an important and crucial task to identify which loopholes lead the software into risk and create some serious harm to the system and how system will respond in this type of situation [1]. Security is something that needs more attention and focus. The information security sector or the software development sector has a different classification of security needs. The security of software and applications is widely exploited by intruders on a huge basis. The situation demands high-security measures and concerns. To achieve this objective, firstly we need to classify and describe various threats that affect security in software. This chapter significantly portrays a threat scenario to readers about software security and displays what are factors that affect security in software and make an application exploitable.

3.1 Objectives

On the successful completion of this chapter, the students will be able to do the following:

- To understand and describe threats and their types in general
- To appreciate the need, importance, and significance of security threats
- To define and understand information security
- To realize the facts related to various information security attributes
- To understand common threats and their exposure's analysis
- To analyze the variety of secure development models to produce secure software
- To understand various models for secure development life cycle and assurance
- To describe the facts related to security threat classifications
- To analyze the threat impact analysis under effective risk assessment process
- To understand various protection and mitigation strategies regarding threats
- To analyze the comparative study based on various threat protection and mitigation strategies

DOI: 10.1201/9781003330516-3

3.2 Threats

Defining threats in software is a process that can be described as hierarchy, and it is a process of categorizing potential harms in different categories [2]. To understand this topic more simply and efficiently let's assume an employee wants some confidential information stored in a computer. The process of undertaking and acquiring that information can be non-intellectual like a malware; on the other hand, there is also a possibility that employee came to office on non-working hours and accessed the information by tempering system physically. This is the biggest reason authors categorize and try to portray the computer threats briefly in categorization point of view. Therefore, to understand the scenario as an overview and identify factors of threat for security, we classify the security threats into the following terms as mentioned in Figure 3.1.

3.2.1 Physical Threat

Physical threat is something that leads the security of the system and computer into the damage of physical loss and harm [2, 3]. In simple words, we can say that it is the incident that causes some physical or asset loss in an organization or system or computer. The physical threat can be categorized into the following types that are discussed in Figure 3.2.

- *Internal Threat*: This includes threats like fire, water supply tunnel blast, power supply-related issues, hardware failure, etc.
- *External Threat*: Mainly this type of physical threat is associated with natural disasters like earthquake, Tsunami, flood, etc.
- *Human Cause Threats*: This type of threat includes theft, intentional errors, accidental errors, and many other human-generated threats that cause security breach.

3.2.2 Non-Physical Threat

This type of threat includes security loopholes that cause exploitation in computers and organizations through non-physical interaction and damage [3]. This type of threat causes information loss, interruption, and delay in business operations, corruption, and alteration in sensitive data, spying, spoofing, and other cyber security threats. Various popular and

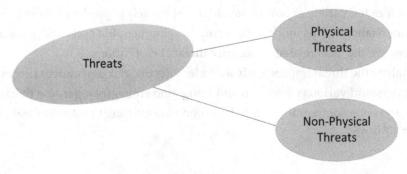

FIGURE 3.1
Types of threats.

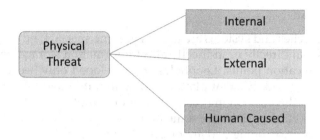

FIGURE 3.2
Physical threat.

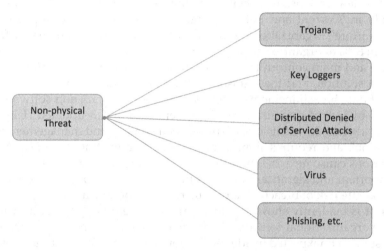

FIGURE 3.3
Non-physical threats.

significant non-physical threats for organizational and computer systems are described by the following terms as depicted in Figure 3.3.

- Trojans
- Key loggers
- Distributed Denial of Service Attacks
- Virus
- Phishing, etc.

All these are potential non-physical threats for security and causes that lead an organization into exploitation situation. Mitigating these threats requires technical expertise as well as logical measures. There is a need to mitigate and prevent these threats and run organizational operations without any threat and interruption.

However, in a nutshell, mitigation of these two types of threats is the most concerned and most significant objective for security management. Moreover, to understand the security threat scenario more effectively and clearly we need to concentrate and understand the information security fundamentals more briefly and descriptively.

3.2.3 Common Threat

Data security approaches and systems are useless in some special kind of attack situations. This type of attack can directly or indirectly affect information storage points, transaction points and communication points. Loopholes are developed only because of continuous non-standard patching and different platform compatibility issues. Accurately extracting possible loopholes is the challenging task because of complex structures and large code lines of applications. Further, there are some potential threats available that did not come into light with one time scanning and are rare in identification.

A specialized attacker of computer systems is a great adopter also. Because a good attack deployment demands brilliant system understanding and behavioral analysis; therefore, it is very significant job for attacker to know at which point the operating system shows warning and review options.. A special cyber attacker is always a great watcher. As per an ongoing study in 'Current and Future Danger: A CSI Primer on Computer Crime and Information Warfare', organizational workers are the most concerning entity for information security in 80% of organizations.

The biggest and main concern that causes information security breach is still unsolved and requires a solution, and these unsolved breaches and attack vectors cause approximately 66% of data breach incidents. Every asset of organization and software contribute in exploitation by lack of responsibility and understanding. Un-updated IT infrastructure also causes 13% breach incidents in enterprise. Data security and management is totally an organizational job and requires significant focus by administrative bodies. Additionally, unknown reasons cause next 10% breach issues. Further, from an organizational point of view, it is important and significant to assess the every asset of organization as a potential threat and evaluate risk of breach on a routine round in organization.

Moreover, it is evidently shown by incidents that there are physical threats also that cause harm in organizational security. There are physical thefts, nature disasters, and various types of sudden unexpected incidents like power cut, etc. There are also possibilities of attacks that combine both physical and digital platforms to conduct and successfully deploy attacks in organization. These attacks target most precious and important information of organization and conduct their attack for a long period of time. To manage and prevent this attack, experts specifically classify them into a new type of attack category named advanced persistent threat.

3.3 Security Threats

A classical definition of threat is as follows: A possible point or issue that has the potential to be a serious risk in future for organization or software is considered as threat. Further for underlining and highlighting the concept of threat in software security or organizational security, it is important to inherit threat from three basic triads of security CIA and critically analyze the use of threat into these security factors. A classification of threat is as follows:

- The threats for businesses are considered as business threats. This type of threat is associated with harm or loss in business functionality as well as any type of delay in the nature of businesses. For instance, assume there is an organization with payroll technique of salary distribution. Now, if the software is unable to extract or provide an employee worksheet then it is very critical for accounts department to prepare employee salary sheet. These types of situations are considered as business threats. Moreover, during the software development process, these types of threat assessments get overlooked because no one is going to analyze additional functionalities of organization and software.

- The second type of threat is system threat that directly affects software and system of organization that is essential to run enterprise properly. Due to its technical attributes and inheritance system, threats are more often grabbed in software development compared to business threats. This type of threat affects software directly.

- As the next type of threat, there are nature-based threats that are associated with various types of natural disasters that can cause organizational and technical infrastructure of enterprise.

- There are technical threats available in threat categorization. Technical threats are potential threats that can be caused by a simple technical fault in system or its sub system.

- Unexpected random threats include power cut, fire-related issues, and many others.

3.3.1 Security Threats Based on Common Security Vulnerability

Security vulnerability is a topic that is associated with various types of attack vectors and attack methodologies of cyber security. There are various techniques and approaches available that perform different types of exploitation by exploiting vulnerabilities in software and applications. A brief descriptive introduction is provided by the author in Figure 3.4 and the following headings:

- *Cross-site scripting*: This is an attack approach that exploits website-based vulnerabilities and performs unusual harmful access gradation or powers. As a process of this attack, an attacker penetrates the website by giving various syntax-based

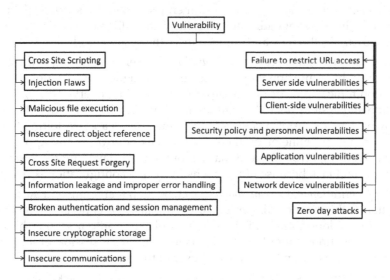

FIGURE 3.4
Vulnerability classifications.

commands and then finds the point that can be exploited. After understanding the point of exploitation, the attacker sends some malicious commands to the hosting website and tricks the server into its command and gets the access of the desired operation. These attacks are associated with and use input functionality for end users as their weapon and conduct their whole attack on this functionality of applications. As a shorter form of representation, various experts and cyber specialists call the attack an injection attack because of its input nature.

- *Injection-based attacks*: The injection character-based attacks utilize input functionality of software and applications and then exploit them as a vector. The injection attacks work on the approach that conduct query response system. In simple words if an end user inputs any type of query to the host system, then it's going to perform as a backend command and try to operate the connected database according to inputted query. This type of attack has a lot of potential and can alter or use as exceptionally compromised system.

- *Malicious file inclusion*: This type of attack uses files as an attack vector and performs malicious code scripted in these files. A badly designed, structured, and prepared web application always has the possibility that it can automatically activate inputted scripts and files functionality without any prior notification. Attackers use this issue as their weapon and deploy malicious file-related attacks. If the inputted script of URL or file has a malicious functionality and attributes, then congratulations your system is compromised.

- *Object-based referencing*: This is an access control issue that arises when there is lack of management in access control. There are various other access control vulnerabilities and attacks available that are caused only because of mismanagement.

- *Cross-Site Request Forgery (CSRF)*: This type of attack uses end user as a victim and vector. The attacker tricks the user into an unexpected situation where end user is bound to perform activity that an attacker wants to perform and gets hacked. The biggest advancement and weapon of attackers is social engineering in this type of attack where they firstly understand and watch the nature of victim like their hobbies, interests, and social activities and then trick them by sending them a malicious interesting topic of their interest. If the victim clicks on that link, the attacker successfully tricks the user and compromises the system easily.

- *Information leakage and improper error handling*: The error handling is the most concerned topic but unfortunately neglected by designers in the development of application topic. An error of any browser or website or server displays the configuration and system-related essential important details. These details can be utilized by hackers to perform cross-site scripting attacks and exploiting the servers easily. In order to define error, there are bundles of error in any application like memory out error, error 404, and many more others. Managing these errors is the most important task because of their sensitivity as a configuration reveal point.

- *Broken authentication and session management*: Session managing and authentication disruption is the most crucial and challenging task for experts to prevent. Some small technical loopholes lead the whole application into a session hijacking or exploiting situation where the attackers clone or hijack session of authenticated users and behave like an authenticated user in front of host server.

- *Insecure cryptographic storage*: This is a storage level breach attack that is caused by exploiting encryption keys. A bad key for encryption is utilized as a good attack vector by attackers. This type of attacks performs small level of breaches and causes information leakage-related incidents.

- *Insecure communications*: This type of vulnerability can cause hijacking, tempering, and confidentiality breach or identity theft-related issues in software. An insecure communication is caused by unencrypted session management without any security protocol like HTTP This type of failure in communication establishment can cause server-to-server or client-to-server relation into some serious integrity loss or security loss situation.

- *Failure to restrict URL access*: This type of vulnerability gives a space to force browsing by unrestrictedly allowing URL operations in system. This type of vulnerability has a potential to compromise your browser that is associated with confidential remarks and information about your personal activity as well as your passwords also in some cases. This kind of vulnerability has the ability to bypass various familiar websites of victim and hijack various sessions of victim just in one click. This type of attack possibility creates a concern about unsecured web browsing.

- Vulnerability vectors that lead a server into trouble or exploitation situation:
  - Poorly structured application
  - Operating system files and operations
  - Unsecured and scheduled backup configuration
  - Lack of secondary servers
  - Bad data storage approaches

- Vulnerability vectors that cause errors related to end-users:
  - Unsecured browsing
  - Mishandling in software
  - Lack of social engineering awareness

- Security policy and personnel vulnerabilities including:
  - Excessive user rights and unauthorized devices
  - Phishing
  - Unencrypted laptops and removable media

- Application vulnerabilities including:
  - Instant messaging applications
  - Peer-to-peer sharing applications

- Network device vulnerabilities including:
  - VoIP servers and phones

- Zero day attacks

3.3.2 Security Threats Based on Security Risk

- *Failure to cover security basics*: The common vulnerabilities and exposures used by attackers in the past year reveal that fundamental security measures are lacking. Cyber criminals use less than a dozen vulnerabilities to hack into organizations and their systems because they don't need more.

- *Not understanding what generates corporate security risks*: Companies often fail to understand 'their vulnerability to attack, the value of their critical assets, and the profile or sophistication of potential attackers'. Security risks are not always obvious. The categories below can provide some guidance for a deliberate effort to map and plan to mitigate them in the long term.

- *Policy-related issue*: Setting up a unified set of regulations and rules is the most concerned and important job for any enterprise in their working model. Attackers are not only penetrating IT industry rather than that they are frequently targeting non-technical sectors because of their low security standards and high possibility of breach incidents. This type of condition leads the higher corporate authorities into trouble and forces them to create highly good security policy standards that can protect their intellectual properties. Moreover, policy creation is essential but the prioritization of these policies and their strict deployment in organization infrastructure is also the most important step that enterprises need to focus on nowadays. To brief the audience about a classical policy for security, authors state some points that need attention during policy development:

  - Risk assessment is the most prioritized and the first step for organizational security in routine.
  - An e-governance model with the blend of security attributes is needed.
  - Every step needs pre-defined set of rules in organization.
  - Technical infrastructure upgradation and proper routine assessment is required.
  - Third party utilities assessment is required to identify the level of risk.
  - A secure supervision to address loopholes frequently is required.

- *Confusing compliance with Security*: Another risk business has to deal with is the confusion between compliance and a security policy. Ensuring compliance with company rules is not the equivalent of protecting the company against cyber attacks unless the rule integrates a clear focus on security, of course. Enterprise risk management requires that every manager in the company has access to the parts of the security system that are relevant to them. Security is a company-wide responsibility, as our CEO always says. As a result, managers (and everyone else) should oversee how data flows through the system and know how to protect confidential information from leaking to cyber criminals' infrastructure.

- *The carbon life form – the weakest link*: There are also other factors that can become corporate security risks. They're the less technological kind. The human factor plays an important role in how strong (or weak) your company's information security defenses are. It turns out that people in higher positions, such as executive and management roles, are less prone to becoming malicious insiders. It's the lower-level employees who can weaken your security considerably. Be mindful of how you set and monitor their access levels. As you can see for this recent statistic, privilege abuse is the leading cause for data leakage determined by malicious insiders.

- *Financial, human resource and skill-based issues*: A growing plant always needs proper care; similarly, a startup or growing business requires good care and management. In this type of concern, financial factors take an important special place and can quickly change the business. Further security is something that needs attention as well as high budget infrastructure for proper application. Further, besides financial challenges, there is challenge of skill proof manpower. There are a lot of unemployed graduates available in the world, but when it comes to skill-based workers, there is lack in this number. So, to manage this type of situation, enterprise owners compromise with their resources and infrastructure and try to operate business under their available funding and resources. All in all, a challenging task is always not an easy cup of cake for any person.

- *Awareness about security and its training*: A trained employee is always beneficial for business. Security is something that requires extra attention, and to prevent serious harms in enterprises, businesses need to aware and train their employees for every new type of attacks and possibilities of risk. Further, to train employees, there are a lot of reference books and best practices available that guide an enterprise about how to train employees perfectly for security assurance.

- **Bad plan for recovery**: To be a big and growing enterprise in the current era, you need to have courage and resources to face big cyber threats and attacks frequently. In order to prepare a business against cyber attacks, it is always essential to manage and have a great recovery plan for any type of error and causality. These plans are the ways for businesses to have their business security assurance.

- *Unexpected evolving risk*: These risks are associated with malicious malwares in consideration and tell us about their harmful effects. Malwares are the key weapon for attackers, and they frequently try to deploy malwares on internet to spread the vulnerability as much as it can be. This is the reason why current enterprises need a special protection factor that prevents malwares and their attacks in business and organization. This factor needs to have an ability to prevent and restrict malicious activities outside the organizational infrastructure and continuously supervise every potential threat portion of enterprise on routine basis. The increasing ratio of cyber attacks and their statics portray a serious situation in front of business, and they require additional security measures to prevent this highly exploitable situation of digitalization.

3.3.3 Software Security Risk

There are various ways to do harm or damage your product, process, business, or application by the attackers. Risk is directly associated with the various ways that interact with business logic. Sometimes it is safer and you don't need urgent attention, but due to malicious or vulnerable entities it may be harm you. There is a possibility that this harm can damage your reputation or it may have no bad consequences. To determine the impact of risk, you evaluate the likelihood of each threat, attack, or weaknesses to their technical pursuit. The overall observation of technical, behavioral, and operational activities can enable you to decide the impact and severity of risk to business, process, or applications that are depicted in Figure 3.5.

FIGURE 3.5
Software security risk estimation model.

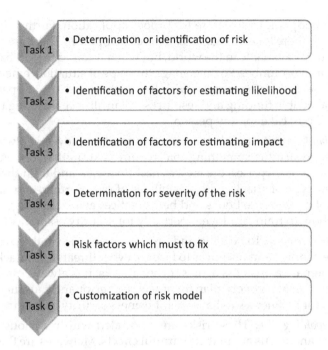

FIGURE 3.6
Steps involved for risk estimation.

Many approaches are available for risk analysis. The Open Web Application Security Project (OWSAP) presents standards risk estimation model on the basis of standard methodology for application security.

$$\text{Risk} = \text{Likelihood} \times \text{Impact}$$

Further, the defined factors are combined to determine the overall security for the risk that may follow the tasks depicted in Figure 3.6.

3.3.3.1 The CWE Top 25

There is another source known as Common Weakness Enumeration (CWE) which is responsible to deliver the details of most impactful issues experienced during software development. These weaknesses are more analyzable to exploit and damage reputation by allowing intruders to perform malicious activities including control over the system, steal data or prevent to access resources. Table 3.1 is responsible to offer the details of Top 25 CWE that are more helpful for developers, testers, managers, academicians, and security professionals. The following key players are structuring 2020 catalog by associating the scores of CVE (Common Vulnerabilities and Exposures) with 'NIST (National Institute of Standards and Technology), NVD (National Vulnerability Database), VCSS (Common Vulnerability Scoring System)' through CWE team members applying methods to the data to assure each vulnerabilities based on pervasiveness and severity.

TABLE 3.1

Top 25 Common Weakness Enumeration (CWE) adopted from Web Address:
https://cwe.mitre.org/top25/archive/2020/2020_cwe_top25.html

Rank	ID	Name	Score
[1]	CWE-79	Improper Neutralization of Input During Web Page Generation ('Cross-site Scripting')	46.82
[2]	CWE-787	Out-of-bounds Write	46.17
[3]	CWE-20	Improper Input Validation	33.47
[4]	CWE-125	Out-of-bounds Read	26.50
[5]	CWE-119	Improper Restriction of Operations within the Bounds of a Memory Buffer	23.73
[6]	CWE-89	Improper Neutralization of Special Elements used in an SQL Command ('SQL Injection')	20.69
[7]	CWE-200	Exposure of Sensitive Information to an Unauthorized Actor	19.16
[8]	CWE-416	Use After Free	18.87
[9]	CWE-352	Cross-Site Request Forgery (CSRF)	17.29
[10]	CWE-78	Improper Neutralization of Special Elements used in an OS Command ('OS Command Injection')	16.44
[11]	CWE-190	Integer Overflow or Wraparound	15.81
[12]	CWE-22	Improper Limitation of a Pathname to a Restricted Directory ('Path Traversal')	13.67
[13]	CWE-476	NULL Pointer Dereference	8.35
[14]	CWE-287	Improper Authentication	8.17
[15]	CWE-434	Unrestricted Upload of File with Dangerous Type	7.38
[16]	CWE-732	Incorrect Permission Assignment for Critical Resource	6.95
[17]	CWE-94	Improper Control of Generation of Code ('Code Injection')	6.53
[18]	CWE-522	Insufficiently Protected Credentials	5.49
[19]	CWE-611	Improper Restriction of XML External Entity Reference	5.33
[20]	CWE-798	Use of Hard-coded Credentials	5.19
[21]	CWE-502	Deserialization of Untrusted Data	4.93
[22]	CWE-269	Improper Privilege Management	4.87
[23]	CWE-400	Uncontrolled Resource Consumption	4.14
[24]	CWE-306	Missing Authentication for Critical Function	3.85
[25]	CWE-862	Missing Authorization	3.77

3.4 Security Threats Classification

Security threat is a concern of perspective. In simple words, there are various security threats for software and secure development. Different researchers have different opinions and suggestions regarding security threat classification. Due to this versatility, the classification of threats is a complex and challenging task for security experts. In the space of security, various kinds of security threat groupings are utilized. The motivation behind why threat characterizations are important originates from the way that if data framework assets ought to be ensured, we need to know the sources and the threats from which we are ensuring it [4, 5]. To understand the threats for security more easily, we categorize and analyze various potential risks that have significance toward security and are discussed by various researchers.

3.4.1 Errors

Errors have a very high significance in software security. Errors create unexpected delays and mishandling of data in a system that causes serious exploitation and loss of situation within the organization. Moreover, to understand the error more easily and exceptionally, we can categorize this into two basic parts that are written in Figure 3.7.

a) Intentional Errors
b) Non-Intentional Errors

a) **Intentional Errors**

Intentional error is the type of error where an employee or user tries to exploit and perform data mishandling with an intention of organizational harm and loss. It is a condition where the possibility of information loss is high and in the situation of danger. It is proven through some previous examples that intentional error in the information of software can cause serious loss to business and software.

b) **Non-Intentional Error**

This is a type of error performed by an employee or user in an accidental condition. In simple words, we can say that when the data mishandling is performed without any intention and reason, only by an accidental situation, then this is called non-intentional error.

3.4.2 Fraud and Theft

Fraud and theft are other types of harms or threats that cause serious exploitation and loss in organizations and software. Fraud is a spoofing activity that is performed to trick an organizational employee into a trap and extract information, revenue, and another sensitive asset from it. Fraud can lead to the theft situation in a business or software. There are two types of frauds and thefts available in software or organizational security that is depicted in Figure 3.8.

a) Physical Fraud and Theft
b) Non-Physical Fraud and Theft

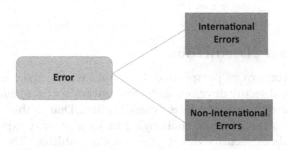

FIGURE 3.7
Types of errors.

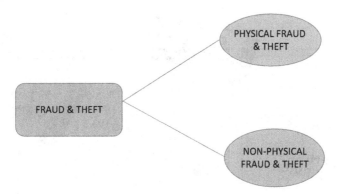

FIGURE 3.8
Types of fraud and theft.

a) **Physical Fraud and Theft**

This is a type of fraud and theft where the attacker or intruder is physically available to perform the threat activity. The physical presence of intruders is necessary for this type of threat. This type of threat is associated with activities like theft of hardware, hard information copies, organization assets, and other activities.

b) **Non-Physical Fraud and Theft**

This type of threat is performed from non-physical interaction with the organizational asset. For instance, consider hacking in organizational servers, which is a perfect example of non-physical fraud and theft. An attacker sends a phishing mail to employees from thousands of kilometer far and tricks the employee in a situation where he downloaded the attachment and gets hacked by the intruder without any physical interaction.

3.4.3 Threat to Privacy

This is an emerging threat in software security and organizational security. There is a heavy amount of data stored and managed by databases, but the condition of security in these databases is not well up-to-date. This type of situation creates exploitable privacy harm to software security and business information. There is a need to restrict access as well as manage the security of these databases and update the security from time to time.

Further, after describing these fundamental threats for the security of software and organization, there is a need to understand the security concept for information security within the organization. Further, to understand the information security condition in organizations and software more easily, we categorize the situation into four basic types of intrusions that are performed on information security.

a) **Intrusion to physical security**:

This type of intrusion is associated with DoS attacks, tapping of wired communication, and various other similar physical accessed intrusions. A brief description of these attacks is displayed in Figure 3.9.

b) **Intrusion to personal security**:

This type of attack includes the threat that targets personal information security in software or organizational security [6–10]. The attacks on personal data security

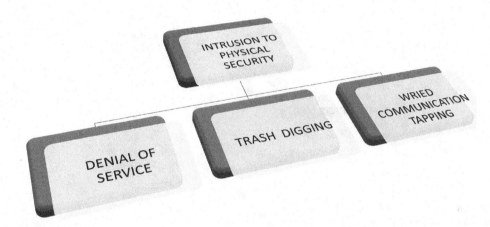

FIGURE 3.9
Physical intrusion.

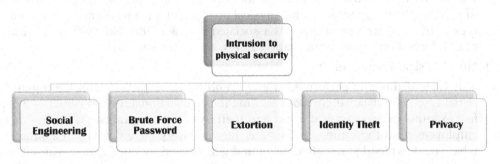

FIGURE 3.10
Private information intrusion.

come under this intrusion. Social engineering, extortions, password brute force, and any other type of attacks come under this heading. The descriptive representation of these attacks is given in Figure 3.10.

c) **Intrusion to communication and information security**:

This type of attacks is associated with intrusion on data security and communication mediums. For instance, attack on data and attack on software is popularly known intrusion on data and communicational mediums [10]. A descriptive portrayal of intrusions is given in Figure 3.11.

d) **Intrusion to operational security**:

These types of intrusion-associated breaches are related to application-level security. These breaches include spoofing, frauds, searching, and many other similar attacks. A graphical representation of these attacks is displayed in Figure 3.12.

All in all, it is proven that there are a variety of security threat classifications available for software, business, and information security. There is a need to understand these threats according to every organization and apply appropriate security measures according to the identified threat.

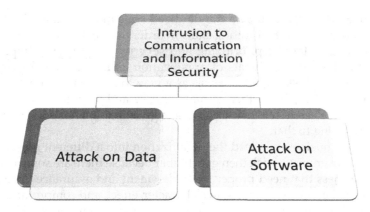

FIGURE 3.11
Communicational and information security intrusions.

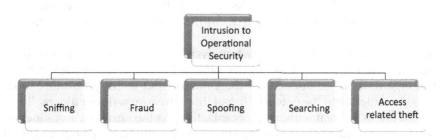

FIGURE 3.12
Operational intrusions.

3.5 Threat Impact Analysis

Danger and effect investigation fill in as a significant piece of the risk evaluation process, just as to guaranteeing powerful business coherence and calamity recuperation [11, 12]. Without a legitimate comprehension of the effect of information misfortune and the conceivable idea of the dangers to the information, it is hard to comprehend the risks in question and to appropriately decide how it very well may be most viably overseen. In this progression, the effect each risk occasion could have on the task is evaluated.

In general, this type of analysis aims to assess which and how the resources and environment affect the organization. In order to apply analysis, it is essential to assess resources and their effects properly for producing effective impact outcome [12]. To get an effective outcome as an impact analysis, it is essentially required to assess every potential risk of organization in this assessment. This type of analysis needs extra efforts and resources as well as techniques to be deployed properly in enterprise environment.

During the impact analysis of threats, it is challenging to assess increasing domain of organization into consideration. To understand this line more properly, remind that impact is always calculated on resource and current available environment of organization. Some extra efforts and vast possibility of growing businesses demands challenging impact analysis and lead an obstacle during analysis process. Garvey [13] provides a multi-criteria decision-making-based framework to analyze impact by associating future expansion.

The given framework also produces a standardized scale of rating that gives a free-hand assessment to examiners and their rating skills in order to rate threats.

Risk assessment is a task of prioritizing and severity analysis [14]. Impact of risk is always inheriting the possible threats of organization and their scaling by given rating parameters. Performing risk impact analysis as a way to assure risk in organizations is a challenging and complex job. Further, to make it easy and acceptable for organizational point of view, there is need to rate risk according to given parameters and perform the scaling of threats according to that.

The expansion of business can lead the organization into a different perspective of risk impact analysis. The impact of risk then gets higher because there are some new attributes gets added to business that need proper risk assessment and assurance. Every new attribute that gets added in business has its own character, effect, and compromise possibilities that need to be shown in risk assessment of organization for proper and effective impact analysis [13]. Further, impact is always based on the imagination and best practices. The new features also demand to assess their future potential as risk and their scope as an exploration vector in organization. After identifying all these factors, it is essentially important task to analyze and then portray impact of threat and risk for organization numerically and qualitatively.

Moreover, to conduct the threat impact analysis four initial steps need consideration and significance. Firstly, we need to identify catalog information and the whole physical asset list of organizations to understand the situation and security position. In the next step, we need to understand the potential threat that can cause serious vulnerability exploitation or can work as a threat within the organization. As the next step, examiners need to assess these potential threats into the terms of quantitative and qualitative. This type of assessment tells the severity of the threat and its impact on organizational security. After doing all this, we need to ensure the effectiveness of the risk management framework for which this impact analysis is performed. These are simple and summarized steps that need consideration during the threat impact analysis process. A graphical illustration of the topic is described in Figure 3.13.

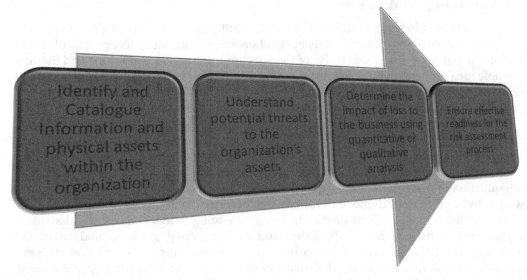

FIGURE 3.13
Threat impact analysis.

3.6 Protection and Mitigation Strategies

The present era of cyberspace has an extra and special place for information or data [15]. Every aspect of internet is producing, using, and storing data as well as information from its level. There are various methods and techniques available and consciously developed by scientists to manage this amount of data systematically. Due to this huge amount of data on internet in the current situation, the first attribute that comes in mind is security. Security is something that is most expensive and essential in this type of situation. To solve this issue various prevention and mitigation strategies are available.

Yet, what would you be able to do to obstruct programmers and relieve data penetrate hazard? The solution of data breaches and security concerns is not an easy task for experts [16]. Further it is also not a process that can be utilized as an individual. Proper and assured security and breach prevention techniques are required for various operations and resources in use. These resources are utilized by security strategies from organizational point of view to assure data security in this terrifying situation of cyber edge.

Moreover, there is a large list available of different measures that inherit threat mitigation strategies in different aspects. To make it summarized, simple, and clear, authors classify these strategies as conclusive topics and discuss them in the following written headings. Authors also specify the mitigation strategies' basic functionality through a graphical image that gives an ideal solution to readers about whether the mitigation strategy helps in protecting or identifying or mitigating or any other terms. The various identified mitigation strategies are mentioned in the following sections.

3.6.1 Software Update and Upgrade Daily

This is an effective step that helps organizations to identify and protect their systems on a daily basis [17]. A daily and frequent upgradation in system configurations and assets can lead the business into a secure architecture and provide a breach free environment within the organization as shown in Figure 3.14. The basic functionality that is provided through this mitigation strategy is identification and protection of software from attacks.

3.6.2 Privacy and Privileges Security of Accounts

Managing the access control system of organization and software can prevent privilege-based exposure to software. This situation can lead the organization and software into some serious issues related to revenue and respect [17]. To manage the privilege-based security within the software, there is a need to protect the access management workflow in software and create administrative restriction-based access management. This mitigation strategy also helps in the identification and protection of software as shown in Figure 3.15.

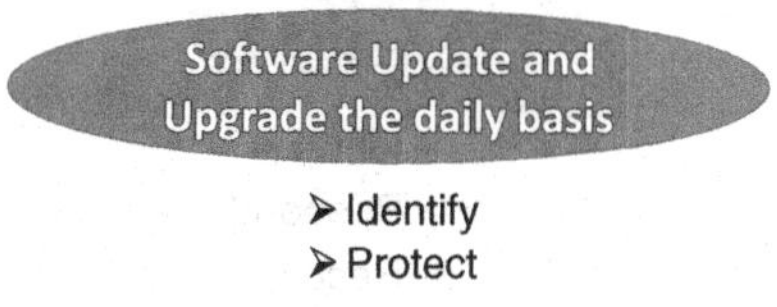

Software Update and
Upgrade the daily basis

➢ Identify
➢ Protect

FIGURE 3.14
Basic functionality of mitigation strategy.

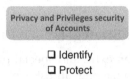

FIGURE 3.15
Functionality of mitigation strategy.

3.6.3 Security Training in Employees

These mitigation measures help most effectively and efficiently. Employees are the most vulnerable and risky asset of an organization that can be easily triggered through effective social engineering attacks [18]. Providing effective and good security training gives an effective countermeasure in identifying, managing, and protecting infrastructure as depicted in Figure 3.16.

3.6.4 Hunt for Network Loopholes Frequently

Network vulnerability is the reason for exploitation maximum times. It is the most necessary and effective part of security mitigation strategies to identify network vulnerabilities daily. That's why the authors include this mitigation strategy on priority. This mitigation strategy gives identification, response, and recovers functionality that helps software and organization most effectively as shown in Figure 3.17.

3.6.5 Implementation of Multifactor Authentication

This type of security management strategy provides extra layer security in countermeasures of the organization against a security threat as shown in Figure 3.18. A multifactor

FIGURE 3.16
Security training.

FIGURE 3.17
Network loopholes.

❖ Identify

❖ Protect

FIGURE 3.18

Implementing multifactor authentication.

TABLE 3.2

Basic Functionality of Different Mitigation Strategies

Strategy/Functionality	Identify	Respond	Protect	Recover
Software update and upgrade on a daily basis	✓		✓	
Privacy and privileges security of accounts	✓		✓	
Security training in employees	✓	✓	✓	
Hunt for network loopholes frequently	✓	✓		✓
Implementation of multifactor authentication	✓		✓	

authentication measure gives complimentary high-level security that is hard to bypass and provides initial security to every aspect of software and organization. The basic nature of this type of security strategy is the identification and protection.

All in all, we can say that these previously discussed mitigation strategies give an ideal solution to software threat and risk effectively. Managing security threats is a challenging task but maintaining the above-discussed strategy can help the organization in counter measuring the exploitation situation effectively. Moreover, to understand the situation of basic functionalities provided by these discussed strategies, we provide Table 3.2 that illustrates different mitigation strategies and their associated basic functionality.

3.7 Conclusion

Software threat is something that has variety and velocity in it. The current era of digitalization opens a door for various security threats that lead organizations into an exploitation situation daily. Managing this situation is a challenging and complex job as a security expert. Authors try to portray a summarized state of situation that is currently penetrating software development strategies and its resources very effectively. The current situation of software development threat tells that there is a need to first classify various threats on the plot of secure development and then analyze their impact as well as after that mitigate them to produce effective and secure software and organizational systems. This chapter aims to provide brief and effective situation awareness related to various threats and their impact on secure development. After that it provides effective mitigation strategy information for tackling security issues in organizational security. Authors strongly believe that this type of effective study gives an appropriate path to the readers and aware the readers about the various threats that can lead an organization into the danger of breach.

Key Terms

- Asset: Something that needs to be secured and preserved by the organization as well as has some worth to business also. The asset might be simply the software or information utilized by that system.

- Attack: The situation where software and any system gets exploited through some vulnerability or loophole.

- Threat: Possible business or software vulnerability/loophole that can lead the organization or system into the situation of exploitation in the future (not currently).

- Vulnerability: A weak or risky point that can cause exploitation and lead the business into immense loss and harm.

- Risk: Risk is an expectation of loss, a potential problem that may or may not occur in the future.

- Malware: A malicious attribute associated application that is developed to perform some harmful operation in system.

- Social Engineering: Understanding, observing, and analyzing victims' social, personal, and private activities that can be utilized as an attack against victim.

Points to Remember

- Attackers' motives
- Root cause of exploit
- Networking and network packet analysis
- Patch management
- End-user training
- Authentication
- Intrusion detection
- Privacy invasion/theft
- Ransomware
- Phishing attacks
- Incident response management

Objective-Type Questions

Q1 **All of the following are examples of real security and privacy threat except:**
   a) Hackers
   b) Virus
   c) Spam
   d) Worm

Q2 **According to the CIA Triad, which of the below-mentioned element is not considered in the triad?**
a) Confidentiality
b) Integrity
c) Authenticity
d) Availability

Q3 **When you use the word _____ it means you are protecting your data from getting disclosed:**
a) Confidentiality
b) Integrity
c) Authorization
d) Availability

Q4 **One common way to maintain data availability in organizations is _____:**
a) Data clustering
b) Data backups)
c) Data recovery
d) Data altering

Q5 **When there is an excessive amount of data flow, which the system cannot handle, _____ attack takes place:**
a) Database crash attack
b) DoS (Denial of Service) attack
c) Data overflow Attack
d) Buffer Overflow attack

Q6 **From the options below, which of them is not a threat to information security?**
a) Disaster
b) Eavesdropping
c) Information leakage
d) Unchanged default password

Q7 **From the options below, which of them is not a vulnerability to information security?**
a) Flood
b) without deleting data, disposal of storage media
c) unchanged default password
d) latest patches and updates not done

Q8 **Compromising confidential information comes under _____:**
a) Bug
b) Threat
c) Vulnerability
d) Attack

Q9 **Possible threat to any information cannot be _____:**
a) reduced
b) transferred
c) protected
d) ignored

Q10 _____ is the practice and precautions taken to protect valuable information from unauthorized access, recording, disclosure or destruction:
   a)   Network Security
   b)   Database Security
   c)   Information Security
   d)   Physical Security

Q11 Every employee of the firm must need to have some basic knowledge of cyber security and types of hacking and how they are done:
   a)   True
   b)   False

Q12 _____ has become a popular attack since last few years, and the attackers target board members, high-ranked officials and managing committee members of an organization:
   a)   Spyware
   b)   Ransomware
   c)   Adware
   d)   Shareware

Q13 If you're working in your company's system/laptop and suddenly a pop-up window arises asking you to update your security application, you must ignore it:
   a)   True
   b)   False

Q14 Collecting freely available information over the internet is an example of _____ type of information gathering:
   a)   active
   b)   passive
   c)   active and passive
   d)   non-passive

Q15 _____ scanning is an automatic process for identifying vulnerabilities of the system within a network:
   a)   Network
   b)   Port
   c)   Vulnerability
   d)   System

Short-Answer Type Questions

Q16 What type of various fundamental threats are present in software security?

Q17 What is intentional and non-intentional error?

Q18 Why employee security training is necessary for organizational security?

Q19 What do you mean by intrusion to personal security?

Q20 What is difference between physical and non-physical fraud and theft?

Descriptive Questions

Q21 What do you mean by threat mitigation strategies? Define with examples.

Q22 What is impact analysis of threat and how it inherits from risk management?

Q23 Define various types of threats and their examples that affect software or organizational security?

References

1. [Online], Available at: https://www.guru99.com/potential-security-threats-to-your-computer-systems.html

2. [Online], Available at: https://www.logpoint.com/en/understand/types-of-cyber-threats/

3. M. Jouini, L. B. A. Rabai, and A. B. Aissa, "Classification of Security Threats in Information Systems", *Procedia Computer Science*, 32, 2014, 489–496. doi:10.1016/j.procs.2014.05.452

4. G. Sandro, H. Željko, Information system security threats classifications. *Journal of Information and Organizational Sciences*. 31, pp: 51–61, 2007.

5. M. Alhabeeb, A. Almuhaideb, P. D. Le, and B. Srinivasan, "Information Security Threats Classification Pyramid", *2010 IEEE 24th International Conference on Advanced Information Networking and Applications Workshops*, Perth, WA, 2010, pp. 208–213. doi: 10.1109/WAINA.2010.39

6. R. Kumar, M. Zaroor, M. Alenezi, A. Agrawal, and R. A. Khan, "Measuring Security Durability of Software through Fuzzy-Based Decision-Making Process", *International Journal of Computational Intelligence Systems*, 12(2), 2019, pp. 627–642. doi: 10.2991/ijcis.d.190513.001

7. R. Kumar, A. Baz, H. Alhakami, W. Alhakami, M. Baz, A. Agrawal, and R. A. Khan, "A Hybrid Model of Hesitant Fuzzy Decision-Making Analysis for Estimating Usable-Security of Software", *IEEE Access*, 8(4), 2020, pp. 72694–72712. doi: 10.1109/ACCESS.2020.2987941

8. R. Kumar, A. K. Pandey, A. Baz, H. Alhakami, W. Alhakami, M. Baz, A. Agrawal, and R. A. Khan, "Fuzzy-Based Symmetrical Multi-Criteria Decision-Making Procedure for Evaluating the Impact of Harmful Factors of Healthcare Information Security", *Symmetry*, 12 (664), 2020, pp. 1–23. Multidisciplinary Digital Publishing Institute (MDPI). doi: 10.3390/sym12040664

9. A. K. Pandey, A. K. Tripathi, A. Alenezi, A. Agrawal, R. Kumar, and R. A. Khan, "A Framework for Producing Effective and Efficient Secure Code through Malware Analysis", *International Journal of Advanced Computer Science and Applications*, 11 (2), 2020, pp. 497–503, The Science and Information (SAI) Organization Limited. doi: 10.14569/IJACSA.2020.0110263

10. A. K. Pandey, A. I. Khan, Y. B. A. Alam, M. M. Agrawal, A. Kumar, and R. A. Khan," Key Issues in Healthcare Data Integrity: Analysis and Recommendations", *IEEE Access*, 8, 2020, pp. 15847–15865.

11. J. Kaur, A.I. Khan, Y.B. Abushark, M.M. Alam, S.A. Khan, A. Agrawal, R. Kumar, and R.A. Khan, "Security Risk Assessment of Healthcare Web Application Through Adaptive Neuro-Fuzzy Inference System: A Design Perspective", *Risk ManagHealthc Policy* 13, 2020, pp.355–371. doi: 10.2147/RMHP.S233706

12. [Online], Available at: https://www.mitre.org/publications/systems-engineering-guide/acquisition-systems-engineering/risk-management/risk-impact-assessment-and-prioritization

13. P.R. Garvey,*Analytical Methods for Risk Management: A Systems Engineering Perspective*, Boca Raton, London, New York: Chapman-Hall/CRC Press, Taylor & Francis Group (UK), 2008, ISBN: 1584886374.
14. K. Sahu and R. Shree, "Software Security: A Risk Taxonomy", *International Journal of Computer Science & Engineering Technology* 6, 2015, pp. 36–41.
15. [Online], Available at: https://www.atlantic.net/hipaa-compliant-hosting/how-to-best-mitigate-cybersecurity-risks-and-protect-your-data/
16. [Online], Available at: https://www.3pillarglobal.com/insights/mitigation-strategies-to-address-it-security-risks
17. [Online], Available at: https://www.nsa.gov/Portals/70/documents/what-we-do/cybersecurity/professional-resources/csi-nsas-top10-cybersecurity-mitigation-strategies.pdf
18. [Online], Available at: https://championsg.com/12-steps-mitigate-cyber-threats

Useful Links

Threat to Security

https://www.igi-global.com/chapter/trends-in-malware-attacks/247286
https://www.guru99.com/potential-security-threats-to-your-computer-systems.html#:~:text=Security%20Threat%20is%20defined%20as,such%20as%20a%20virus%20attack.
https://www.reveantivirus.com/in/computer-security-threats

Organizational Threat

https://cyberthreatportal.com/types-of-security-threats-to-organizations/
https://www.ccsinet.com/blog/common-security-risks-workplace/
https://www.insightsforprofessionals.com/it/security/types-of-security-threat

Threat Impact

https://prisminfosec.com/services/threat-and-impact-analysis/#:~:text=Identify%20and%20catalogue%20information%20and,for%20the%20risk%20assessment%20process

Secure Development

https://techbeacon.com/security/secure-development-lifecycle-essential-guide-safe-software-pipelines
https://www.microsoft.com/en-us/securityengineering/sdl
https://www.synopsys.com/blogs/software-security/secure-sdlc/

Threat Mitigation

https://www.carbonite.com/blog/article/2016/02/11-ways-to-mitigate-insider-security-threats
https://study.com/academy/lesson/it-threat-mitigation-definition-strategies.html
https://medium.com/@patrickkijek/threat-mitigation-techniques-for-web-application-security-f0ab917db694
https://www.infoblox.com/glossary/threat-mitigation/

4

Software Security Metrics

There's no point in being exact about something if you don't even know what you're talking about.

John von Neumann

Metrics are the quantifiable measurement of software or system properties. It is an effort to know the impact of investment on process or product. It is very helpful to determine the increased accountability, compliance, and security estimation quantitatively or qualitatively. As per the report of the RSA conference, 50% feel that current metrics provide limited value for security changes, IT risk, threat prevention, and effectiveness of people/process/technology. Sixty-nine percent feel current metrics do not align with business objectives. Security is multidimensional, emergent, and irreducible. It is an endeavor to accomplish the quantitative and objective basis of security assurance with the help of security metrics. The Institute of Information Infrastructure Protection (I3P) reported that security metrics will emerge as the most influencing research area for the next decade [1, 2].

For the most part, a security issue emerges because of the absence of inalienable safety efforts. Estimating security is tied in with utilizing presence of mind. Administrators need to figure out what to gauge, sort out the factors that make them sensible and significant, and manufacture repeatable recipes that show the preview status of security and how it changes after some time. Scientists and industry experts are making significant endeavours to make sure about programming. However, it might for the most part experience the ill effects of deferred security appraisals, which tallies intensely toward security and quality affirmation measures. Exertion regarding ahead of schedule and exact security assessment should be embraced for beneficial software development. It seems inescapable to have a possibly robust methodology ahead of schedule throughout the software development life cycle and precise security assessment [3–5].

Metric specialists and experts have various sentiments on the estimation/assessment of software security utilizing single and coordinated metrics. Nonetheless, the analyst firmly feels that a solitary coordinated security metric may prompt a bound together proportion of security, instead of by doing the subjective and unavoidably emotional translations for security through a scope of single measurement, which gives part astute estimations. It is unequivocally felt that industry individuals just as the experts would prefer not to have diverse part safety efforts, however, are more intrigued by a brought together measure. Security measurements are the proportion of security approaches, cycles, and items. Security administrators search for an enchantment equation that figures danger and viability in lessening hazard, yet security measurements aren't unreasonably straightforward. [11, 12, 25, 26]

DOI: 10.1201/9781003330516-4

Only few security metrics available may be utilized in the beginning phase of the development. There is a need to build a security development structure to build up a negligible arrangement of the metrics or coordinated metric.

In addition, such training may end up being profoundly productive for some reasons, including the following:

- Vulnerabilities discovery early in the ancient period produced in the underlying periods of the life cycle (detail and configuration archives);
- Decrease the cost of change – late recognizable proof and alleviation of vulnerabilities are a lot costlier than prior ones;
- Security monitoring from the initial stages of the software is good;
- Quantitative examination of applied methods and processes;
- More precise arranging of asset distribution depends on the framework's anticipated blunder inclination and its constituent parts.

Based on the justification for early use of security metrics to estimate software security, there might be an immense arrangement of exploration addresses that ought to be tended too. A portion of the appropriate ones are expressed as follows:

- Which are the variables that directly have impact on the software security?
- Will any standard framework be available for developing security metrics?.
- Would we be able to build up a coordinated or insignificant arrangement of security metrics that joins all the parts of the whole security factor?
- Can the security of software be assessed effectively at each degree of SDLC?
- Could exertion of assessing the security decreased through great estimation tools?
- Can a security metric utilization be truly helpful and dependable, without guaranteeing hypothetical and empirical validity?
- Can we get security metrics, which may be used in the initial development phase of the system?
- Is it conceivable to extricate quantitative highlights from the portrayal of software design to empower us to anticipate the level of viability of a software framework?
- Is it conceivable to remove quantifiable highlights from the portrayal of software design to empower us to anticipate the measure of exertion needed to construct the made sure about software depicted by that plan?
- What properties of software measures are required to decide the security of a design?
- How general are the lessons learned in this examination? Would they be able to be applied in circumstances including different measurements for two associations with diverse operational settings?

The thought is to give a method for evaluation to applications that associations can utilize to help give them knowledge about the security risk of software. Nonetheless, such a measurement can't be outright given that the importance of security differs depending on the setting. [20–23]

4.1 Objectives

On the successful completion of this chapter, the students shall be able to accomplish the following:

- Understand and describe the security metrics in general.
- Appreciate the need, importance and significance of software security metrics at each level of development.
- Realize the facts related to different software security metrics.
- Identify measurable security characteristics, partner sub-sets of security qualities to software framework substances.
- Create or utilized technique to survey the security quality of framework substances.
- Enumerate and realize efforts made in the development of software security metrics.
- Adaptation of best software security metrics suite.

4.2 Software Security Metrics

Emphasizing the minimal availability of quantitative measures of security, A.J.A. Wang says, 'security measurement is largely ad-hoc and the security metrics are usually qualitative'. S. L. Pfleeger et al. believes that some current measurements can help portray the invulnerability and strength of the system, but more research is needed. Estimation has been a foundation of good science for quite a long time. Indeed metrics enable us to learn more about and do more in the world around us. Quantitative measurement is the backbone to build secure software. Its behavior acts as a balancing wheel between targeted and achievable security levels. Based on quantitative assessment, it is easy to address the impact. Impact analysis based on certain metrics is a more appropriate mechanism to counter the problem and execute decisive metrics as the true enabler for countermeasures by quantifying certain characteristics of system-related issues. A measure is a measurement looked at against a norm. It will help to choose other alternatives. It promotes software engineers' enhanced access and distinguishes risk during the software development process. It is fundamental to have the option to characterize the genuine importance while security is estimated. A security metric is an arrangement of related measurements empowering evaluation of the level of opportunity from the chance of experiencing harm or misfortune vindictive assault. A comprehensive audit of works of writing on programming security uncovers that the field of characterizing security measurements efficiently is too youthful to even consider having an all-around acknowledged definition. The issue behind the adolescence of security measurements is that the current act of programming security is as yet a profoundly assorted field, and comprehensive and broadly acknowledged methodologies are as yet missing. A lot of work has been done in characterizing and proposing security measurements. Different security measurements exist in writing and are broadly utilized by the security network. The majority of the measurements are proposed to miss the mark regarding meeting the set goals of evaluating the measures, just as experimentally characterizing the equivalent. Many considerations have been dedicated to measurements focusing on the operational security of conveyed frameworks, decomposing imperfection rates, known and un-patched vulnerabilities, and framework configuration. Security measurements are difficult to evaluate because the teach itself is still in the beginning phases of advancement. There isn't yet a typical jargon and relatively few archived best practices to follow. Security measurements allude to the quantitative estimations of trust demonstrating how well a framework meets the security necessities [6–10].

4.3 Defining Good Security Metrics

Without measurement, it is impossible to align security policies and mechanism of implementation to enhance security. Metrics are the more authoritative tools for software security practitioners to estimate strength, their level, furthermore, preparation to address the security issues they are confronting. Metrics can likewise help recognize framework vulnerabilities, giving direction in organizing remedial activities and raising the degree of security mindfulness inside the association. After some time, they give important patterns and are valuable in following execution and guiding assets to start execution improvement activities. Numerous creators have recommended various methods of acknowledging great measurements which are referenced in Figures 4.1, 4.2, and 4.3. Attributes of good security metrics ought to incorporate the following: [7, 19, 25–27, 35]

- A great security metrics ought to have the option to quantify the proper thing for which it has been composed.
- It should likewise give a quantitative estimation to settle on certain choices.
- It should be sufficiently fit to be estimated precisely.
- A decent metrics ought to be approved prior to its utilization.
- Metrics ought to be more affordable.
- It ought to be accessible in the beginning phase of software development.
- It ought to have the option to anticipate in the general security of software and vulnerability of software being worked on.
- The security metrics ought to have the option to be refereed freely.

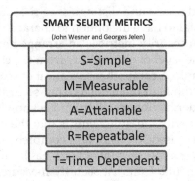

FIGURE 4.1
Smart security metrics.

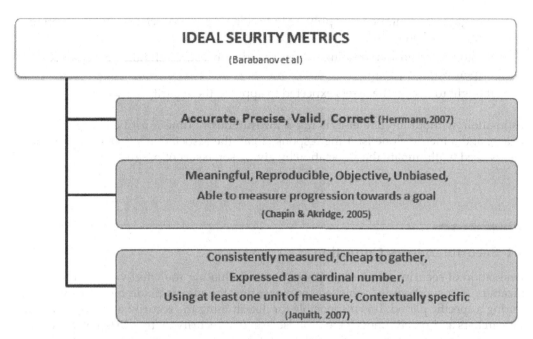

FIGURE 4.2
Ideal security metrics.

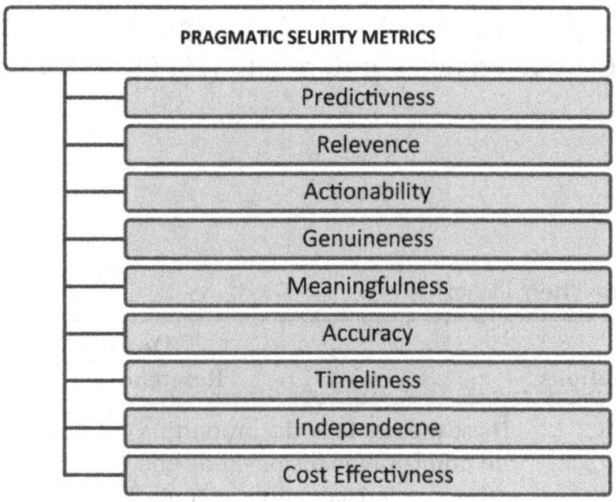

FIGURE 4.3
Pragmatic security metrics.

- It ought to be repeatable so the outcomes are autonomous of the expert playing out the estimating.
- Good security metrics should be adaptable from little single-PC frameworks to huge country scale venture organizations.
- It should create reproducible and legitimate estimations.
- It should gauge something of significant worth to the association.
- It ought to have the option to decide genuine advancement in security pose.

- It ought to be equipped for applying to a wide scope of associations while creating comparative outcomes.
- It should aid in determining which security measures should be deployed in response to a request.
- It ought to decide the assets expected to apply to the security software.

Estimation, without anyone else, is not a measurement. Time must be brought into the image, and a metric alone isn't the response to all the association's issues. The measurements need to illuminate the association by giving some sort of progress.

4.4 Security Metrics Collection

Evaluation of security efforts is responsible for evaluating the effectiveness of any organization. It is successfully achieved by measuring the efforts made by security metrics during a specific period. It is responsible for determining the security of the organization. Researchers and practitioners have proposed several security metrics listed in Table 4.1.

Security metrics are an emerging field in software security. Numerous product ventures, specialists, and professionals have created security measurements. These measurements are identified with various periods of the product advancement life cycle. An efficient audit on the security metrics is accessible for various periods of software development. The security metrics for prerequisite phase, plan stage, coding/execution stage, testing stage, and support stage are referenced underneath [16] (Tables 4.2–4.5).

TABLE 4.1

List of Security Metrics and Their Description

Security Metrics	Abbreviations	Description Reference [24, 28–35]
Computer viruses per malicious code	VPMC	These metrics tally the proportion of the quantity of PC viruses to add up to number of malicious code got: The adequacy of this metric proportion of computerized antivirus controls.
Relative attack surface quotient	AS	Microsoft designed it. This metric quantifies the attack capacity of a framework, i.e., the probability that an assault on the framework will happen and be effective. It is determined by finding the root attack vectors, which are highlights of the focused on framework that emphatically or contrarily influence its security.
Relative vulnerability metric	VM	This metric analyzes the determined proportion of exploitable vulnerabilities identified in a framework's software segments when an interruption. counteraction framework (IPS) is available against a similar proportion determined when the IPS is absent.
Security incidents and investigations	SI&I	These measurements check the quantity of security episodes and examinations performed to discover such an occurrence. These metrics help with observing security occasions.

(Continued)

TABLE 4.1 *(Continued)*

List of Security Metrics and Their Description

Security Metrics	Abbreviations	Description Reference [24, 28–35]
Cost of security breaches	CSB	This metric appraises the overall expense of security breaches. It gives a measure to genuine business misfortune identified with security disappointments.
Time and materials	TM	This assigns a value to the time and materials allotted to security functions. It demonstrates the actual commercial cost of maintaining a security program.
Security compliance	SC	This metric estimates consistency with security rules. It produces level of consistency coordinating security program objectives.
Static analysis tool effectiveness metric	SATEM	The metric consolidates the genuine number of defects with the instrument's bogus positive and bogus negative rates and afterward loads the outcome as per the target group for the subsequent estimations.
Predictive undiscovered vulnerability density metric	PUVDM	This metric is the extrapolation of Vulnerability Discovery Rate measurements. It offers measure to unfamiliar or theoretical vulnerabilities.
Flaw severity and severity-to-complexity metric	FSCM	These metrics rate the detailed software imperfections as a basic, high, medium, or low seriousness. It likewise decides if it is conceivable to make an immediate relationship between the number and seriousness of recognized vulnerabilities and bugs and the unpredictability of the code that contains them.
Security scoring vector (S-vector) for web applications	SSV	This metric is utilized to rate a web application's usage against its prerequisites for specialized capacities, basic insurance, and procedural strategies to create a general security score for the application. Martin recorded another arrangement of measurements in his paper on software security assessment dependent on a top-down Mc Call-Like Approach.
Inalterability metrics	IM	This metric characterizes the trouble of unlawful code change by a likely hacker.
Physical difficulty metrics	PDM	This metric measures the physical difficulty of code modification.
Checksum efficiency metrics	CEM	Efficiency of the checksum algorithm measures by this metric.
Self-test validity metrics	SVM	This metric characterizes the trouble of illicit code adjustment by an expected hacker.
Diversity metrics	DM	The diversity of code assess by this metric.
Number of versions	NoV	These metrics tally the various variants of a similar system. The code is troublesome in each rendition, yet the usefulness continues as before.
Diversity factors	DF	These metrics tally the various renditions of a similar system. The code is troublesome in each form, yet the usefulness continues as before.
Multiplicity metrics	MM	This measurement evaluates the quantity of summons of a similar instrument. The more a mechanism is utilized, the more troublesome it will be to bypass.
Multiplicity factor	MF	This metric quantifies the trouble of adjustment of the code actualizing the component.
Frequency of use	FoU	These metric gauges how regularly the instrument is utilized.

(Continued)

TABLE 4.1 *(Continued)*

List of Security Metrics and Their Description

Security Metrics	Abbreviations	Description Reference [24, 28–35]
Isolation metrics	IM	This metric is utilized to evaluate the segregation of the instrument from the remainder of the application and framework.
Code isolation	CI	These metric surveys the physical disconnection of the code portion actualizing the instrument.
Data isolation	DI	This metric addresses the information section of the product actualizing the instrument.
Data reuse	DR	This metric tends to the trouble of altering the operational boundaries of the system when it isn't being used.
Context isolation	CI	The proposed metric deals with the segregation given from the specific situation.
Interruptibility metrics	IM	These proposed metrics are designed to protect the instrument from hinder-driven attacks.
Mandatory mediation	MM	The proposed metric surveys the component utilized each time it could.
Mediation factor	MF	This metric builds up the proportion between the successful utilization of a component and its possible use.
Mediation efficiency	ME	This metric gauges the productivity of utilization, considering that this proficiency is identified with the circumstance of the instrument in the complete framework.
Number of mediation	NoM	For each capacity utilizing the component, this metric gauges the occasions it is utilized.
Audit ability metrics	AAM	This metric is intended to survey if the product leaves auditable hints of its utilization.
Listing of access denial	LAD	It is responsible to assess the presentation of the system when it denies an entry or some activity.
Alarm triggering metrics	AMT	This metric assesses the exhibition of the alert setting off system.
Non-standard behavior detection	NSBD	This metric targets evaluating the productivity of such frameworks, distinguishing when a subject's conduct goes amiss from its norm.
Listing of granted access	LGA	This metric analyzes the framework's presentation by keeping track of the permissible requests.
Access vector	AV	It quantifies how the weakness is misused, for example, locally or distantly. The more distant an aggressor can be to assault a data resource, the more noteworthy the weakness score.
Access complexity	AC	It gauges the intricacy of the assault needed to abuse the weakness, once an assailant has accessed the objective framework. The lower the necessary intricacy, the higher the vulnerability scores.
Authentication	AU	It gauges the occasions an assailant must verify to an objective to misuse vulnerabilities. The less the validation cases required, the higher the weakness score.
Confidentiality impact	CC	It calculates the number of occasions an attacker must verify an objective in order to exploit the vulnerability. The less the confirmation cases required, the higher the weakness score.
Integrity impact	IC	It quantifies the effect on the integrity of an effectively misused vulnerability. Expanded respectability sway builds the weakness score.
Availability impact	AC	It quantifies the effect on the accessibility of an effectively abused vulnerability. Expanded accessibility sway builds the weakness score.

TABLE 4.2

Security Metrics for Requirement Phase

Security Metrics	Abbreviations	Description Reference [13, 14]
Number of least priority security requirements	NLPSR	The number of security necessities that have less need than the other and the considered prerequisites won't influence the framework much or there will be no impact on it.
Number of priority security requirements	NPSR	This metric for the quantity of security necessities that have more need than the others and consider the prerequisites which, because of assaults on the framework, will most influence or devastate the framework.
Security requirements recorded deviations	SRRD	This metric is utilized to give the quantity of deviations from security necessities.
Security requirements stagesecurity errors	SRSSE	It gives the number of security mistakes that are the aftereffect of deficient or inaccurate security necessities.
Security requirements gathering indicators	SRI	It gives markers on prerequisites social event and investigation stage, which clarifies the effect of security necessities on the quantity of security breaches/violations.
Total number of securityrequirement	TNSR	It expects to gauge the quantity of security necessities distinguished/discovered during the investigation stage.
Ratio of security requirements	RoSR	This gives the proportion of necessity that directly affects security to the all-out number of prerequisite. $Rsr = ISRI/IRI$ Where, SR is denoted for the set of security requirement for the system. R is denoted for the setof the entire requirement assigned to the system.
Number of omitted securityrequirements	NoSR	It gauges the quantity of security necessity that has been not measuredthroughout the examination stage.

TABLE 4.3

Security Metrics for Design Phase

Security Metrics	Abbreviations	Description Reference [13–15, 18]
Percent of security coding aspects	PSCA	This shows the level of security perspectives considered during coding as indicated by plan.
Percent use of coding standard	PCS	It shows the utilization of coding guidelines for ensuring the turn of events and will be upheld in recognizing the thought of security norms during code usage.
Number of security errors	NSE	This measurement demonstrates the imperfections communicated as the whole of coding mistakes and the blunders from other library code.
Stall ratio	SR	This measurement expects to gauge the proportion of the quantity of lines of non-reformist articulations tuned in to the absolute number of lines in a circle. SR is being used for calculating the Lines of non-progressive statement in a loop/Total lines in the loop
Coupling corruption propagation	CCP	It is characterized as the quantity of youngster strategies call with the parameter(s) that depend on the parameter(s) of the first summon.

(Continued)

TABLE 4.3 *(Continued)*

Security Metrics for Design Phase

Security Metrics	Abbreviations	Description Reference [13–15, 18]
Critical element ratio	CER	This expects to give the proportion of basic information components in an item to the absolute number of components in the article. It quantifies the manners in which noxious data sources can contaminate a program. CER is responsible to measure the *Critical Data Elements in the Object/ Total Number of Elements in the Object*
Precision	P	It relates the genuine imperfect segments to the absolute number of segments anticipated as faulty. *Precision = TP/TP + FP* where TP and FP are for true positive and false positive.
Recall	Rc	It is characterized as the proportion of genuine damaged parts to the all-out number of faulty segments. *Recall = TP/TP + FN* where TP is true positive and FN is false negative.
F-measure		Utilized to connect the exactness and review as a symphonious mean. $$F - measure = \frac{2 \times Recall \times Precision}{Recall + Precision}$$
Accuracy		It is utilized to gauge the general precision of the expectation. $$Acc = \frac{TP + TN}{TP + TN + FP + FN}$$
Ratio of implementation errors thathave direct impact on security	Reerr	This gives the proportion of the quantity of mistakes that directly affect security to the complete number of blunders in the execution of the security. Rserr = *Nserr/Nerr*
Security metrics	Abbreviations	Description
Percent of security coding aspects	PSCA	This indicates the percentage of security aspectsconsidered during coding according to design.
Percent use of coding standard	PCS	Secure development uses coding standards by identifying security standards during code implementation.
Number of security errors	NSE	Metric values are responsible for counting coding errors and other library codes to indicate the total flaws.
Stall ratio	SR	The proposed metric value is the simple ratio between the number of lines of non-progressive statements in the loop to the total number of lines in a loop. SR is being used to count the lines of non-progressive statements in a loop/total lines in the loop
Coupling corruption propagation	CCP	It is defined as the number of child methods calledwith the parameter(s) based on theoriginal invocation parameter(s).
Critical element ratio	CER	The proposed metric value is achieved by calculating the ratio of the critical data elements in an object to the total number of elements of an object to measure the malicious inputs that have the possibilities to infect the program. CER is responsible for counting the Critical Data Elements in the object/ total number of elements in the object

(Continued)

TABLE 4.3 *(Continued)*

Security Metrics for Design Phase

Security Metrics	Abbreviations	Description Reference [13–15, 18]
Precision		This is the ratio of the true defective components and the total number of components predicted as defective. Precision = TP/TP + FP where TP and FP are true positive and false positive.
Recall		It is defined as the ratio of true defective components to the total number of defective components. *Recall = TP/TP + FN* where TP and FN are true positive and false negative.
F-measure		It is used to combine the precision and recall as a harmonic mean. $$F - measure = \frac{2 \times Recall \times Precision}{Recall + Precision}$$
Accuracy		It is used to measure the overall accuracy of the prediction. $$Acc = \frac{TP + TN}{TP + TN + FP + FN}$$
Ratio of implementation errors that have direct impact on security	Reerr	It is responsible for measuring the number of errors that directly impact security to the total number of errors in implementing the security. Rserr = Nserr/Nerr

TABLE 4.4

Security Metrics for Testing Phase

Security Metrics	Abbreviations	Description Reference [13, 14]
Security requirements considered for testing	SRCT	It tends to be shown by the proportion of the security necessity tried, and the quantity of security prerequisite assembled (NSRG).
Process effectiveness	PE	The proportion of the quantity of security weakness found (NVD) to the quantity of modules gone through security testing (MST) tends to be spoken to. PE = (N_{VD})/ (M_{ST})
Security testing ratio	STR	This shows the proportion of modules gone through security testing to the entire number of modules. STR = (M_{ST})/M
Ratio of security test cases thatfail	Rtcp	This plans to give the proportion of quantities of experiments that neglect to distinguish execution mistakes to the quantity of experiments uncommonly intended to recognize the security issues. Rtcp = |TF| / |TP| + |TF|

TABLE 4.5

Security Metrics for Maintenance Phase

Security Metrics	Abbreviations	Description Reference [13, 14]
Mean time to complete security changes	MTCSC	This intends to give the proportion of various patches delivered to deliver security weakness to the complete number of patches of the framework. MTCSC = MTTSF + MTTR
Percent of changes with security exceptions	PCSE	It is assessed by the extent of counts of completed changes with security exclusions and completed changes expanded by 100.
Ratio of patches issued to addresssecurity vulnerability	Rp	This means giving the proportion of various patches delivered to deliver security weakness to the absolute number of patches of the framework. Rp = Nsp/Np
Number of security incidentsreported	Nsr	It expects to quantify the quantity of episodes that are worried about security.

4.5 Security Metrics Development Process

A successful metric development process is helpful to decide what to measure. The metric development program is an effective mechanism to evaluate organizations' past and current security investments with proper justification. It will also provide wisdom for the decision-making process for future endeavor. It indicates a good understandability, common beliefs to ensures program effectiveness and mission support that what is the security policies have been created and implemented through security metric assistance. The following steps should be taken care at the time of developing a security metric process:

a) The goals and objectives of the metric development program must be discussed and well defined.
b) If there is any relevant metrics available, the validity of metrics must be checked through various aspects.
c) Establishment of a strong correlation between the values of matrices with core stakeholders.
d) Valid approach to generate metrics.
e) Establishment of benchmarks for proper validation and targets.
f) Metric reporting based on pre-tryout and post-tryout.
g) If, any stabile action needed to upgrade, prepare a valid plan for execution.
h) Establish a formal program review.

Without any standard system for distinguishing and creating security measurements, it gives off an impression of being worthwhile to put forth an attempt to plan such an improvement cycle to carryout security measurements right off the bat in the advancement life cycle. This facilitates tailoring security metrics to a specific organization and different stakeholder groups. It finally assesses how effectively these metrics associate with the predefined objectives of the overall security plan.

4.6 Security Metrics Development Framework

Security metric development framework is the mechanism for reliable estimation of software security quantitatively or qualitatively at the various stages of software development. A dependable quantitative or subjective assessment of programming security is profoundly attractive, and it very well may be effectively accomplished through creating security measurements at different stages. The measurements' advancement cycle includes six stages along with prescriptive strides for each and has been portrayed pictorially in Figure 4.4. This system has been proposed based on necessary and fundamental segments for planning great security metrics. The main stage begins with the conceptualization. Making arrangements for the ideal metrics is treated as a significant errand. It has been advanced as a subsequent stage, trailed by the stages named as improvement, hypothetical approval, and trial approval and bundling. An endeavor has been made to emblematically speak to the soul of planning a security metric and make the structure prescriptive followed by a concise portrayal of every of the stages containing the portrayed strides in the unique reference to advancement of metrics.

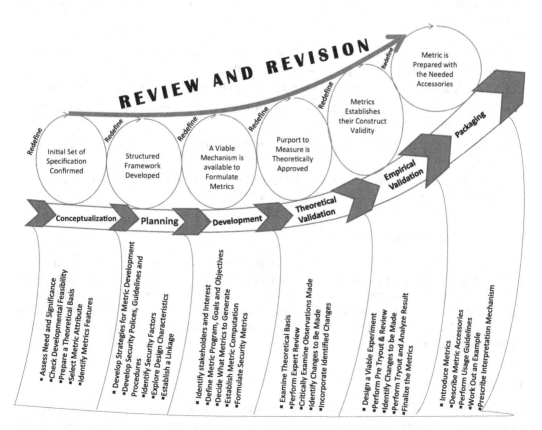

FIGURE 4.4
Security metrics development framework.

4.6.1 Premises

The accompanying premises have been viewed as when the structure is proposed to measure object-situated plan security accepting unpredictability as a key boundary:

- A basic arrangement of highlights for wanted measurements might be utilized to frame the reason for its turn of events.
- Assure consistence/adherence to gather a by and large acknowledged arrangement of attributes that great plan has.
- A coordinated methodology is needed to distinguish and persevere with all the security-explicit issues engaged with programming improvement life cycle stages.
- Identify strategies and guidelines as a wellspring of programming security measurements.
- Assure to control some way or another all the incidental and mediating factors that may influence the result-based forecast.

4.6.2 Generic Guidelines

The rules before following the cycle for evaluation of security might be recorded as follows:

- Assure consistence/recognition to gather the regular arrangement of basic and alluring highlights of the proposed philosophy.
- Identify and endure all security components to be estimated at different stages.
- Properly connect recognized credits with their characteristic property to frame related measurements.
- There is no generally settled definition for every one of the significant level security factors.
- The set of security ascribes utilized to improve the structure has been characterized operationally in the unique situation. [17]

4.6.3 Conceptualization

The comprehensive platform to address the problems and optimized solution through healthy logical screening is the foremost challenge of the conceptualization phase. Initial ideas may be assessed through various parameters to realize the problem related to facts. Facts must be validated logically, and metrics' importance comes under the existence. The development feasibility will also be evaluated that helps to build a strong theoretical basis for the preparation of metrics.

4.6.4 Planning

This phase helps find out the problem-solving solutions to succeed. It provides a complete guidance for designer and developer to work on given roadmap. This will help design and develop metrics based on strategic planning and policies on securities and procedures that are carefully reviewed to remove the anomalies. Security factors are recognized and plan qualities are investigated. Linkage between security factors and design properties are maintained for higher availability.

4.6.5 Development

There is urgent need to establish a viable mechanism to formulate metrics. It is a basic aspect of the condition of-the-practice in software security designing. All around planned metrics with reported goals may assist the association with moderating the vulnerabilities. Metrics program objectives and destinations are characterized. A metrics calculation is set up lastly assecurity metrics is planned.

4.6.6 Theoretical Validation

The fundamentals of validation are to check whether the developed models and metrics measure what they are supposed to measure. Firstly, it is responsible for taking care of the activities or steps involved to build the right product. Theoretical validation aims to ensure a theoretical basis through literature survey and analysis. Secondly, the values of used metrics are the accurate indicator for proving valid measures for design constructs and help in providing the foundation for empirical study.

4.6.7 Empirical Validation

The second step 'Experimental Validation' is to play out a tryout with sensible information to demonstrate that the created models are legitimate proportions of the ideal attributes. The approval segment is not concurred that consistency, operability, and adequacy are the shrouded factors for model advancement procedures, and mix of three proper highlights like master instinct, genuine framework estimations, and hypothetical outcomes/ investigation are the noteworthy imperatives for the level of legitimacy. In software building research, hypothetical and experimental examinations are essential to assess proposed strategies and practices to fathom how and when they work for development. Approval of models against the outcomes or conduct of different models is a procedure that should be utilized with care. Both may be invalid since they do not precisely correlate to the behavior of the basic framework. Thus, it is important to put the created security metrics under testing. Changes are distinguished and the tryout is performed. The outcome from tryout is investigated and, as an end, metrics is finished.

4.6.8 Packaging

This is the final step in the metric development process. During this phase, the developed metric is equipped with the essential amenities to become a functional product. Metrics are defined, and all of their constituents are discussed. A usage guideline is specified, along with a concise overview. Finally, a technique for implementation is suggested.

4.7 Conclusion

The participated segments for building the hypothetical structure and reflection on security measurements improvement reach following determinations:

- Security measurements improvement structure in reasonable system might be evaluated as an accumulation of the systems' individual security ascribes.
- A negligible arrangement of measurements is needed to cover all the parts of the security-related issues.

- Metrics ought to be characterized so that various individuals at various occasions or spot get similar qualities for similar frameworks.
- The improvement measure assists with assessing the nature of programming and giving the product ventures quotes, which encourages the assessment and arranging of the new exercises.
- Informal survey and updates ought to be done throughout whole periods of programming security appraisal measure.

So as to give a huge improvement that is expected to assess security, some critical issues concerning security metric advancement system are as per the following:

- The proposed system sets up an approach to relate quantifiable attributes to programming security, and further it likewise builds up a relationship between different security issues and its elements.
- The proposed structure may frame a reason for security ordering of programming item.
- The proposed structure might be utilized as a source of perspective for the analysts working in the region of programming security to create other philosophy for measuring security through the advancement life cycle.
- Industry experts might utilize the proposed structure to put a security rating of their items.
- The business specialists might utilize the proposed structure to rank the business in the light of security, like quality confirmation or rating.

Key Terms

Software Security, Security Metrics, Security Metric Framework, Security Metric Development Process.

Point to Ponder

1. Development of secure programming which can withstand assaults is a developing requirement for the present condition.
2. Without evaluation nothing can be anticipated. Thus, evaluation of security and weakness is essential to help anticipate the insusceptibility and versatility of the product.
3. Quantification of programming security at a beginning phase empowers the assessment and appraisal of security and provides the premise for evaluating

security innovations. Evaluation of security will assist with compromising security objectives and cost.

4. A security metric is an arrangement of related measurements empowering evaluation of the level of opportunity from the chance of experiencing harm or misfortune malignant assault.

5. A security measurements achievability model understands the sufficient degree of prerequisites, and this level is subject to the capacity of the dynamic for security measurements. It closes as the attainability levels accentuate the believability of security measurements, their pertinence to be used, the estimation approach, and their adequacy for the planned use.

Objective-Type Questions

1. Intruders are the most common sort of security threat, and they are as follows:
   a) To account access
   b) To data access
   c) Hacker
   d) To computer access

2. What must be recognized in terms of risk identification?
   a) All the threats
   b) Consequences
   c) Vulnerabilities
   d) All of the above

3. What is jeopardizing the software's quality and timeliness?
   a) Business risks
   b) Project risks
   c) Known risks
   d) Technical risks

4. What is a flaw in a computer-based system that may be exploited to produce loss or harm?
   a) Attack
   b) Various Threats
   c) Vulnerabilities
   d) Exposure

5. A chemical plant system may detect high pressure and operate a relief valve to lower it before an explosion happens. What type of dependability and security concern is stated in the example?
   a) Hazard avoidance
   b) Damage limitation
   c) Hazard detection
   d) Hazard detection and removal

6. The components of pragmatic security metrics are
   a)   Accuracy
   b)   Cost effectiveness
   c)   Relevance
   d)   All of the above

7. Security testing ration indicates
   a)   Ratio of modules undergone security testing to the total number of modules
   b)   Ratio of the security requirement tested, and the number of security requirement gathered
   c)   Measure the number of incidents that are concerned with security
   d)   All of the above

8. Which are the security metrics for design phase?
   a)   Critical Class Coupling
   b)   Critical Class Extensibility
   c)   Classified Methods Extensibility
   d)   All of the above

9. What are the phases of security metric development process?
   a)   Conceptualization
   b)   Validation
   c)   Routing
   d)   None of these

10. What are the security metrics for coding and implementation phase?
   a)   Stall Ratio
   b)   Percent of Security Coding Aspects
   c)   Number of Security Errors
   d)   Security Testing Ratio

Short-Answer Type Questions

1. What answer will you get from the developed security metrics?

2. What decisions will be supported from security metrics?

3. What will be the environmental context for the development of specific security metrics?

4. Write down the procedure for the collection of data regarding measurement.

5. How the developed security metrics are matured and are they capable to reduce risk?

6. Identify the factors for good security metrics and bad security metrics.

7. What percentage of the applications has been reviewed with respect to the acceptable level of security?

8. Define the mechanism to identify the reference point used for comparison.

9. Write down the involved steps to provide the accuracy of given security metrics.

10. Write down the goals and measurement process for SMART security metrics.

Descriptive Questions

1. What will be the level of software security metrics coverage to comply with security policies?

2. What are the existing software security metrics used for different phases of software development life cycle?

3. Write down the various factors and steps involved in the development of software security metric development.

4. What do you mean by security metrics? Explain about the components of SMART, IDEAL, and PRAGMATIC security metrics?

5. What do you understand by absolute measurement? In which context software security metrics are helpful to finalize the potential solution for self-assessment and risk management?

6. 'Security metrics are the best tools for quantification and decision making process'. Justify your answer.

7. Write down the appropriate security metrics for object-oriented software at design phase.

8. What are the advantages and limitations of security metrics? Why does a project manager need to estimate through various metrics?

9. Suppose you are developing a project and you have estimated various analyses through object-oriented security design metrics. Can you predict that quantified values of security are strong or weak hypothesis?

10. What problem you face when you are developing several versions of the same product? How these metrics are helpful? Justify your answer.

References

1. G. McGraw,*"Software Security": Building Security*, Addison-Wesly, 2006.
2. S. Islam and P. Falcarin,"Measuring Security Requirements for Software Security",*10th International Conference on Cybernetic Intelligent Systems (CIS)*, IEEE, 2011, pp. 70–75, ISBN 978-1-4673-0687-4, DOI: 10.1109/CIS.2011.6169137.
3. G. McGraw and B. Potter,"Software Security Testing",*IEEE Security & Privacy*, 2(5),2004, 81–85.
4. D.S. Herrmann, *Complete Guide to Security and Privacy Metrics*, Auerbach Publications, ISBN: 0-8493-5402-1, 2007.
5. M. Swanson, N. Bartol, J. Sabato, J. Hash, and L. Graffo, "Security Metrics Guide for Information Technology Systems", NIST Special Publication 800–55, National Institute of Standards and Technology, 2003.
6. J. A. Chaula, L. Yngstrom, and S. Kowalski, "Security Metrics and Evolution of Information Systems Security", *Proc. of the 4th Annual Conference on Information Security for South Africa*, 2004.
7. S. C. Payne, *A Guide To Security Metrics*, SANS Institute Information Security Assignment version 1.2e, 2006, Web reference: https://www.sans.org/white-papers/55/, Last Access 20 June 2022.
8. P. Goodman, *Software Metrics: Best Practices for Successful IT Management*, Rothstein Associates Inc., August 2004.

9. B. Alshammari, C. Fridge, and D. Corney, "Developing Secure System: A Comparative Study of Existing Methodologies", *Lecture Notes on Software Engineering*, 2(2), May 2016, 139–146, DOI: 10.7763/LNSE.2016.V4.239.

10. R. M. Savola, "A Security Metrics Development Method for Software Intensive Systems", *Advances in Information Security and its Application, Communications in Computer and Information Science*, 36, Springer, 2009, 11–16.

11. J. A. Wang, H. Wang, M. Guo, and M. Xia, "Security Metrics for Software Systems", *In the Proc. of ACMSE*, March 19–21, Clemson, SC, USA, 2009.

12. P. K. Manadhata and J. M. Wing, "An Attack Surface Metric," Technical Report. School of Computer Science, Carnegie Mellon University (CMU), 2005,CMU-CS-05-155.

13. S. Jain, and M. Ingle, "Security Metrics and Software Development Progression," *Journal of Engineering Research and Applications*, 4(5), ISSN: 2248–9622, 2014, (Version 7), 161–167.

14. K. Sultan, A. En-Nouaary, and A. H-Lhadj, "Catalog for Assessing Risks of Software throughout the Software Development Life Cycle,"*The Proc. of International Conference on Information Security and Assurance*, IEEE, 2008, pp. 461–465.

15. I. Chowdhury, B. Chan, and M. Zulkerine, "Security Metrics for Source Code Structures," *Proceedings of the Fourth International Workshop on Software Engineering For Secure Systems*, ACM, 2008, pp. 57–64.

16. S.A. Ansar, R.A. Khan and Alka, "A Phase-wise Review of Software Security Metrics", *Networking Communication and Data Knowledge Engineering* (pp. 15–25), January 2018. DOI: 10.1007/978-981-10-4600-1_2.

17. A. Agrawal and R. A. Khan. Software Security Metric Development Framework (An Early Stage Approach). *American Journal of Software Engineering and Applications*, 2(6), 2013, 150–155. DOI: 10.11648/j.ajsea.20130206.14

18. V. H. Nguyen and L.M.S. Tran, "Predicting Vulnerable Software Components with Dependency Graphs," *Proceedings of the 6th International Workshop on Security Measurements and Metrics*, 2010, ISBN: 978-1-4503-0340-8, DOI: 10.1145/1853919.1853923.

19. O. S. Saydjari, "Risk: A Good System Security Measure," *Proceedings of the 30th Annual International Computer Software and Applications Conference (COMPSAC'06)*, 0-7695-2655-1/06 $20.00, IEEE, 2006.

20. S. Naqvi and M. Riguidel, "*Quantifiable Security Metrics for Large Scale Heterogeneous Systems,*" 1-4244-0174-7/06/$20.00, IEEE, 2006, pp. 209–215.

21. W. Qu and D. Zhang, "Security Metrics Models and Application with SVM in Information Security Management," 1-4244-0973-X/07/$25.00, IEEE, 2007, pp. 3234–3238.

22. A. Ozment, "Software Security Growth Modeling: Examining Vulnerabilities with Reliability Growth Models," *Quality of Protection: Security Measurements and Metrics*, Dieter Gollman, Fabio Massacci and Yautsiukhin (Eds.), Artsiom.

23. J. M. Wing, "Software Security," *First Joint IEEE/IFIP Symposium on Theoretical Aspects of Software Engineering (TASE'07)*, 0-7695-2856-2/07 $20.00, IEEE, 2007.

24. Software Security Assurance, "State-of-the-Art Report (SOAR) Information Assurance Technology Analysis Center (IATAC) Data and Analysis Center for Software (DACS) Joint endeavor by IATAC with DACS," July 31, 2007.

25. A. J. A. Wang, "Information Security Models and Metrics," *43rd ACM Southeast Conference*, ACM, March 18–20, Kennesaw, GA, USA, 2005, pp. 178–184.

26. J. Hallberg, A. Hunstad, and M. Peterson, "A Framework for System Security Assessment," *Proceedings of the 2005 IEEE Workshop on Information Assurance and Security, United States Military Academy*, West Point, NY, 2005, pp. 224–231.

27. O. S. Saydjari, "Is Risk a Good Security Metric?" *QoP'06*, ACM 1-59593-553-3/06/0010, Alexandria, VA, October 30, 2006, pp. 59–60.

28. D. A. Chapin and S. Akridge, "How Can Security Be Measured?" *Information Systems Control Journal*, 2,2005.

29. C. Cowan, "Relative Vulnerability: An Empirical Assurance Metric," Presented at the *44th International Federation for Information Processing Working Group 10.4 Workshop on Measuring Assurance in Cyberspace*, Monterey, CA, 25–29, June 2003.

30. F. Stevens, Validation of an Intrusion-Tolerant Information System Using Probabilistic Modeling, MS thesis, University of Illinois, Urbana-Champaign, Illinois, 2004, Web reference: https://www.perform.illinois.edu/people/fabrice-stevens/, Last access: July 2022.

31. O.H. Alhazmi, Y. K. Malaiya, and I. Ray, "Security Vulnerabilities in Software Systems: A Quantitative Perspective," *Proceedings of the IFIP WG 11.3 Working Conference on Data and Applications Security*, Storrs, CT, August 2005.

32. R. R. Barton, W. J. Hery, and P. Liu, "An S-vector for Web Application Security Management," Working Paper, Pennsylvania State University, University Park, PA, January 2004.

33. S. Martin, "Software Security Evaluation Based on a Top-Down Mc Call-Like Approach," *IEEE*, 1988, pp. 414–418.

34. D. B. Aredo, "Metrics for Quantifying the Impacts of Monitoring on Security of Adaptive Distributed Systems," Master Thesis Proposal – II, December 2005.

35. R. Savola, "Towards Security Metrics Taxonomy for the Information and Communication Technology Industry," *International Conference on Software Engineering Advances (ICSEA 2007)*, 0-7695-2937-2/07,2007, IEEE.

Useful Links

https://www.csoonline.com
https://www.educause.edu/focus-areas-and-initiatives/policy-and-security/cybersecurity-program/resources/information-security-guide
https://www.networkworld.com
http://www.cisoplatform.com
https://www.bsimm.com/framework/governance/software-security-metrics-strategy.html
https://www.securitymetrics.com/pci
https://misti.com/infosec-insider/selling-security-metrics-to-the-board-of-directors

5

Software Security Estimation

Simple can be harder than complex: You have to work hard to get your thinking clean to make it simple. But it's worth it in the end because once you get there, you can move mountains.

Steve Jobs

The present age is an era of Digitalism; every sector and industry is regulated by a software-based digital automated system. Technology is used everywhere in everything you use and run in everyday life as from your phone, a wireless wristband to automated parking lots [1]. In its very heart, the world has felt an explosive effect of software and the IT industry, and the need for security design in people's everyday lives has made it imperative that new designs and new security technologies be built so that advanced technology can be implemented in a variety of applications. Security engineers' assigned work is changing very rapidly, reflecting developments in technology as well as growing new specializations that continue to develop in this sector along with employers' priorities and practices [2]. This type of global technological use and adaptation generates high-risk factors for these systems that are commonly used for transacting and controlling, as well as storing sensitive public and private data in everyday life. Software security is a mechanism that relies on a pro-active approach, i.e. in order for software developers to achieve high protection, pro-active approaches to security that build and enforce information security elements [3]. Furthermore, the pro-active approach to software development implies that the primary and successful impact of software and the protection of software are recognized.

In any sector, digitalization is not only important today, but it is also the best way to increase income for any sector [4]. The key benefits of the digital revolution were fast communication and convenient access at manageable costs and time investments. In any kind of digital presence of an organization, software has a central function. Through its secure architecture, software is built to meet the structural needs of the company. In cases of data violation accidents, however, growing software dependence also leads to doubtful growth. A cyber security evaluation study shows that nearly 54% of the organizations acknowledged that at least one violation of their organization was recorded last year [4, 5]. The study also states that the data ratio can be much higher as many businesses have not reported violations. Many businesses believed that such a disclosure would impact their customers' confidence and cause revenue loss as well as damage to the brand image. In another article, British Airways reported that its software failure problem had been hampered in 2019 [6, 7]. The failure caused approximately 100 aircrafts to be cancelled while the schedule for other 200 airways flights was interrupted. This scenario has increased the demand for the production and maintenance of applications with enhanced safety in order to protect user and organizational data. The instances of data breaches have put huge pressure on developers to build safe software that is protected from breaches. Security is a difficult and dynamic challenge because of the complexity of protection to ensure and sustain stupidity.

DOI: 10.1201/9781003330516-5

Software security is a dynamic measure since it relies on multiple variables and strategies. It is a crucial job to analyze these factors to handle software protection. Therefore, the developers concentrate on designing stable applications from the software's very design stage to achieve this objective. Since the design phase, the developers have been trying to incorporate safety features and identify potential infringement risks in software. The software is therefore designed in line with built security requirements and design models. Moreover, to underline this problem, this chapter effectively tries to portray a description of various factors and risk attributes of software that create loopholes and exploitation possibilities in software from its design phase.

5.1 Objectives

- Understanding and portraying a general understanding about the software security concept, its different techniques, and obstacles that appear in the path of security management.
- Identifying the factors that directly influence security of software.
- Underlining a technique of pointing out application design analysis that gives an additional technique to examiners for identifying loopholes in software's.
- Identifying directly influencing factors of the vulnerability of object-oriented software design.
- Discovering the standard framework available to minimize vulnerability propagation in design phase.
- Portraying a systematic approach for evaluating security assurance and condition of security in software.
- Providing information about different techniques of security evaluation.
- Underlining the concept as an informative manner the chapter gives an additional informative character where reader can utilize the knowledge of chapter into their expert use.
- Identifying different threats and vulnerabilities of software from its development phase.

5.2 Security Estimation

The level of security assurance and survey execution needs a software security assessment [7]. Bothersome dangers exploit equipment and software shortcomings or weaknesses that can affect the infringement and the breakdown of accessibility, honesty, secrecy, and non-repudiation just as different parts of software security, for example, confirmation, protection, and encryption. And IT industry endures shocking harms because of the absence of security assessment before a software release. The security policies and estimation groups can work together during the structure stage to make software secure.

During the structure stage, the software is in incredibly pliant stages. In order to associate financial expansion and security concerns during the rearranging of software is an ideal domain that needs attention. Expansion of security attributes in software development is a matter of comparative analysis [8, 9]. Authors believe that security expansion and implementation in software is a matter of planning and experimental results. A systematic plan and result sensitivity can help the experts in achieving highly secure and diverse software. Tempering the security planning and management of software development can produce errors and issues in software development. A systematic process of security expansion and development is immense need for software developers. Different attributes of software and security are directly and indirectly always affecting the security of software and its development. This type of situation always creates sensitivity and challenging task for software developers.

5.2.1 Software Security Estimation

Structuring secure software depends on the use of secure software plan standards. These standards will be examined in this part and structure is the major reason for software affirmation. Software security confirmation has been given numerous definitions, and it is critical to comprehend the idea. The reason for increasing legitimate certainty that software will reliably display everything properties needed to guarantee that the software, inactivity, will keep on working constantly notwithstanding the nearness of supported flaws. In pragmatic terms, such software must have the option to oppose most assaults, endure, however many as could be expected under the circumstances of those assaults it can't avoid, and contains the harm and recoup to a typical degree of activity at the earliest opportunity after any attack it can't avoid or endure.

Moreover, a secure software theory is only implemented by a secure architecture and design of software. To understand the concept of secure software more clearly and descriptively authors categorize different attributes of security software in following headings [10, 11]:

- **Confidentiality**: It refers the ability of the system or software to maintain information privacy at any cost.
- **Integrity**: This ability refers the quality of software that can prevent unauthorized alteration and modification of information.
- **Availability**: It is an ability that helps the software in managing continues data availability and maintains authorized access to data.
- **Authentication**: A process to identify the authorized user identity in software.
- **Authorization**: It is a process to identify the access grants for any user.
- **Accounting**: Managing the history of data transactions and travel in between software users.
- **Non-Repudiation**:It gives ability to software for managing the accountability of every user. It means that no user can deny his activity on software if it is genuine.

All these are various attributes of secure software that play a key role in maintaining security in between software. But that's not all the security implementation which can prevent software security. Whether, there are various other types of models for secure software which can enhance the security performance of software and manage the data security in software architecture. Some significant and key models are written following.

A. Access Control Model

This type of models helps the software developers in managing access of data inn software [12].

- **Bell-LaPadula Confidentiality Model**–This model directly inherit the security of software attributes and works on them. Two rules by using which Bell-LaPadula works are: the Simple Secured Property and the Security Property. "No read up" are there is stated by the simple security. An object at a higher classification level is not read by a subject at a specific classification level. "No write down" is the * Security Property. A lower classification level is not written by a subject at a higher classification level.

- **Take Grant**–I this type of access control the authorized user gives his rights to a guest user or another user as a grant for some special condition or time. This access control system works on a right to manage flow i. e. the granted user only have the permission which are allowed by real authorized user and cannot over flow his permission as well as all the management rights are always available for authorized user.

- **Role-Based Access Control** During this access manage system every user or end node has its own permission and rights according to their responsibility and role in organizational infrastructure. These provided rights and permission are totally inherited by the actual responsibility of user and does not allow them to overwrite or get uncased information or permissions.

- **MAC (Mandatory Access Control) Model**–It is a totally automated system of access management where the deciding of permission is not subject to owner of system whether it is a job of operating system to allow and restrict permission according to requirement.

- **DAC (Discretionary Access Control) Model**–This is a just opposite to the MAC model here owner of system has the rights to assign permissions and access instead of operating system.

B. Integrity Models

This type of system gives a quality of software in managing data integrity and originality in software [13].

- **Biba Integrity Model** – It is a first model that assures integrity in any type of system. It is a model with two rule simple rule and integrity simplicity model. The simple integrity model gives a secure data alteration where lower level of data does not have permission and rights to alter higher level of data. The supporting objective of this type of system is that the system of integrity management provides unauthorized alteration of data from lower level of data. This type of integrity model provides a layering security by restricting low level of data to alert and modify higher one.

- **Clark-Wilson**– This model also works on the two rule policy where the first rule is an object related classification and second one is categorization of data in system. The model ensures integrity of system by providing a security at an execution time via referring application layer of system.

C. Information Flow Model

Data transaction between two points of communications is considered via this type of systems [14].

The Chinese Wall Model– This type of model gives a security to data transaction in system or infrastructures. The system works on a mediator less model. In simple words during this type of system there is no data mediator policy available that restricts data for some amount of time and verifies it. The model gives a secure verification process at sending and receiving points for assurance only.

- **Estimation Model**

Approximately every developed and developing country has its own estimating policies and standards to evaluate security. The USA has its own;Canada has its own; and the European Union also has its own high data criteria standards. An extremely effective and useful policy of data scanning and verification is added by Finnish authorities that is later adopted by approximately every country in world. Security estimation of software's is a combined process of metrics, models and attributes. Attributes has a unique and significant role in measuring the security of software. It is always necessary during security certification any software to measure its attributes condition and security effect. Moreover, the security of the software is ensured if formal and numerical techniques are utilized, yet it makes the framework building so perplexing cycle that the conventional strategies are only sometimes used to improve framework security. Formal Methods ought to be perceived during framework security building to give devices to more profound security investigation whenever required.

It is a long-recognizable worldview that an activity or movement cannot be controlled in the event that it cannot be estimated. Software security additionally comes in this rubric. As of not long ago, the security appraisal measure is done after the improvement of software utilizing subjective rules by security specialists, which is a costly issue. The issue lies in, knowing how and when it ought to be estimated. To underline the summarized concept of software security estimation briefly and provide solid facts, we give a three-phase model that can effectively help in measuring software security is directed in Figure 5.1.

Phase 1: Input Process

- High level Diagram (HLD)/Low Level diagram (LLD)

Phase 2: Security Estimation Process

- Identify Security Factors
- Identity/Design Metric
- Suite Validate Metric Suite
- Quantify Security Factors
- Estimate Security

Phase 3: Output Process

- Qualitative Analysis
- Overall Security analysis

FIGURE 5.1
Software security estimation.

As a working culture of proposed model inn this heading first phase is an initial start level of assessment where examiner develop the basic flow chart and diagrams that are required for estimation. Further, as second step of evaluation examiner apply the adopted approach of estimation and assess factors, and level of security in system. After identifying all these required information's and data now as third and most important phase of estimation examiner analyze the whole overview of security in system as numerically and conceptually.

- **Different Security Models**

Data and its security quintessence ensure level of standards in system. The existence where information has been just accessed in physical documents is a distant memory. The focal point of physical information security is moved to digital information security. In any case, know: Crucial standards of hundreds of years of physical information assurance are as yet important today. Particularly standards identified with the elusive delicate issues when information is shared. It is evidently prove that a strong prevention mechanism is needed for tackling various types of cyberattacks like identity theft, access over ruling and many others. More specifically, the easiest and most important measure of attack is confidentiality loss where the data is not private only for authorized one. Authors strongly believe that managing confidentiality can only be achieved by applying security standards from every aspect of system. Moreover, applying security standards is not an easy cup of cake right now and it is also important for experts to manage and understand existing security matrices.There are various security evaluation and analysis models are available in present and some are described below.

- **Privacy-Management Reference Model**

The main and most significant objective of this framework is written in following bullet points:

- Overlooking the standards of security and privacy in system by outlining every node and aspect of possible loopholes.
- Selecting and adopting some special type of tools and techniques that have the ability to apply extra expansion of security in system and prevent future vulnerability exploitation.

This type of framework is essentially used and beneficial for evaluating existing systems and useful in assess effectiveness of security.

- **NIST Security Framework**

At whatever point you want to draw a cycle with respect to a security or danger measures: oppose the allurement! The US based NIST association is a notable administrative association that offers incredible distributions on all conceivable subjects with respect to security is shown in Figure 5.2. This type of framework for estimation gives ability to examiner for fetching every aspect of system security. In simple wordings the framework is easy to access and underline every node of security requirements and report them in final estimation. In the event that you ever want to make your own security system, reconsider. Generally, required steps for assessment are associated in this model and every step that is associated in framework has its own specific functionality and need.

- **Software Assurance Maturity Model**

This framework is developed and managed for estimating security in software's and numerically quantify the standards of their security clearly. This is a helpful asset in the event that you are dealing in software security as its attribute. Figuring measures isn't profitable, so utilize this important wellspring of data as opposed to wasting time. The main attributes and significance of model is written down and shown in Figure 5.3.

- Understanding the present standards and techniques of security in enterprise by assessment.
- After identifying the security standards and policies in software now it's time to develop new policies based on current assessment.
- Develop supplementary material for helping developed security metrics in organization.
- Routinely assess and identify security loopholes in organizational security.

FIGURE 5.2
NIST security framework.

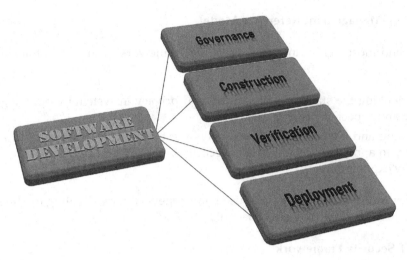

FIGURE 5.3
SAMM model.

5.2.2 Security Risk Estimation

Risk assessment is a process that produces potential report on possible loopholes in security [15]. This process applies various standards and analysis techniques in order to assess potential vulnerability points in organization security. The process associates with every node and asset of organization in consideration as well as applies security standardization in security factoring. These associated factors are organizational projects, time taken in execution of projects, works their flow of work and many other same points.

Whenever, the risk assessment report get fails to bridge a proper security factoring and classification in organization there is need to apply more standardized and systematic evaluation process.

   I. *Identification*: Apply assessment of basic assets and functionality of organization.

  II. *Assessment*: Rate every process; asset and function of organization in a standard of possible threat for quantitatively measure their impact and future possibilities.

 III. *Mitigation*: After rating the asset and every other attribute of organization it is a step which combines the remedy of risk which has more sever scale in the comparison of less sever.

 IV. *Prevention*: This phase of evaluation associate possible countermeasures and prevention techniques that an organization adopts after identifying and mitigating risk.

5.2.2.1 Significance of Risk Estimation

In order to secure organization software risk estimation model helps a lot. Risk estimation processes give an ideal path to organize in order to protect their following assets:

- Organization asset analysis and severity level identification.
- Risk profile for every specific asset in organizing.
- It is also important for organization to assess that what type of harm a risk factor can give to organization.

- Risk report and assessment ratings significantly contribute inn business policy making and their future use.
- The risk evaluation also has significant contribution in employee management an employee assessment report helps the organization in identifying possible harmful employees in organization.

This is a significant point for organizational security that risk assessment and repotting is not only for once in an organizational life. The process is a routine rotation process which combines every aspect of organization every time. A routine checkup in risk assessment is very beneficial for organization.

5.2.2.2 Software Security Risk Estimation

Risk defines a situation involving exposure to danger. It implies future insecurity about divergence from expected sources.It can be assess through indentifying, estimating and prioritizing risk on operational and organizational behaviors by using information system. It can be done using mentioned factors like the knowing the asset risk, by knowing the criticality of risk and what will be the impact of this vulnerability into the system. Proper assessment of above mentioned logical constructs can be represented as a formula for risk estimation.

$$\text{Risk} = \text{Asset}^*\text{Threat}^*\text{Vulnerability}$$

Various ways available to collect information for assessing risks are as follows:

- To conductinterview from data owners and other employees
- To analyze systems and other infrastructure
- To review document and other relevant sources for information gathering

The following steps are highly required for risk assessment depicted in Figure 5.4

Step 1: Find out all assets which are most valuable for organization to protect from harm under threats. These are as follows:
  - Data Servers
  - Customer credentials
  - Transaction data
  - Trade Agreement documents
  - Website

Step 2: Now find out the potential consequences that can damage our asset including data loss and legal consequences.

Step 3: Next step to identify threats and their impact level. Some examples are given as follows:
  - System Failure
  - Malicious actions
  - Natural disasters
  - Accidental human interfaces

Step 1 • Finding of valuable assets

Step 2 • Identify potential consequences

Step 3 • Identify threats and their level

Step 4 • Identify vulnerabilities and assess the likelihood

Step 5 • Assess risk

Step 6 • Create a risk management plan

Step 7 • Create a strategy

Step 8 • Define mitigation processes

Step 9 • Event → Response → Analysis → Mitigation

FIGURE 5.4
Steps for risk assessment.

Step 4: All weaknesses must be identified that can harm an asset. First of all Identify vulnerabilities and assess the likelihood to know the impact and mitigation mechanism can be applied to minimize damages.

Step 5: Risk assessment will specify that arising vulnerability having potential to lead monetary loss against exploitation. By using logical formulas we may categories these risk into various severities like high, moderate, and low along with estimates of its cost.

Step 6: An example to understand the risk management plan according to threat, vulnerability, asset and consequences, risk, and their solution is depicted in Figure 5.5.

Step 7: Build policyfor information technology infrastructure improvement to diminish the most considerable vulnerabilities and find administration sign-off.

Step 8: This step highly required the mitigation process to improve information technology security infrastructure by identifying the least harmful consequences.

Step 9: An example of simple mitigation process defined for a server failure is shown in Figure 5.6.

Threat	Vulnerability	Asset and Consequences	Risk	Solution
High	High	Critical	High	Instant Action Required
High	Low	Critical	High	Need Protection
Moderate	Very Low	Critical	Very Low	No Action Needed
High	Low	Moderate	Low	Continue with full observation

FIGURE 5.5
Example on risk management plan.

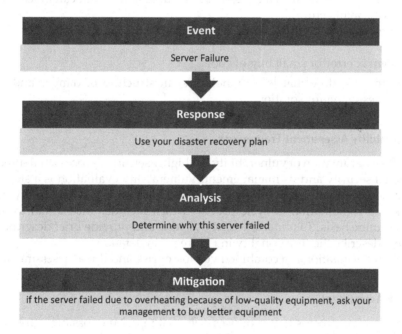

FIGURE 5.6
An example of simple mitigation process.

5.2.3 Vulnerability Assessment

This is an evaluation process which includes assessment of vulnerability in organization. Vulnerability is generally referred for a point of issue in organization that has potential to be a harmful exploitation possibility in future. Vulnerability points and issues get changed according to the nature of businesses and organizations. The potential of vulnerabilities are also different and diverse in every organization based on their resources and environmental needs. The growing rate of vulnerability is a matter of high rate in digitalization with low-rate infrastructure. The loopholes in technical structures and designs create possibilities of exploitation in organizational security.

A vulnerability assessment model can provide following significant contributions toward security.

- Assessment of basic assets and functionality of organization.
- Risk profile for every specific asset in organizing.
- It is also important for organization to assess that what type of harm a risk factor can give to organization.
- Risk report and assessment ratings significantly contribute inn business policy making and their future use.
- The risk evaluation also has significant contribution in employee management an employee assessment report helps the organization in identifying possible harmful employees in organization.

Thereafter, discussing about the fundamentals about vulnerability now it is important and significant to discuss about the characteristics of vulnerability that can give an ideal overview to security architecture.

Classifying vulnerability in security perspective has the following possibilities:

- Code syntax error or small bug of code.
- A design level flow that leads whole system structure in danger and requires reverse designing for solution.

5.2.4 Vulnerability Assessment Framework

As stated above, evaluation of vulnerability is a highly sensitive process that directly affects organizational security and its management. Vulnerability evaluation is a step of various phases that associate initiation to management classifications. Vulnerability assessment framework is a combination of cycle process which includes idea initial to monitoring phase on a routine basis. To underline all the aspects and provide brief description of process, authors describe the functionality in Figure 5.7 in detail.

Vulnerability evaluation is a combined version of risk and threat assessment.

5.2.4.1 Risk Assessment

Risk assessment is a process that produces potential report on possible loopholes in security. This process applies various standards and analysis techniques in order to assess

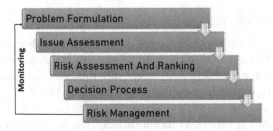

FIGURE 5.7
Vulnerability assessment model.

potential vulnerability points in organization security. The process associates every node and asset of organization in consideration as well as applies security standardization in security factoring.

5.2.4.2 Risk Minimization or Management

It is a process that uses ratings of assessment phase and then categorizes it based on the severity level of risk. More harmful risk points are considered as highly sever and low possible risk points are considered as low sever in rating of risk phase. After rating, those examiners apply management and mitigation optioning on them based on their specific ratings.

5.2.4.3 Monitoring and Adaptive Management

The phase compiles routine checkup and management of risk in a cycle process.

5.2.4.4 Some Other Security Estimating Procedures

It is evidently proven that a strong prevention mechanism is needed for tackling various types of cyberattacks like identity theft, access over ruling and many others. More specifically, the easiest and most important measure of attack is confidentiality loss where the data is not private only for authorized one. Authors strongly believe that managing confidentiality can only be achieved by applying security standards from every aspect of system. Some other famous approaches are described in the following sections:

- **NIST Security framework**

At whatever point you want to draw a cycle with respect to a security or danger measures: oppose the allurement! The US-based NIST association is a notable administrative association that offers incredible distributions on all conceivable subjects with respect to security. This type of framework for estimation gives ability to examiner for fetching every aspect of system security. In simple wordings, the framework is easy to access and underlines every node of security requirements and reports them in final estimation. In the event that you ever want to make your own security system, reconsider. Generally, required steps for assessment are associated with this model, and every step that is associated with framework has its own specific functionality and need.

- **Privacy-Management Reference Model**

The main and the most significant objective of this framework is written in the following bullet points:

- Overlooking the standards of security and privacy in system by outlining every node and aspect of possible loopholes.
- Selecting and adopting some special type of tools and techniques that have the ability to apply extra expansion of security in system and prevent future vulnerability exploitation.

This type of framework is essentially used and beneficial for evaluating existing systems and useful in assess effectiveness of security.

- **Software Assurance Maturity Model**

This framework is developed and managed for estimating security in software and numerically quantify the standards of their security clearly. This is a helpful asset in the event that you are dealing in software security as its attribute. Figuring measures isn't profitable, so utilize this important wellspring of data as opposed to wasting time. The main attributes and significance of model is written down.

- Understanding the present standards and techniques of security in enterprise by assessment.
- After identifying the security standards and policies in software, now it's time to develop new policies based on current assessment.
- Develop supplementary material for helping developed security metrics in organization.
- Routinely assess and identify security loopholes in organizational security.

5.3 Security Profiling

Profiling of software is something that needs to be available at software development life cycle process. It opens a door for designer to understand other attributes and functionality of software that are hidden because of some reasons. There are a lot of features and use of software available that come into existence after its development, but unfortunately software has no abilities to compile their platforms and utilities properly. This type of situation mostly creates software crash situations. Proper profiling and classification of software is a complimentary step that associates risk modeling and assessment in it. A great profiling can produce effective and useful software to industry that can open wings to developers in developing profile-based software development. Figure 5.8 depicts a profiling plan with the following components.

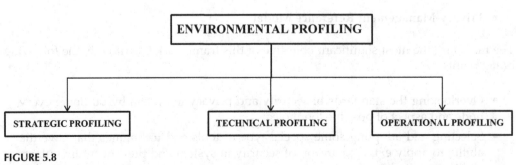

FIGURE 5.8
Profiling plan.

5.3.1 Environmental Profiling

It is always necessarily required by examiners and analysts to identify physical, virtual, and non-materialistic components of organization for assessment. It is always hard to classify and collect every piece of asset properly in identification process because of its diverse nature. Environmental profiling gives additional components in organization structure by separating every environmental need at one lace that is useful in every type of assessment and development is depicted in Figure 5.9.

Environmental profiling is a process that is performed by a profiler's team and it associate every requirement and assessment needs of examiners as well as organization. This type of situation and process ensures update condition of assets and assure the environmental needs are highly compatible to organizational requirements. A standard process of profiling and adopted approach security profiling has its own set of predefined rules for associating environmental profiling in organizations. Some steps are described below:

- Special Profiling tool needed;
- Any other profiling needs;
- The capturing or profiling process does not intent to harm organizational needs and perform any unwanted activity in it,

To make it more easier and adoptive for developers, experts try to provide a more real feeling in profiling they adopt highly configured tools and approaches to perform profiling and measure its sensitivity in the comparison of real development processes. To understand the concept in more simple words, consider that if a system is designed for compatibility work on different platforms then in a profiling section of it the system choose whether to include all compatible platforms in profiling or run with only risky ones.

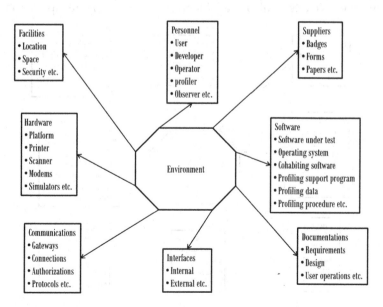

FIGURE 5.9
Environmental profiling.

5.3.2 Strategic Profiling

This heading includes all the needy information's and requirements needed for understanding the profiling concept in security. Strategic profiling is a process of underlining the whole profiling process and developing its needy requirements and framework for flow.To conduct profiling at each phase should be explained with the context of particular phase, every step has its own input and output standard as well as path in framework for smooth flow of operations. This section of chapter provides a whole concept of profiling and its requirements in brief as well as it also pose the steps associated in profiling for development.

Considering every aspects and functionality of software's is essentially required for profiling steps. These considerations develop a systematic strategy for profiling that can reduce effective results and provide a strategic outcome in order to produce organizational security on priority.

The standard for the profiling strategy is developed and send to strategic profiling section as a pre-process before it starts. It is required to set some mile stones or point of verification that gives an idea about which process is completed or which is not yet. For example, consider that there is a project that associate checking of some processes in which the profiling is only done for 80% of processes and remaining processes are on standby. Now to provide a clear and systematic process to examiner it is require having a milestone gap that gives an idea about running status of operation. Figure 5.10 illustrates some typical influences on strategic decision.

5.3.3 Technical Profiling

Another major issue in profiling specification that should be addressed is the selection of appropriate tools and automation. Tools are the most significant and beneficial factor for profiling team that gives an additional power to them. A good tool selection helps them in producing highly effective result whether, if the selection of tool is wrong then there are so very serious aversive effects also available in profiling. There are applications and tools

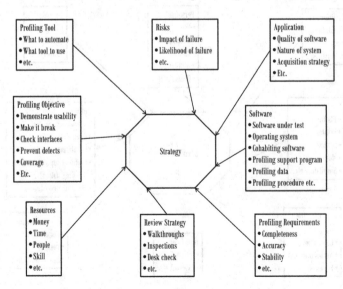

FIGURE 5.10
Strategic profiling.

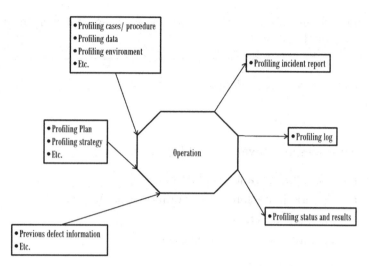

FIGURE 5.11
Operational profiling.

available that has their reuse instruction which says that use them with calm mood and run in a free platform with extra time because good items take long time to be created. Further, in order to select tool it is always important to classify examiners requirement. Tools are totally based on the requirements and there is also no tool available which allow a user to achieve all his requirements because of the diverse nature of requirements. This type of situation creates a condition for examiners where they have to use same kind of more than one tool at a same time for getting different perspectives and results in order to achieve great results.

5.3.4 Operational Profiling

This is a profiling step which associate information about the every profiling operation and monitor them on a routine cyclic process basis. The association of operational information includes every type of information about profiling operations and their status also whether they are in run or standby condition is described in Figure 5.11. To make a documentation for operational profiling examiners need to prepare test result reports, logs and much other documentation that need extra efforts and time investment.It is a popular phrase in profiling industry that only 40% of efforts are required in testing and remaining all the efforts are needed for borrowed resources and testing post procedures.

In order to collect profess against your finding you have to associate every result of test and incase of tools performed testing then they automatically have their records of input and results. Further, for manual process of testing examiner have to prepare result documentation with verified input datasets to assure its effectiveness and validity.

5.4 Operation Ability

Profiling testing is a process that has always a question mark on considered datasets for testing. It is always essential for examiners to carry every specific evidence of testing to validate their results in case file. A good assessment and evolution process has every information about the organization and also has evidence against every result taken from testing in organizational platform

- Past Data/Past Experience
- Accessible Documents/Knowledge
- Suppositions
- Recognized Risks

The four essential strides in Software Project Estimation are

- Estimate the size of the advancement item.
- Estimate the exertion in person-months or individual hours.
- Estimate the timetable in schedule months.
- Estimate the venture cost in concurred cash.

Software Estimation Observation

- Estimation need not be a one-time task in an undertaking. It can occur during
    - Getting a Project.
    - Arranging the Project.
    - Execution of the Project as the need emerges.
- Undertaking degree must be perceived before the assessment cycle starts. It will be useful to have recorded Project Data.
- Task measurements can give a verifiable point of view and important contribution for age of quantitative appraisals.
- Arranging requires specialized supervisors and the product group to make an underlying duty as it prompts obligation and responsibility.
- Past experience can help enormously.
- Use at any rate two assessment procedures to show up at the appraisals and accommodate the subsequent qualities. Allude Decomposition Techniques in the following segment to find out about accommodating evaluations.
- Plans should be iterative and permit changes over the long haul and more subtleties are known.

The Project Estimation Approach that is generally utilized is Decomposition Technique. Decay methods adopt a partition and overcome strategy. Size, Effort and Cost assessment are acted in a stepwise way by separating a Project into significant Functions or related Software Engineering Activities.

Step 1: Understand the extent of the software to be fabricated.

Step 2: Generate estimate of the software size.

- Start with the announcement of degree.
- Deteriorate the product into capacities that can each be assessed separately.
- Figure the size of each capacity.
- Infer exertion and quotes by applying the size qualities to your standard efficiency measurements.
- Join work evaluations to create a general gauge for the whole undertaking.

Step 3: Generate a gauge of the exertion and cost. You can show up at the exertion and quotes by separating an undertaking into related programming designing exercises.

- Recognize the grouping of exercises that should be performed for the task to be finished.
- Gap exercises into undertakings that can be estimated.
- Estimate the exertion (in person hours/days) needed to finish each errand.
- Join exertion appraisals of assignments of action to deliver a gauge for the action.
- Get cost units (i.e., cost/unit exertion) for every action from the information base.
- Register the complete exertion and cost for every action.
- Join exertion and quotes for every action to create a general exertion and quote for the whole undertaking.

Step 4: Reconcile gauges: Compare the subsequent qualities from Step 3 to those got from Step 2. In the event that the two arrangements of assessments concur, at that point your numbers are exceptionally dependable. Something else, if generally dissimilar assessments happen direct further examination concerning whether –

- The extent of the venture isn't satisfactorily perceived or has been misconstrued.
- The capacity and additionally action breakdown isn't precise.
- Chronicled information utilized for the assessment strategies is unseemly for the application, or old, or has been twisted.

Step 5: Determine the reason for difference and afterward accommodate the assessments.

5.5 Security Measurement Process

We can't construct quality programming, or improve your cycle, without estimation. Estimation is fundamental to accomplishing the essential administration targets of forecast, progress, and cycle improvement. A frequently rehashed express by DeMaro remains constant; "You can't oversee what you can't quantify!" All cycle improvement must be founded on estimating where you have been, the place you are presently, and appropriately utilizing the information to anticipate where you are going. Gathering great measurements and appropriately utilizing them generally prompts measure improvement!

5.5.1 Measures, Metrics, and Indicators

Product estimation is a quantifiable measurement, property, or measure of any part of a programming project, item, or cycle. It is the crude information which is related with different components of the product cycle and item. Table 5.1 gives a few instances of helpful the board measures.

Different approaches and rules are developed to evaluate various functionality of software's that gives an ideal condition analysis situation to developers experts:

- Monitor requirements,
- Predict development resources,
- Track development progress,
- Understand maintenance costs.

TABLE 5.1

Example Management Indicator

Area	Measure
Requirement	CSCI requirements
	CSCI design stability
Performance	Input/output bus throughout capability
	Processor memory utilization
	Processor throughout put utilization
Schedule	Requirements allocation status
	Preliminary design status
	Code and unit test status
	Integration status
Cost	Person-months of effort
	Software size

Measurements are utilized to look at the present status of your program with past execution or earlier gauges and are gotten from before information from inside the program. They show patterns of expanding or diminishing qualities, relative just to the past estimation of a similar measurement. They moreover show regulation or breeches of pre-set up limits, for example, admissible inert deformities. Measurements are additionally valuable for deciding a "business technique" (how assets are being utilized and devoured). For instance, in delivering equipment, the board takes a gander at a lot of measurements for scrap also, modify. From a product viewpoint, you will need to see a similar data on how much cash, time, and labor the cycle devours that doesn't add as far as possible item. One way a product program may devour an excessive number of assets is if mistakes made in the necessities stage were not found and revised until the coding stage. Not exclusively does this make modify, yet the expense to address a mistake during the coding stage that was embedded during prerequisites definition is roughly half higher to address than one embedded and revised during the coding stage. The key is to get blunders as quickly as time permits (i.e., in a similar stage that they are prompted).

The board's measurements will be estimations that help assess how well the securing office is continuing in achieving their obtaining plan or how well the contractual worker is continuing in achieving their Software Development Plan. Patterns in the board measurements uphold estimates of future advancement, early difficulty discovery, and authenticity in plan modifications. Programming item credits are estimated to show up at item measurements which decide client fulfillment with the conveyed item or administration. From the client's point of view, item credits can be dependability, convenience, practicality, specialized help, responsiveness, issue space information and comprehension, and viability (innovative answer for the difficult space). Item ascribes are estimated to assess programming quality components, for example, effectiveness, honesty, dependability, survivability, convenience, rightness, viability, undeniable nature, expandability, adaptability, compactness, reusability, and interoperability. Cycle measurements are utilized to check associations, devices, methods, and techniques used to create and convey programming items. Cycle ascribes are estimated to decide the status of each period of advancement (from prerequisites examination to client acknowledgment) and of assets (dollars, individuals, and timetable) that's way each stage.

There are five classes of measurements by and large utilized from a business point of view to quantify the amount and nature of programming. During improvement specialized and imperfection measurements are utilized. Reseller's exchange measurements are then gathered which incorporate client fulfillment, guarantee, and notoriety.

5.5.2 Technical Metrics

Technical Metrics are utilized to decide if the code is all around organized, that manuals for equipment and programming use are sufficient, that documentation is finished, right, and up to-date. Specialized measurements likewise depict the outside attributes of the framework's execution.

Defect Metrics are utilized to discover that the framework doesn't wrongly deal with information, does not strangely end, and doesn't do the numerous different things related with the disappointment of a product serious framework.

End-user satisfaction metrics are utilized to portray the worth got from utilizing the framework.

Warranty Metrics reflect explicit incomes and uses related with rectifying programming abscond dependent upon the situation. These measurements are affected by the degree of deformities, eagerness of clients to approach with grievances, and the readiness and capacity of the programming engineer to oblige the client.

Reputation Metrics are utilized to evaluate apparent client fulfillment with the product and may produce the most worth, since it can emphatically impact what programming is procured. Notoriety may contrast altogether from real fulfillment:

- Because singular clients may utilize just a little part of the capacities gave in any programming bundle; and
- Because promoting and publicizing regularly impact purchaser view of programming quality more than genuine use

5.6 Conclusion

The challenge of software is something with variety and pace. The present digital age opens the door to a range of security threats that daily lead businesses into exploitation. It is a complicated and difficult task as a security specialist to manage this situation. The authors attempt to provide a summary of the current situation in which software development techniques and tools are penetrating very effectively. Conduct a vulnerability assessment to review the effectiveness of previous security measures within the SDLC. For instance, an organization that teaches developers properly to secure coding and conducts safety architecture and source code reviews is most likely less vulnerable than a non-speaking organization. The current situation of the risk to production of software suggests that it is important first to identify and then evaluate the effects of various threats, and then to minimize the threats, so that software and organizational structures are productive and stable. The proposed chapter aims to raise awareness of various threats and their effects on secure development in a brief and effective manner. This offers useful information on the mitigation approach to resolve security concerns in the area of organizational safety. Authors believe strongly that such a successful study offers the reader a suitable direction and makes readers aware of the diverse threat an entity may pose in the danger of infringement.

Key Terms

- Auditing: Records historical events on a system.
- Attack: The situation where software and any system gets exploited through some vulnerability or loophole.
- Threat: Possible business or software vulnerability/loophole that can lead the organization or system into the situation of exploitation in the future (not currently).
- Vulnerability: A weak or risky point that can cause exploitation and lead the business into immense loss and harm.
- Track: Monitor the risks and mitigations plans.
- Control: Has all the rights and permission grant by authority.
- Confidentiality: Privacy of information from unauthorized spy on data.
- Auditing: Records historical events on a system.

Point to Remember

- Software building is a designing control that is worried about all parts of software creation.
- Software development happens when you change existing software frameworks to meet new necessities. Changes are consistent, and the software must develop to stay valuable.
- Risk management is a process that gives wings to business security and helps the organization to identify and mitigate potential business and technical risks.
- Security engineering is a pre-active inclusive approach that combines with SDLC and produces sustainable and secure software.

Review Questions

1. What are the points need attentions in defining security for software?
2. What is significance of vulnerability analysis?
3. What is the basic security attributes for secure software?
4. Why Software Security is most concerned topic?
5. Do we need to review security at each phase of the software development lifecycle?
6. What is the basic security attributes for secure software?
7. What is significance of risk analysis?
8. Why security engineering needed?

Objective-Type Questions

1. According to the CIA Triad, which of the below-mentioned element is not considered in the triad?
   a) Confidentiality
   b) Integrity
   c) Authenticity
   d) Availability

2. When you use the word _____ it means you are protecting your data from getting disclosed.
   a) Confidentiality
   b) Integrity
   c) Authorization
   d) Availability

3. One common way to maintain data availability in organizations is _____
   a) Data clustering
   b) Data backup
   c) Data recovery
   d) Data Altering

4. When there is an excessive amount of data flow, which the system cannot handle, _____ attack takes place.
   a) Database crash attack
   b) DoS(DenialofService)attack
   c) DataoverflowAttack
   d) Buffer overflow attack

5. From the options below, which of them is not a threat to information security?
   a) Disaster
   b) Eavesdropping
   c) Information leakage
   d) Unchanged default password

6. From the options below, which of them is not a vulnerability to information security?
   a) Flood
   b) Without deleting data, disposal of storage media
   c) Unchanged default password
   d) latest patches and updates not done

7. Compromising confidential information comes under _____
   a) Bug
   b) Threat
   c) Vulnerability
   d) Attack

8. _____ is the practice and precautions taken to protect valuable information from unauthorized access, recording, disclosure or destruction:
   a) NetworkSecurity
   b) DatabaseSecurity
   c) InformationSecurity
   d) Physical Security

9. Every employee of the firm must need to have some basic knowledge of cyber-security and types of hacking and how they are done.
   a) True
   b) False

10. _____ has become a popular attack since last few years, and the attacker target board members, high-ranked officials and managing committee members of an organization:
    a) Spyware
    b) Ransomware
    c) Adware
    d) Shareware

11. If you're working in your company's system/laptop and suddenly a pop-up window arise asking you to update your security application, you must ignore it.
    a) True
    b) False

12. Which attribute is not part of CIA triad?
    a) Confidentiality
    b) Integrity
    c) Authenticity
    d) Availability

13. Risk management process is used to identify and mitigate potential organizational risk?
    a) True
    b) False

14. Security engineering is an supporting process for software engineering?
    a) True
    b) False

15. Confidentiality refers for continues data availability?
    a) True
    b) False

16. Steps associated inn NIST security model?
    a) 6
    b) 5
    c) 4
    d) 12

Short-Answer Type Questions

1. Why software security is significant?
2. What are steps initially taken by an organization to manage software security in the organization?
3. What is the extensibility issue in software, define?
4. What is NIST?
5. Why security engineering is an inclusive approach?

6. What type of various fundamental threats present in software security?
7. What is intentional and non-intentional error?
8. Why employee security training is necessary for organizational security?
9. `What do you mean by intrusion to personal security?
10. What is difference between physical and non-physical fraud and theft?

Descriptive Questions

1. What do you mean by threat mitigation strategies define with examples?
2. What is impact analysis of threat and how it inherits from risk management?
3. Define various types of threats and their examples that affect software or organizational security?
4. What is Security engineering, why it is important?
5. Describe various software security models?

References

1 G. McGraw, *Software Security: Building Security*. Boston,MA: Addison Wesley Professional, 2006.
2 M.A. Sasse and I. Flechais, "Usable Security Why Do We Need It? How Do We Get It?", 2005. Available online: https://www.researchgate.net/publication/316236669 (accessed on 15 November 2019).
3 J. Ryoo, B. Malone, P.A. Laplante, and P. Anand, "The Use of Security Tactics in Open Source Software Projects", *IEEE Transactions on Reliability* 65, 2015, 1195–1204.
4 G. Pedraza-Garcia, H. Astudillo, and D. Correal, "A Methodological Approach to Apply Security Tactics in Software Architecture Design", *Proceedings of the 2014 IEEE Colombian Conference on Communications and Computing (COLCOM)*, Bogota, Colombia, June 4–6,2014, pp. 1–8.
5 F. Osses, G. Márquez, M.M. Villegas, C. Orellana, M. Visconti, and H. Astudillo, "Security Tactics Selection Poker (TaSPeR) a Card Game to Select Security Tactics to Satisfy Security Requirements", *Proceedings of the 12th European Conference on Software Architecture: Companion Proceedings*, Madrid, Spain, September 7, 2018, pp. 1–7.
6 J. Kaur, A. I. Khan, Y. B. Abushark, M. M. Alam, S. A. Khan, A. Agrawal, R. Kumar and R. A. Khan, "Security Risk Assessment of Healthcare SoftwareThrough Adaptive Neuro-Fuzzy Inference System: A Design Perspective", *Risk Management and Healthcare Policy*, 13, 2020, pp. 355–371. doi: 10.2147/RMHP.S233706
7 [Online], Available at: https://www.mitre.org/publications/systems-engineering-guide/acquisition-systems-engineering/risk-management/risk-impact-assessment-and-prioritization
8 P.R. Garvey, *Analytical Methods for Risk Management: A Systems Engineering Perspective*. Boca Raton, London, New York: Chapman-Hall/CRC Press, Taylor & Francis Group (UK), 2008, ISBN: 1584886374.
9 [Online], Available at:https://www.atlantic.net/hipaa-compliant-hosting/how-to-best-mitigate-cybersecurity-risks-and-protect-your-data/
10 [Online], Available at:https://www.3pillarglobal.com/insights/mitigation-strategies-to-address-it-security-risks

11 [Online], Available at: https://www.nsa.gov/Portals/70/documents/what-we-do/cybersecurity/professional-resources/csi-nsas-top10-cybersecurity-mitigation-strategies.pdf

12 [Online], Available at: https://championsg.com/12-steps-mitigate-cyber-threats

13 R. Kumar, M. Zaroor, M. Alenezi, A. Agrawal, and R. A. Khan, "Measuring Security Durability of Software through Fuzzy-Based Decision-Making Process", *International Journal of Computational Intelligence Systems*, 12 (2), 2019, pp. 627–642. doi: 10.2991/ijcis.d.190513.001

14 R. Kumar, A. Baz, H. Alhakami, Baz M. Alhakamiw, A. Agrawal, and R. A. Khan, "A Hybrid Model of Hesitant Fuzzy Decision-Making Analysis for Estimating Usable-Security of Software", *IEEE Access*, 8 (4), 2020, pp. 72694–72712. doi: 10.1109/ACCESS.2020.2987941

15 R. Kumar, A. K. Pandey, A. Baz, H. Alhakami, W. Alhakami, M. Baz, A. Agrawal, and R. A. Khan,"Fuzzy-Based Symmetrical Multi-Criteria Decision – Making Procedure for Evaluating the Impact of Harmful Factors of Healthcare Information Security",*Symmetry*, 12 (664), 2020, pp. 1–23. doi: 10.3390/sym12040664

Useful Links

Secure Development

https://techbeacon.com/security/secure-development-lifecycle-essential-guide-safe-software-pipelines
https://www.microsoft.com/en-us/securityengineering/sdl
https://www.synopsys.com/blogs/software-security/secure-sdlc/

Threat Mitigation

https://www.carbonite.com/blog/article/2016/02/11-ways-to-mitigate-insider-security-threats
https://study.com/academy/lesson/it-threat-mitigation-definition-strategies.html
https://medium.com/@patrickkijek/threat-mitigation-techniques-for-web-application-security-f0ab917db694
https://www.infoblox.com/glossary/threat-mitigation/

Software Engineering

https://dinus.ac.id/repository/docs/ajar/Sommerville-Software-Engineering-10ed.pdf

Security Engineering

https://www.cl.cam.ac.uk/~rja14/Papers/SEv2-c01.pdf

Risk Management

https://us-cert.cisa.gov/bsi/articles/best-practices/risk-management

Software Security Problem

https://www.sciencedirect.com/science/article/abs/pii/S1361372320300427

6

Secure Software Architecture

Securing a computer system has traditionally been a battle of wits: the penetrator tries to find the holes, and the designer tries to close them.

Gosser

With the rapid expansion of the Internet, the convergence of ICT is reflected through many notable developments in our society. The increase in the use of information and communication systems led to an impressive development in relation to reliability with the perspective of security, cost, and software functionality. Security problems associated with computers and software are repeatedly, extensive and serious. In an era plagued by asymmetric cyberattacks, proclaim regarding the reliability, integrity, and security of the system must also incorporate requirements for the essential security of accomplished software. Software security is an idea that still requires evident description. Understanding the nature of software is important when developing methods to measure software security. The most adequate means is to find different dimensions including confidentiality, integrity, availability, authentication, and authorization. It is evident from literature that most of the time the complex nature of software is responsible for security flaws. At a given acceptance level, more complex applications are harder to recognize and intruders take advantage of unmanaged enough complexity to violate security issues.

The term *'architecture'* is a multifaceted conception that can have various descriptions in the field of information technology. Architecture refers to the conceptual essence of an application, the principal decisions regarding its design, and the key abstractions that characterize the application. The contextual peculiarities and different perspectives of enterprises are explored in different sections of this chapter. It is a summary of the essence and essential of the application. By architecture we mean the major design decisions made about the system. There are various types of architecture which are as follows:

- Business architecture
- Information technology (IT) architecture
- Information security architecture
- Application (software) architecture
- Security architecture

Architecture estimation is preserved through several phases of a software development process. They can be used to contrast and recognize stability and limitations in architectural alternatives during the preliminary design phase. They can also be practiced to estimate present systems in preparation for maintenance or uninterrupted development. The evaluation helps the software developers to make sure that the software architecture will be proficient to convene the quality requirements and numerous approaches have been proposed for the assessment of the software architecture. The approaches can be alienated into four major groups, namely, based on experience, based on simulation, based on mathematical modeling, and based on scenario.

DOI: 10.1201/9781003330516-6

6.1 Objectives

Aim of the chapter:

- To develop better understanding about software architecture.
- Appreciate the need, importance and significance of security estimation at risk perspective.
- Define and understand security architecture, models, process and components.
- Enumerates and realize numerous software security estimation models and techniques.
- Visualize the different perspectives of software security estimation.
- Realize the importance and significance of software security architecture.

6.2 Software Architecture

As per the lines of codes increases, the complexity of software increases. Enough complexity of the software is itself a crisis. It reflects the negative effect on the software quality and security after compromising certain threshold values of software attributes. Software architecture provides an optimal solution to deal with design complexity by controlling body of methods and techniques through proper integration with methodologies and models with appropriate analysis. A research article written by Perry and Wolf [1] discusses the fundamentals of software architecture which defines software architecture is the collection of all associated components, the various structures, and underlying principles.

$$\text{Software Architecture} = \{\text{Elements}, \text{Form}, \text{Rationale}\}$$

Another study about software architecture by Garlan & Shaw [2] produced the following definition: *'Software architecture is the computational components, or simply components, together with a description of the interactions between these components, the connectors'*. Security architecture is a subset of software engineering discipline. On the above cited observation on security architecture, it is well formulated association of components and connectors of the particular software system. Abstraction and encapsulation are the key properties which are more helpful to establish the association and interaction among the respective components of the software system. Figure 6.1 shows the software architecture evolution.

6.2.1 Essential Qualities for Architecture Evaluation

Recognition of the important attributes for the development of the software is known as software architecture. Various quality attributes, including efficiency, performance, maintainability, etc., have an intensive impact on the architecture of software. This is very evident for the fulfillment of quality attributes based on healthy software architecture. Sophisticated methods are important prerequisite for the evaluation of software

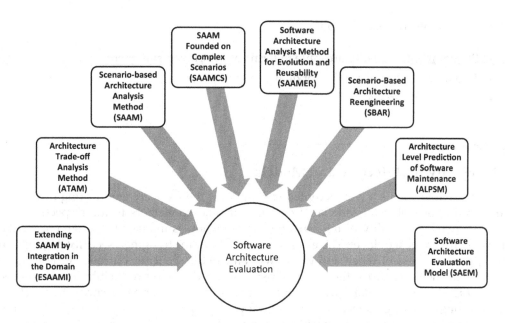

FIGURE 6.1
Software architecture evolution.

architectures on the basis of quality attributes. Several quality characteristics and/or trade-off methods estimating studies are particularly notable. There is an increased number of published articles for an assessment method of software architecture that refers to the concurrent use of multiple attributes. Numerous techniques for estimating software architecture have been illustrated to help developers to build up software architecture that will have the ability to meet requisite on the system. These properties are important for organizations working in the field of software development with relevance to developing software in a real-time system domain using a software-line approach. However, an industrial system usually has requisite on many quality characteristics of the system. Consequently, architecture assessment techniques that trace several properties characteristics, such as performance, maintenance, testability, and portability would be more valuable. This study focuses on the essential properties of software architecture assessment that draw attention on more than one quality attributes: [3–5]

- Performance
- Availability
- Modifiability
- Reliability
- Security
- Functionality
- Portability
- Variability
- Subset ability
- Conceptual Integrity

Output of architecture evaluation:

- Requirement of quality attribute in terms of prioritized statement
- To map with the approaches of quality attributes
- Risks and non-risks

6.3 Security Architecture and Models

Security architecture is a well-accepted expansion of the software engineering discipline. Architecting describes all associated components and connectors to the respective software systems. Rationality of the functional components is managed through encapsulation at software design level. The essential requirement to strengthen security depends on the appropriateness of when and where we can use the security controls. These security controls can help to address the potential risk associated with reproducible design process. Such unified security design process in a certain scenario describes security architecture. Architecting the design specifications to achieve appropriate stability among the components signifies the strong relationship and dependencies. Primarily security architecture and design is a multilevel domain. It manages hardware and software at primary level to get the secure system. The next level keeps logical models and the upper level preserve evaluation methods through quantification to know the actual impact of security. The key attributes of software security architecture in Figure 6.2 are as follows: [4, 5]

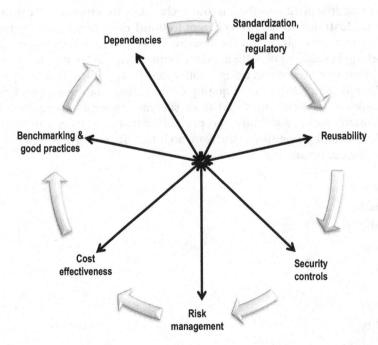

FIGURE 6.2
Key attributes of software security architecture.

- Dependencies
- Standardization, legal, and regulatory
- Reusability
- Security controls
- Risk management
- Cost effectiveness
- Benchmarking and good practices

6.3.1 Security Models

Security is one of the most influential factors for software quality which needs to upgrade itself to enhance the life of software products and process. Enhancing security is one of the exceptionally imperative strides toward long life expectancy of security at an early level of software development [6]. Various studies have been done in this regard and few relevant observations are mentioned below to understand about security and its related issues, and their solutions are mentioned in Table 6.1.

TABLE 6.1

Various Assessment and Estimation Models for Security

S. No.	Security Models	Characteristics	Key Properties	Reference
1	Lattice Models	Multilevel and multilateral security	It is a mathematical framing foundation of which is built upon the set of elements, fractional ordering information with holding the properties for elements with least upper bound and greatest lower bound.	[7, 8]
2	State Machine Models	Integrity Assessment	A mathematical modeling which holds behavior of the system to various inputs or sequences. It describes variables, various transition states, and respective functions to maintain the integrity of the system.	
3	Noninterference Models	State Analysis	User's action in one security domain cannot affect with the users in another security domain.	
4	Bell–LaPadula Confidentiality Model	Multilevel State Analysis, Confidentiality aspects of accesses	Different classification level must be verified through proper authentication to get the necessary security clearance. The confidentiality of information must be protected through various rules, including *no-read-up rule, no-write-down rule, strong star property rule, tranquility principle.*	
5	Biba Integrity Model	Integrity Assessment	To preserve integrity of data, it holds lattices, information flow form one level to another via proper rules including *no-read-down* which not allowed reading data from lower integrity level. *No-write-up rule* allowed not writing data from higher security level and the invocation property does not allow calling subject to higher level.	

(Continued)

TABLE 6.1 *(Continued)*

Various Assessment and Estimation Models for Security

S. No.	Security Models	Characteristics	Key Properties	Reference
6	Clark–Wilson Integrity Model	Integrity of Information	This model prevents unauthorized user to make further modification via separation of duties assigned to respective users. The model preserves the consistency at internal and external level via primitive read/write operations which is specially derived from different vendors.	
7	Access Control Matrix	Access Control	A common model used in any operating system and applications to control the accesses.	
8	Information Flow Models	Multilevel State Analysis, Authorization Checking	Information is the primary source which should be compartmentalized into classification and knowledge.	
9	Graham–Denning Model	Multilevel State Analysis, Access Control	Graham–Denning Model is defined with the set of eight primitive protection rules to safe and secure functionality. These rules are wrapped for creation, deletion, and access rights for read, grant, and transfer.	
10	Harrison–Ruzzo–Ullman Model	Integrity of Access Rights	An algorithm-based security model which explores the potential and restrictions of the system for confirming safety to the system. It confirms the access rights of the user to preserve integrity of the information or system.	
11	Brewer–Nash (Chinese Wall)	Multilevel State Analysis, Access Control	Users access controls rights are controlled dynamically on the basis of his previous actions. It will help to protect the conflict of interest between the various users' access rights. Flow-based information system discontinues the flow on the raise of any conflict of interest.	
12	Take Grant Model	Confidentiality Model	Confidentiality-based security model performs four most important operation including take, grant, create and revoke.	
13	Wang &Wulf Model	Proposed security measurement framework and perform quantitative assessment of software security	Under the aegis of SM framework first it defines software security and then selection of various unit and scale and use of estimation methodology and performs validation of metrics.	[8]
14	User System Interaction Effect (USIE) Model	A framework on service oriented architecture (SOA) for quantitative analysis of software security	The proposed model analyzes and mitigates software attackability by influencing the subsequent internal attributes. Internal security metrics are being proposed to predict impact of software attackability factors. Theoretical validation is available for the suite of metrics. Correlation between internal security metrics and attackability must be established and empirical validation conducted to verify the relationship between the valid security metrics and software attackability concepts.	[9]

(Continued)

TABLE 6.1 *(Continued)*

Various Assessment and Estimation Models for Security

S. No.	Security Models	Characteristics	Key Properties	Reference
15	M.U.A. Khan Model	Security quantification methodology on SDLC artifacts.	The various aspects of security vulnerabilities are exposed and quantifiable results are being presented to know the actual impact analysis. The identified vulnerabilities are as follows: • To find out the number of errors • Trace number of vulnerabilities • To establish correlation between errors and vulnerabilities • Demanding security requirements for error removal • Identify risks • Cost analysis for implementing security requirements • Assets, values of assets, and the damage	[10]
16	B B Madan Model	Modeling and quantification of security attributes of software systems	A semi-Markov model for an intrusion tolerant for modeling and quantification of security attributes. This security quantification analysis describes the attacker behavior and solved the semi Markov process for security attributes by using some common distribution functions like reliability theory, deterministic, exponentials, hyper-exponentials, hypo-exponentials, weibull, gamma, and log-logistic. This can be helpful to investigate the steady state availability and the mean time to security failure.	[11]
17	Fuzzy Inference System	Modeling process is defined through Implementation	The proposed study identifies the limitations of existing prioritization techniques with respect to security attributes analysis. It recommends the need of prioritization techniques to identify the most underutilized attributes and block them for further insecurity. The proposed framework takes the security model as the input and uses fuzzy inference system to use linguistic terms.	Davoud Mougouei [12]
18	Multi-dimensional scaling	Security Threat	Identification of security threat-response pairs via expert interviews, surveys and examined security threats including security performance degradation, identify theft, and data loss. Mapping between security behavior and performance was taken under consideration with the help of individuals' security behaviors and analyzed them using multi-dimensional scaling.	Robert E. Crossler [13]
19	Survey-based report	Critically examined the security and software architecture	A novel work was carried for automation purpose for software security requirements. Precise review targeting security requirements for distributed applications and protection methods of software is presented in the proposed work. An architectural view was discussed to protect attacks on smart houses.	Friedrich Praus et al. 2016 [14]

(Continued)

TABLE 6.1 *(Continued)*

Various Assessment and Estimation Models for Security

S. No.	Security Models	Characteristics	Key Properties	Reference
20	Survey-based report	Main reasons of security failures are addressed	A very essential part for any organization which is known as software security assurance plan is being discussed with its four major supports, including strong focus on security awareness and education, secure development practices and procedures, automation of security testing, and ongoing security assurance program.	Sarah Vonnegut 2016 [15]
21	Technical report cum dissertation based on security problems	Software security assurance program to incorporated in development life cycle	The basic necessity of software security assurance program under software engineering is to produce vulnerable free software. The researcher integrating learning curriculum on software assurance program which is recommended by its stakeholders. This should be strictly followed while developing application software.	Robert Evans 2015 [16]
22	Technical report based on security problems	Guidelines are provided	This report confirms about how to build effective assessment plan. It discusses the procedures of security and privacy controls for conducting assessments which will be implemented in the development phases of software life cycle. This will provide guidelines to analyze and assess security and privacy of software systems during their development phases with risk management perspective.	National Institute of Standards and Technology (NIST) 2014 [17]
23	Research paper based on security problems	Framework for security patch management	Security patch management framework was proposed, including vendor notification, tracking, risk assessment, packaging, and deployment based on authoritative standards which is similar to the process of defect management in SDLC. It uses the best practices for software development and useful for development process, including policy, risk management, standardization.	Michael Hoehl 2013 [18]
24	Research paper based on security goals and threats	Framework for early integration of security in software-development process is given.	Proposed framework for secure development with incorporation of security development life cycle to overcome the repercussion of late software development effort with comparison to early software development strategies. The author identified a framework which eliminates this problem by engaging security requirements in the all stages of development. The identified design attributes affecting security requirements were also prioritized and a security design template was prepared by this research.	Kakali Chatterjee et al.2013 [19]

(Continued)

TABLE 6.1 *(Continued)*

Various Assessment and Estimation Models for Security

S. No.	Security Models	Characteristics	Key Properties	Reference
25	Model-driven methodology	Proposed a development framework to enhance security through assessment	Author in his research raised the issue of security problems due to design complexities. The author described that cost and time to inbuilt security in software at the last stage of development is high. Hence, this research focused on securing software during the design of software. Design complexity invites bugs and so it is advised in this paper to consider complexity attributes in design to improve the security of software. In this work author identifies security complexity factors in perspective to its impact on object-oriented factors. It provides a development framework which incorporates design complexity attributes into the development to enhance security. This framework includes premises and generic guidelines to be followed for securing the software. The framework is then validated by quantitative study of an experiment and given three models consisting confidentiality integrity and availability quantification model.	S. A. Khan [20]
26	Model-driven methodology based on vulnerability assessment	Proposed a framework for vulnerability minimization	Vulnerability flaw in the design of software is the main reason for security issues. A framework for object-oriented design was proposed to encounter vulnerable design with the help of security metrics. Complexity of design and attributes such as confidentiality, integrity and availability play a foremost role in software security assurance.	Alka Agarwal et al. 2011 [21]

6.4 Security Architecture Process

It will provide support for executives for reliable configuration of choices during whole IT landscape. Business goals must be designed strategically for highest support to organization. Numerous components are involved, including training, technology, identity, and configuration management and elements fit for the domain of security, etc., are described for planned security architecture in Figure 6.3.

- **Architectural risk assessment**

The architectural risk assessment is responsible for prioritization and allocation of various security risks with all associated components and connectors to the respective software systems. It is also responsible to find out the vulnerable areas or high risk zones which are

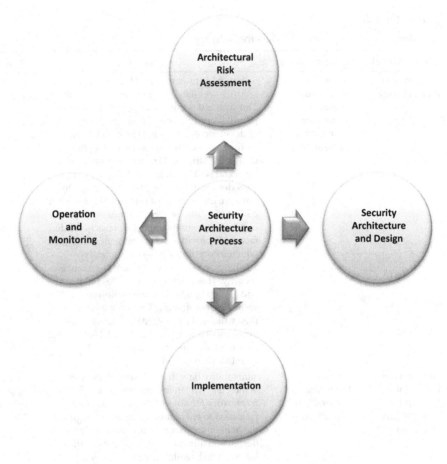

FIGURE 6.3
Security architecture process.

more susceptible to attack. From architectural risk assessment, the following information can be easily identified:

a) Categorization of information
b) Potential risk identification
c) Security audits

- **Security Architecture and Design**

This section is responsible for the design and development of various security services at architectural level, which are the primary sources for the risk related to business.

- **Implementation**

This section discusses the various ways of security services and process implementation. It will provide the complete overview regarding the actual functioning among services and components, their operations, and controlling mechanism. It will ensure that the implemented services are carefully managed as per the assured security policies, standard, security architecture decisions, and risk management in the real runtime implementation.

- **Operations and Monitoring**

This step is responsible for security threats and vulnerability mitigation and provides the suggestive measures explaining about their impact and operational state. The proper monitoring will help to find out the comprehensive solutions.

6.5 Components of Security Architecture Process

Combination of people, process, and effective tools are three proficient components of security architecture for the protection of organizational assets. It is evident from the definitions of security architecture that policies must be driven to follow the performance expectations that align with management decisions regarding implementation and enforcement of architecture as depicted in Figure 6.4.

Characterization of the system: Identification of features is the primary step of most of the problem-solving activities. This stage is responsible for the development of the concept

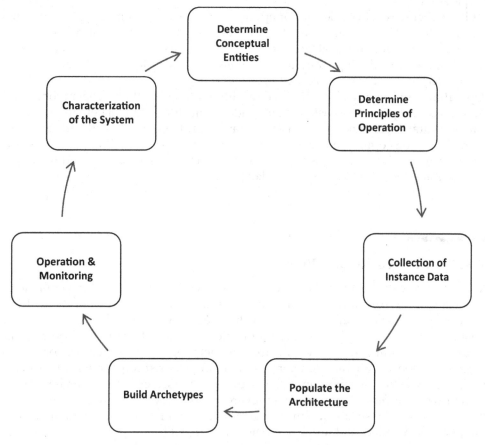

FIGURE 6.4
Components of security architecture process.

and key solutions as well as related facts. The major intention of primary stage is to identify factors which are more appropriate for user's needs, information sensitivity, and upcoming threats.

Determine conceptual entities: User's need refers to the requirement or expectation of client from the safety of software. The identified factors are further treated as key elements and help to make a roadmap for security architecture process.

Determine principles of operation: The next step is responsible to understand its theoretical assumptions for the purpose of successful operational ability. This is responsible to examine the possible options, various scopes, availability of information, and supporting tools. Such an action turns into inevitability, as it can inspire the developer to build such a model that is more apprehensive in it than would be preferred.

Collection of instance data: This phase of process reckons with the pattern of theoretical and empirical viability of information or data for analysis and development of security architecture process. It is also responsible to explore the compatibility of data with best practices with the development process and proposed mechanism to focus on internal structure that reveal of each individual entity and on external factors that determine the interactions among entities.

Populate the architecture: Another step also emphasizes the collection of significant features or inherent characteristics which are best suited for security architecture development paradigm.

Build archetypes: After selection of optimized perquisite information, the next step is responsible to build the security architecture. Substantial concepts are also design properties that may be thoroughly analyzed by examining the internal and exterior arrangement, relationship, and functioning. Commonly accepted set of security attributes are rearranged as per the requirement of development process.

Operations and monitoring: This will ensure the applicability of operations is complete, correct, and provides constant result under some degree. It will help to ensure about the architectural dependency and consistency analysis at design phase. It will be helpful to explore the various dimensions of operational characteristics including performance and its associated functions and its nonoperational characteristics including modifiability and business-related features like time to market [22–24].

6.6 Software Security Best Practices

A research observation is carried out by Saltzer and Michael Schroeder for comprehensive high-level security principles in context of safety measures derived from the real-world scenario to build secure software. It will facilitate developers to build and deploy secure software. There are many detailed design practices available that are the best guidelines for safety design principles. These practices will help regardless of platform or language to architectural-level software decisions. It is highly required to get advantages of security professionals to frame most appropriate questions based on software architecture and design to avoid the most widespread and severe defects. Novelty of this presented concept is the key principle for secure design. The security design principles are built upon an idea of simplicity, separation, and restriction. The summarized list given in Table 6.2 will act as the best security principles that require higher attention for reducing the risk of the software posted by security issues to software architects and designers [23–29].

TABLE 6.2

Comparative Chart for Software Security Best Practices

Reddwine and Davis	John Viega and Gary McGraw	Saltzer and Schroeder	P. Razvan	D. Wheeler
Abuse cases	Secure the weakest link	Least privilege	Relevancy and the weakest links	Validate all input
Security requirement	Practice defense in depth	Failing securely	Clarity	Avoid buffer overflow
Risk analysis	Fail securely	Securing the weakest link	Quality	Secure the interface
External review	Follow the principle of least privilege	Defense in depth	Involve all stakeholders	Separate data and control
Risk-based security tests	Compartmentalize	Separation of privilege	Technology processes	Minimize privileges
Static analysis	Keep it simple	Economy of mechanism	Fail safe operation	Minimize the functionality of a component
Risk analysis	Promote privacy	Least common mechanism	Defense in depth	Configure safely and use safe defaults
Penetration Testing	Very hard to hide secrets	Reluctance to trust	Principle of appropriate privileges	Load initialization values safely
Security breaks	Be reluctant to trust	Never assuming that your secrets are safe	Interacting with users	Fail safe
	Use your community resources	Complete mediation	Trust boundaries	Avoid race conditions
		Psychological acceptability	Third-party software	Trust only Trustworthy channels
		Promoting privacy	Manipulation of sensitive data	Setup a trusted path
			Attack first. On paper!	Use internal consistency
			Always think 'Outside of the Box'	Self-limit Resources
			Be humble	Prevent cross site malicious content
			Declarative vs. programmatic	Foil semantic attacks
			Reviews are your best allies	Be Careful with data types
				Carefully callout to other resources
				Send information back judiciously

6.7 Conclusion

Architecting software is very tensile stage of development. Security breaches are responsible not only for financial loss but also for the trust and integrity of the software design and development industry Developing a system with the necessary functionality and higher efficiency to mitigate against malicious intruder attacks involves secure design and deployment. The purpose of addressing security issues at the design stage is to protect applications from external threats and attacks. Security should be incorporated in the software-development cycle from the beginning and continue until the product is available. There is an urgent requirement to minimize the frequency of defects for security enhancement through protecting perceived nature of uncontrolled complicity. Efforts are being made to increase security by reducing the frequency of flaws by analyzing the overall software-development process, taking into account complexity.

Key Terms

Software Architecture, Security Architecture & Models, Security Architecture Process, Software Security Risk, The Top 10 OWASP vulnerabilities, Top 25 Common Weakness Enumeration, Software Security Risk Estimation

Points to Remember

- •. A versatile concept with a variety of details in the field of information technology which we refer to as the term 'architecture' having key abstraction for specifications and decision-making process.
- •. Software architecture description is an example of interconnected elements, form, and justification.
- •. Obligatory transformation on the complete design of the system is imposed through taxonomy of architectural pattern, including data-centered, data flow, call and return, object-oriented and layered architecture.
- •. Economy, visibility, spacing, symmetry, and emergence are the most appropriate considerations to provide support for architectural decisions to software professionals.
- •. Common weakness enumeration (CWE) is accountable for detailing the most effective issues practiced throughout software development.

Review Questions

1. The term *'architecture'* is a multifaceted conception that has various descriptions in the field of information technology. Explain this concept with appropriate case study.

2. By architecture we mean the major design decisions made about the system. Discuss with suitable case study for the various types of architectures.

3. Visualize the different perspectives of software security estimation with their relative impact analysis on the software development.

4. Describe the essential qualities for architecture evaluation of software.

5. Discuss the solution for risk-management plan according to threat, vulnerability, asset, and consequences with respect to risk.

Objective-Type Questions

1. Which model is responsible to raise the issues regarding confidentiality of information?
   a) Bell-LaPadula Model
   b) Biba Model
   c) Clark-Wilson Model
   d) Confidentiality Model

2. What is the first step of risk-estimation model?
   a) Determine severity of risk
   b) Risk identification
   c) Impact estimation
   d) Customization of risk Model

3. User System Interaction Effect (USIE) Model is commonly accepted for _____ in early development stage.
   a) Security estimation
   b) Risk identification
   c) Risk analysis
   d) Security verification

4. User System Interaction Effect (USIE) Model is _____ capable for quantitative assessment at the architectural level.
   a) Object oriented
   b) Object based
   c) Service oriented
   d) Function based

5. User System Interaction Effect (USIE) Model where internal metrics are being used for prediction using appropriate abstraction of security measures for?
   a) Software quantification
   b) Software analyzability
   c) Service security
   d) Software attackability

Short-Answer Type Questions

1. Prove that architecture refers to the conceptual essence of an application.
2. What are the essential properties of software architecture assessment that draw attention on more than one quality attributes?
3. Discuss the output of architecture evaluation.
4. What are the key attributes of software security architecture?
5. Which type of information is required for architectural risk assessment?
6. What are the various components of security architecture process?
7. What are the top 10 vulnerabilities of Open Web Application Security Project for the year 2017–2018?

Descriptive Questions

1. Define various assessment and estimation models for security.
2. Briefly describe the Case study on User System Interaction Effect (USIE) Model.
3. What do you mean by software security risk estimation? Discuss the various models in details.
4. Discuss the common weakness enumeration (CWE) which is responsible to deliver the details of most impactful issues experienced during software development.
5. What do you mean by risk? Discuss the Steps involved for risk assessment.
6. Explain with suitable example of simple mitigation process defined for a server failure.
7. Provide the complete list for Top   10 OWASP vulnerabilities and their comparative chart published in different time frame.

References

1. D. E. Perry and A. L. Wolf, "Foundations for the Study of Software Architecture", *ACM Sigsoft Software Engineering Notes*, vol 17 no 4 Oct 1992 Page 40
2. David Garlan and Mary Shaw, "An Introduction to Software Architecture". In V. Ambriola and G. Tortora (ed.), *Advances in Software Engineering and Knowledge Engineering, Series on Software Engineering and Knowledge Engineering*, Vol. 2, World Scientific Publishing Company, Singapore, pp. 1–39, 1993.
3. https://www.techopedia.com/definition/72/security-architecture
4. https://www.orbussoftware.com/resources/videos/iserver-product-videos/security-architecture/
5. http://www.opensecurityarchitecture.org/cms/foundations

6. https://owasp.org/www-community/OWASP_Risk_Rating_Methodology

7. https://media.techtarget.com/searchSecurity/downloads/29667C05.pdf, Last access 15 June 2022.

8. C. Wang and W. A. Wulf, "Towards a Framework for Security Measurement", *Proceedings of National Information Systems Security Conference*, Baltimore, October 7–10, 1997, pp. 522–533.

9. M. Yanguo Liu, "Quantitative Security Analysis for Service-Oriented Software Architectures", Ph.D Thesis, Department of Electrical and Computer Engineering, University of Victoria, 2008.

10. M. U. A. Khan and M. Zulkernine, "A Survey on Requirements and Design Methods for Secure Software Development", *Technical Report No. 2009–562*, School of Computing, Queen's University, Kingston, Ontario, Canada, August 2009.

11. B. B. Madan, K. Gŏseva-Popstojanova, K. Vaidyanathan and K. S. Trivedi, "Modeling and Quantification of Security Attributes of Software Systems", *Proceedings of the International Conference on Dependable Systems and Networks (DSN'02)*, IEEE, 2002, pp. 505–514.

12. D. Mougouei, PAPS: A Scalable Framework for Prioritization and Partial Selection of Security Requirements, Cornell University Library, 2017, Publication Number, eprint arXiv: 170600166.

13. R. Crossler and F. Bélanger, "An Extended Perspective on Individual Security Behaviors: Protection Motivation Theory and a Unified Security Practices (USP) Instrument", *Advances in Information Systems, ACM SIGMIS*, 45(4), 2014, pp. 51–71.

14. F. Praus, W. Kastner and P. Palensky, Software Security Requirements in Building Automation, Sicherheit 2016 - Sicherheit, Schutz und Zuverlässigkeit, 2016, pp. 217–228.

15. S. Vonnegut, Need-to-Know AppSec News Stories, 2016, Available https://www.checkmarx.com/2016/04/21/need-know-appsec-news-stories-april-2016/ Last visit April 2018.

16. R. Evans, Integrating Security in to the Undergraduate Software Engineering, Curriculum, UN F Thesis and Dissertations, 600, 2015.

17. B. E. A. Plans, *Assessing Security and Privacy Controls in Federal Information Systems and Organizations*, NIST Special Publication, 800, 53A, 2014.

18. M. Hoehl, *Framework for Building a Comprehensive Enterprise Security Patch Management Program*, STI Graduate Student Research, SANS, 2013.

19. K. Chatterjee, D. Gupta and A. De, "A Framework for Development of Secure Software", *CSI Transactions on ICT*, (1),2013, pp. 143–157.

20. S. A. Khan and R. A. Khan. "A Framework to Quantify Security: Complexity Perspective", *International Journal of Information and Education Technology*, 2 (5), 2012, p. 439.

21. A. Agrawal and R. A. Khan, "A Framework for Vulnerability Minimization: Object Oriented Design Perspective", *Computer and Communication Technology*, 2011, pp. 499–504.

22. SaaS Industry Market Report: Key Global Trends & Growth Forecasts. 2018. Available at: https://financesonline.com/2018-saas-industry-market-report-key-global-trendsgrowth-forecasts/ Last Visit on 04 Sep 2018.

23. P. Razvan, "Best Practices for Secure Development", October 2001.

24. S. T. Redwine, Jr. and N. Davis, "Process to Produce Secure Software", *Nation Cyber Security Summit*, March 2004.

25. J. Viega and G. McGraw, "Building Secure Software", Addison-Wesley, 2002. ISBN 0-201-72152-x.

26. P. Martin and C. Gail, "Concern Graphs: Finding and Describing Concerns Using Structural Program Dependencies", *In the proceedings of ICSE*, 2002.

27. H. Michael, "Secure Systems Begin with Knowing Your Threats – Part I", http://security.devx.com/upload/free/Features/zones/security/articles/2000/09sept00/mh0900[2]-1.asp, visited on 20 April 2007.

28. D. Evans and D. Larochelle, "Reported Flaws in Common Vulnerabilities and Exposures Database", *IEEE Software*, January 2002.

29. D. A. Wheeler, "Secure Programming for Linux and Unix HOWTO", *GNU Free Documentation License*, March 2003.

Useful Links

https://www.cloudflare.com/learning/security/threats/owasp-top-10/
https://github.com/OWASP/www-project-top-ten/blob/master/index.md
https://www.veracode.com/security/owasp-top-10
https://sucuri.net/guides/owasp-top-10-security-vulnerabilities-2020/

7

Software Security Assurance

It is very difficult to make a vigorous, plausible, and job-risking defense of an estimate that is derived by no quantitative method, supported by little data, and certified chiefly by the hunches of the managers.

Fred Brooks

National Defense Authorization Act (NDAA) incorporated a policy on software security (in Section 932, Strategy on Computer Software Assurance) which serves as the initial cybersecurity law of 2011 that assists the U.S. Department of Defense to develop an approach to ensure the security of software applications. Software Security Assurance, a collection of observations to ensure proactive application security, is the base for constructing applications acquiescence. A decisive assurance on technology has brought with it an increased level of accountability to protect information resources from malicious risk or damage. Ineffective software security management is responsible for financial failure and tarnishing the reputation of software security industries. Controlling and improving security is the foremost concern in software security assurance. This assurance of safety is planned in advance. It is clear from various security literatures that applying the security assurance procedure reveals all the qualities necessary to ensure that the software, in operation, will continue to function reliably despite the presence of intentional defects.

Software security assurance is an imperative mechanism for protecting the software's design, production, and support. Software security assurance establishes resistance tendency for recovery to a normal level of software functioning against malicious attacks or damages. This permitted level of trust is strongly connected to desired software characteristics such as quality, correctness, reliability, usability, interoperability, safety, fault tolerance, and, most importantly, security. Software security assurance activity is responsible for developing secure software products by detracting exploitable software weaknesses and addressing means to enhance capabilities that typically expand, acquire, and deploy resilient software. An effective software security assurance activity is responsible for:

- Ensuring that the practiced information system has appropriate, sensitive defense mechanisms to deal with malicious acts.
- Specifying SSA technologies and actions that could promote defects deterrence emboldens and efficient recovery mechanism to support security tools and data.

Software security assurance program benefits secure development projects by saving money and time. The emphasis of software security assurance is product assurance. What is essential – process or product? A secure product is associated with securing the development process of the product. The emerging conception of software security assurance focuses on appraising the processes by which products are developed. The main purpose of the software assurance program is to confirm that the secure software development

DOI: 10.1201/9781003330516-7

and software assurance process follow security assurance plans and standards and recommend process improvements. The process evaluates the current state of software security and builds a remedial program for the software development life cycle. It identifies the specified risk and threats to software and assesses the code for vulnerabilities throughout development. Another core objective is to test and verify the design and code for vulnerabilities and measure the success of the security plans so that process can be repeatedly enhanced [1].

7.1 Objectives

Upon successful completion of this chapter, the students would be proficient at accomplishing the following:

- Understand and define software security assurance
- Appreciate the components and responsibilities of SSA
- Realize the importance of software security assurance program
- Understand and establish the standards and procedures
- Realize the need for software security metrics and models
- understand the basics of software security assurance activities
- Categorize the possible questions that may be asked during walkthrough and inspection

7.2 Software Security Assurance

A planned and systematic pattern of events necessary to ensure security in software is called software security assurance. The term security assurance incorporates the following:

- The actions are taken to ensure that the design and developed software is helpful to minimize the risk to an organization.
- Systematic activities that reduce and control risk may include data integrity, data leakage, data misuse, and website malfunctions.
- The input, update, manipulation, and output are the essential parts used for sustainable measures for the enterprises. Furthermore, policies, procedures, and systematic measures are recognized in the enterprise to provide and sustain specified degrees in terms of efficiency, risk reduction, security scalability, cost reduction, compliance, and clarity – of sight through the system development life cycle.
- It is an application of risk management techniques all over the software development life cycle.
- It is a technique for successfully executing and enforcing software security policies and standards throughout the software development life cycle.

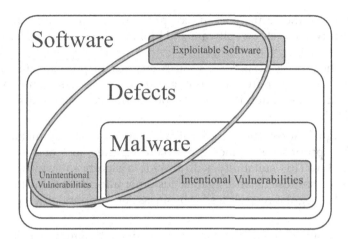

FIGURE 7.1
Exploitable Software versus Vulnerability.

- Responsible for the dependability of software security in the vendor environment.
- Software security initiatives to improve the security of all developed software.

National Information Assurance Terminology refers to software security assurance as to the level of trust designed or inserted as part of software throughout the life cycle, intentionally or unknowingly, as a software work objective and free from vulnerabilities. Figure 7.1 shows how different kinds of vulnerabilities may be helpful to breach security assurance through software exploitation [2–4].

7.2.1 Goals

The fundamental aim of software security assurance is to ensure that software is designed and developed to reduce risks to an organization. Risks can include data integrity, data leakage, data misuse, website deflection, etc. The potential in the organization to promise the software is securely built throughout SDLC. The important features as follows:

- Establish the Software Security
- Build the Software Security Group
- Develop strategy, policies, and standards
- Integrate SDLC checkpoints
- Analyze the application portfolio and establish metrics
- Conduct training and awareness activities

7.2.2 Responsibilities

Software security assurance is an essential administration responsibility. The role of vulnerabilities in software may generate deficits in terms of secure and reliable information, robust processes, and reporting. The purview of the managerial level always makes an effort to mitigate such vulnerabilities, which may lead to sensitive information disclosure.

The responsibilities of the security assurance program are to identify the priorities that have direct or indirect impacts on software and build controls over cost and values.

- **Assertion:** The process of software security ensures the prerequisite control mechanism and derives force from defending significant processes and data management. Valid documentation is a reliable source for asserting control over external or internal behavior.

- **Cost and Significance:** The significant way for vulnerability management is to provide the appropriate balancing between expected loss and occurrence rate of vulnerability. This suitability will provide a significant way of thinking for researchers to compose balance against customer information, business best practices and rules, regulating policies for business and support, and reputation of the organization.

- **Risk evaluation:** Evaluating criteria is a significant component of a successful review. To develop a mechanism for lowering the rate of vulnerabilities occurrences is to rectify vulnerability first against successful attacks and estimate losses in a probabilistic manner.

- **Vulnerability management:** This is the best way to protect your application to discover the weaknesses as soon as possible. These management skills provide a great space between risk and threats. This phenomenon prepares appropriate action to eradicate the risk.

- **Security standardization:** The concept behind standardization provides a foolproof mechanism to control the possibilities of vulnerability occurrences in the software at the design or coding phase especially. The automated tools for security assessment mechanisms are readily available to verify and prevent the intended vulnerabilities within the application for correct functionality.

- **Assessment tools:** The best way to control functionalities within their threshold is to provide specific auditing through enabling reviews, monitoring, and acceptable qualitative or quantitative assessment mechanism [3–5].

7.3 Establishing Software Security Assurance Program

Several increased security breaches and their financial predicaments are well-known valid indicators for substantial changes in the security backdrop. There is a need to revitalize a range of software security assurance programs to reinforce the concept of governance, construction, verification, and deployment according to security standards as depicted in Figure 7.2. Numerous techniques are available to mitigate software anomalies to assure their intended functionality as per their execution, but the security assurance program provides sustainability through compliances, reactionary, and security [5–10].

A proposal to the forgoing references shows that early security standardization, architectural reviews, vulnerability management, and metrics in software security assurance programs are critical factors to endowed orientation and a foremost feature for reducing the projected risk. Moreover, such exercise may prove to be highly prolific for many reasons, including the following mentioned in Figure 7.3.

FIGURE 7.2
Software Security Assurance Program.

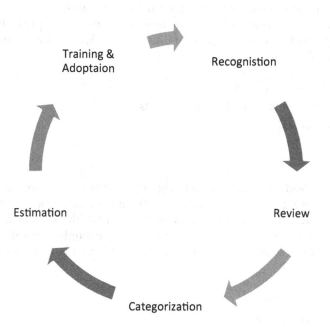

FIGURE 7.3
Components Involved in Security Assurance Program.

- To set the goals based on predefined security standards and requirements for security architecture.
- To provide a robust review mechanism for coding, security testing, and architectural review.
- To bridge the gap through environmental hardening vulnerability management and penetration testing to establish an assurance program.
- Quantitative or qualitative measurement provides a significant reason to manage or control.
- Security estimation metrics provide a significant way to deploy techniques, policies, and guidelines.
- Precise scheduling of resource distribution based upon the envisaged error occurrences of the system and its constituent parts.

A comprehensive review based on software security assurance programs suggested by various researchers and practitioners indicating the critical player to control or mitigate security risk are requirements standardization, strong code review, vulnerability management, security testing, progressive policy mechanism, and appropriate metrics. Thereby, it may indicate that the assurance program can be completely managed through these factors.

7.3.1 Recognition

Recognition is the elegant solution to any problem or opportunity based on some influential environment. The best way to establish refined security standardization for requirements and architectural perspective, there is a need to appropriately scan the environment repeatedly to fix the anomalies, whether they have internal or external influences on the decision-making process. This will provide the best support to improve the actual conditions targeting the root causes of security failures. The identified influencing factors that must be evaluated are as follows:

- Security policies and procedures
- Standards addressing security requirements
- Vulnerability management

7.3.2 Review

The regress review portion is helpful to bridge the gap between construction or recognition platforms targeting secure architectural refinements based on inconsistent security requirements. This review mechanism is beneficial to provide security assurance to keep fixing the security issues after verifying and validating through code review, security testing, and architectural analysis. The review mechanism is highly coherent with the following entities.

- Fault tolerance mechanism
- Intrusion detection mechanism
- Security evaluation
- Efficiency and effectiveness checking

7.3.3 Categorization

To sustain the assurance for security, there is a need to categorize all the pre-requisite information into one bucket according to their technical specification and way to control. This will provide the best way to support higher-level management to identify the standards and process to justify the need in a critical situation as soon as possible across their software assortment. This will result in a classified, measurable, consistent approach to address significant security solutions against their reputation. The following term must be evaluated at the time of categorization to sustain the event accordingly:

- Possibilities of vulnerabilities against prescribed standards
- Categorization of data according to their sensitiveness
- System/process/metrics/units which do not routinely reach the acceptable level of security assurance

7.3.4 Estimation

Quantitative or qualitative assessment is an effective approach to figure out the actual scenario against specific benchmarks. This will generate a significant understanding through different groups of researchers, academicians, industry experts, and higher-level management according to proposed metrics to control the security issues related to operational, functional, legal, and regulatory compliances. This provision provides a way to control and improve initiatives according to serviceability. Moreover, such observation might be highly profitable for many causes, including:

- This reduces the cost of change, as late detection and mitigation of vulnerabilities are much more expensive than before.
- This helps in better security monitoring of the software under development.
- This will support software practitioners in the empirical refinement of the process.
- This will help to minimize the efforts in developing secure software.

7.3.5 Training and Adaptation

Estimation provides rethinking possibilities against the assessment benchmarking. This will give a way to control the issues by properly adjusting security parameters and attributes. It will help to minimize the gap between actual and projected data. This will bring certainty that the proportion of security vulnerabilities is under minimization. It will help build new strategies and training programs to meet the expected security assurance goals. This will be much helpful in the following ways:

- Arrange training policies and compliances to cover all respective issues for security assurance.
- Need to develop security metrics to know the actual impact.
- Prepare strategic guidelines to minimize the impact and guide users and developers for greater sustainability.

7.4 Information Security Assurance Framework

An information security assurance framework measures the security assurance program and promotes enterprise strategic planning to control the organization's risks. Preservation of a secure and resilient environment by identifying specific domains and characteristics is the significant contribution of such comprehensive information security assurance frameworks. There are several information security assurance frameworks available, including ISO 27001, NIST Special Publication 800-53, AICPA Trust Services Principles and Criteria, COBIT (Control Objectives for Information and Related Technologies), HITRUST CSF, and PCI DSS (PCI Security Standard Counsel) with some common standards and multiple compliance requirement together. This standardized framework addresses all the information security issues under the security risk and assurance program shown in Figure 7.4. This security framework should be streamlined and incorporated with the precise coverage areas and associated industry values preferred by security assurance requirements, internal audit, and/or compliance. [6–8, 11–15]

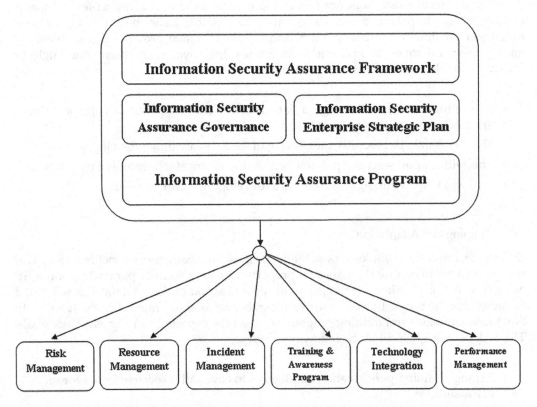

FIGURE 7.4
Information Security Assurance Framework.

7.4.1 Risk Management

One of the most critical information security assurance framework components is risk management. It is responsible for reducing risk possibilities through proper identification of vulnerabilities. The three major components directly associated with risk management are data protection, application support, and vendor management. This component enables the security team to rethink risk across the domain in more comprehensive aspects. This framework in Figure 7.5 facilitates the team to believe an extensive variety of risks in diverse realms and locate the segment for a comprehensive risk assessment. In any risk management, administration and assurance effort is a compulsory early stage. The following components are useful to control the process of risk management.

- **Data Protection Mechanism**

The concept of data protection is directly associated with risk management. It critically examines that data are processed correctly and fundamental rights are protected. Authenticity will play a vital role in protecting the data set. It is involved that information is accessed by whom and how the information will be protected in case of any data alteration. This mechanism creates a protective environment against malicious actors on the network. Protection will work two-fold, including data in rest and data in transit.

- **SDLC Application Support**

Application support is related with services. It enables software development application services to required customers with the relevant business process. The following attributes are essential for greater support.

- Understanding of knowledge domain
- Applicability of applications
- Maximum technical support
- Support tool knowledge

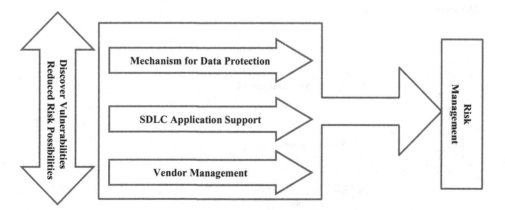

FIGURE 7.5
Risk Management Analysis.

- **Vendor Management**

It is one of the alternative plans of risk management that the activities of the vendor are under observation. Regular auditing is one of the suitable ways to control financial decline. The vendor risk assessment factors of different business nature are as follows:

- Strategic
- Observational
- Reputation
- Safety

7.4.2 Resource Management

What do you mean by resource? It is the fundamental question, but the answer is quite simple. Completion of any task is highly dependent on the resource. It can be anything like material, facility, human, or more. But the obvious questions regarding resources are whether these can be effectively utilized or not? It requires strategic planning for effective utilization. In the context of information security assurance, a reliable partnership among all resources and risk reduction programs are the critical conditions of controlled management. The following factors in Figure 7.6 are needed to be explored for better understanding:

- **Prerequisite Fulfillments**

It is highly required that all the resources must be available at the time of need in a very effective and efficient way. In terms of software, the prerequisite fulfillment may be financial, human expertise, information technology, software requirements, hardware knowledge, and variables for security assurance. Knowledge is required about the various aspects which are directly or indirectly associated with prerequisite fulfillment:

- Resource Scheduling
- Decomposition
- Resource Allocation

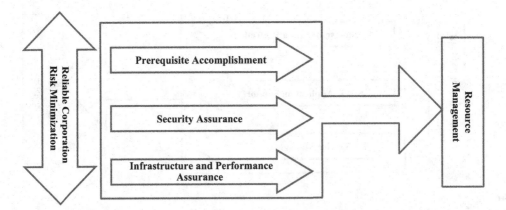

FIGURE 7.6
Resource Management Analysis

- Resource Dependency
- Assignment
- Utilization

- **Basic security Structure Assurance**

The basic security structure assurance signifies that predefined requirements on security have been fully fulfilled under proper observation. The specified activities of any process are successfully achieved. There are plenty of ways to determine the considerations that need to be addressed.

- Information technology system
- Security and business policies
- Security requirements
- Target environment

- **Infrastructure and Performance Assurance**

The infrastructural growth is the primary building block of any development. The evaluation of performance is directly connected with this growth. Performance is correlated with the experience of users. Performance issues need appropriate support and time for mitigation and enhancement. Performance risk can be evaluated by measuring the ability of application and architecture to meet customer performance.

7.4.3 Incident Management

One of the most challenging phases of the security assurance program is incident management. It requires a high-quality training program to deal with security incidents in daily life. Figure 7.7 discusses the various components of incident management. These are about the different security breaches, threats, and vulnerability responses. All issues are verified through proper digital forensics, and digital evidence must be collected for records.

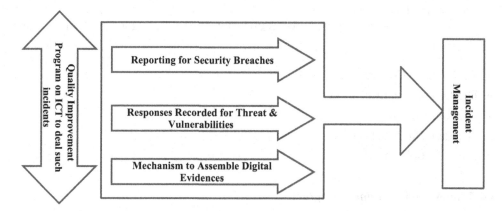

FIGURE 7.7
Incident Management Analysis

- **Security breach reporting**

Reporting of violations comes under the realm of security breach reporting. This violation has sufficient reasons, including unauthorized access to data, networks, applications, and support to devices. Incidents of security breaches bypass the underlying security mechanism. A security violation occurs when an individual or an application illegitimately enters a private, confidential, or unauthorized logical IT perimeter. The following key players are the active components in security breach reporting.

- An early stage of a security attack
- Security policy violation
- Protection through firewalls
- Need security administrator

7.4.3.1 Threat and Vulnerability Responses

Vulnerabilities are the weaknesses in software security design that threats can exploit. They can take advantage of these loopholes to gain unauthorized access. Software design gaps cerate entry points for hackers to breach the security. As per the definitions of asset, threat, and vulnerabilities, researchers have developed the equation of risk which is mentioned below:

An asset (A) is what we're trying to protect.
A threat (T) is what we're trying to protect against.
Vulnerability (V) is a weakness or gap in our protection efforts.
Risk (R) is the intersection of assets, threats, and vulnerabilities.

$$R = A + T + V$$

7.4.3.2 Collection of Digital Evidence

The collection of evidence is the primary task to establish the correlation between crime and digital data. Cyber forensic people are cable to recreate the crime plot to identify the victim and crime based on digital evidence. These acts explore the role of collecting, identifying, and preserving digital evidence in one row. The following issues come under this section.

- Digital Data Collection
- Digital Data Identification
- Digital Data Analysis
- Digital Data Preservation
- Integrity of Evidence

7.4.4 Training and Awareness Program

Training and awareness program is an important section of the security assurance framework. The best way of protection is to educate them about threats, loopholes, nature of the

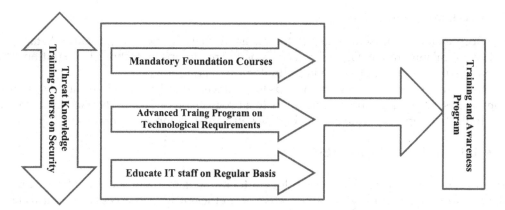

FIGURE 7.8
Components of Training and Awareness Program.

attack, and social and technological impact. Figure 7.8 focuses on training and awareness practices which are mentioned below:

- Foundation training program for newcomers
- A technological advancement training program
- Education for IT staff on a periodic basis

- **Foundation training program for newcomers**

The area of secure software development is a very specialized job profile. It requires a unique training program tailored for newcomers, especially with the involvement of the latest security components. This program aims to provide complete awareness of security threats and their role in application development.

- **A technological advancement training program**

It requires a more appropriate training program with a deeper impact on its employees. Specialized programs must be developed according to the latest research in security and assurance. Security development firms should start specialized bridge courses with the help of security experts to upgrade their employees in the relevant area. It requires a variety of programs, including:

- Induction training
- Orientation program
- Bridge course on the latest technology
- Tailored training

- **Education for IT staff on a periodic basis**

Again, our responsibility is to educate our IT staff on a periodic basis for better consistency in that particular area of specialization. It motivates IT staff in two foil manner. The first fold ensures that employees get the latest knowledge in the relevant area and encourage their juniors to learn more.

7.4.5 Technology Integration

How professionals infuse technology to upgrade society is one of the advanced stages of technological integration. Figure 7.9 focuses on the roadmaps for technical integration. The primary step is to reduce the gap in technological overlapping.

The use of technology integration helps to enhance, extend, or enrich the latest scientific approaches. Technology integration refers to a progression of purposely selecting technology tools that improve strategies during the software development and business process.

- **Information Technology Exposure**

The primary building block for technology integration is to know about the latest dimensions of technology. It provides an effective and efficient way to access different technological aspects of business processes. Various activities are helpful to combine technologies for optimal social uses. It helps in multiple aspects including:

- Linking information technology
- Knowledge management
- Strategic experimentation
- Dynamic modeling

- **Technological Gap Analysis**

Performing gap analysis is a concept for greater understanding between the strength and weaknesses of the technology. It is best to analyze the resources for optimal allocation. It will help to prioritize problems for the better interest of targeted audiences. The following steps are required for gap analysis:

- Conducting gap analysis on a particular area
- Identification of potential circumstances
- Analysis of existing scenario

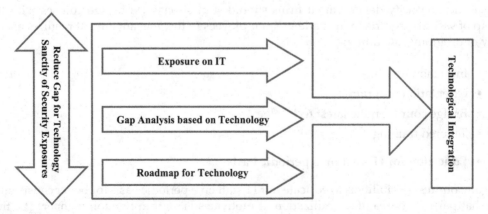

FIGURE 7.9
Components of Technology Integration.

- Comprehensive plan to bridge the gap
- Gap analysis report

- **Technological Roadmap**

Technological roadmap sketches what, when, why, and how technology will be implemented to get maximum benefits to their respective organization. Roadmap brings the ultimate solution of what technological aspects will be implemented. The following steps are needed to visualize the technical roadmap:

- Define the objectives
- Planning
- Methodology
- Measurement
- Real-time analysis
- Validation

7.4.6 Performance Management

Performance is understood as the organization's accomplishment concerning its predefined purposes. It must be evaluated in terms of a qualitative or quantitative manner to know the actual status for further improvements. 'If you want to control, you have to measure' is the famous statement of Lord Kelvin that behaves true in the case of performance management. It is highly required to measure the impact with dedicated metrics. If metrics are not available, first, researchers have to develop metrics accordingly and use those metrics after proper validation. The nature of metrics should be SMART in practice. The components of performance management are depicted in Figure 7.10.

- Specific
- Measurable
- Achievable

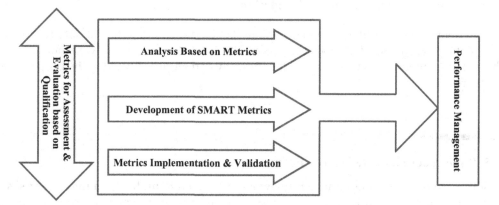

FIGURE 7.10
Components of Performance Management.

- Realistic
- Time-related

- **Metric Analysis**

Metrics are the best tools to analyze the past and present. The quantitative nature helps to examine the scenario. The critical observation is very much helpful to forecast future performance. As discussed by the National Institute of Standards and Technology (NIST), metrics are tools that facilitate decision-making and improve performance and accountability through the collection, analysis, and reporting of relevant performance-related data. The following aims can be achieved by metric analysis:

- Assessment for mission criticality
- Attack risk analysis
- Ensure business continuity
- Minimize causes of failures
- Impact analysis of incidents
- Preventive measurement

- **Metrics Development**

What is the purpose of metrics development? The reason is apparent. Metrics are supportive tools designed to improve performance and the decision-making process. It ensures the different criteria of the performance evaluation process, including data collection, analysis, and reporting. The following points must be ensured at the time of metric development.

- Visibility
- Accountability
- Management
- Support

- **Metrics Implementation and Validation**

It is evident from other literature that implemented metrics should be validated by means of statistical instruments for good correlation. The latest research on software metrics states that software metrics can be validated theoretically and empirically using the properties of measures.

7.5 Cybersecurity Assurance Framework

Deloitte Advisory cyber assurance framework is adopted to understand the cyber risks in an organization. No standardized framework is available to address all aspects of cybersecurity assurance in Figure 7.11. Inclusive cyber assurance frameworks are developed to aid internal audit and/or compliance and can be adapted to an organization's specific needs and environment. [11–13, 14]

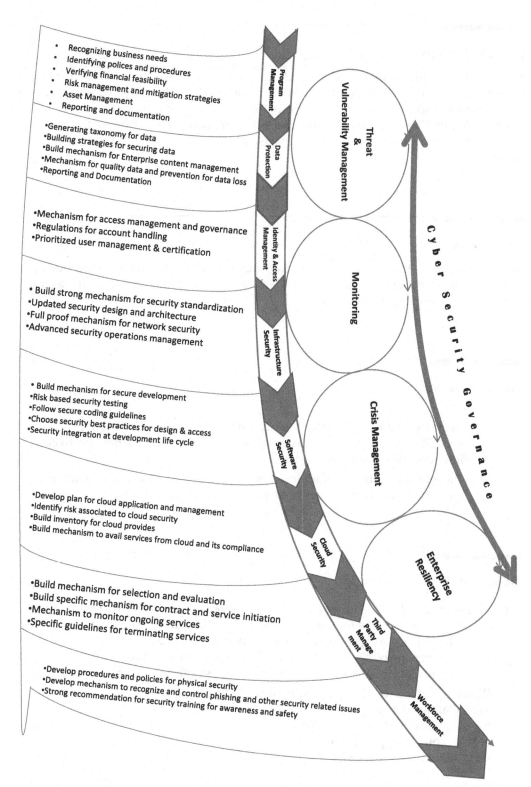

FIGURE 7.11
AComprehensive Cybersecurity Assurance Framework.

7.6 Conclusion

Security is a multidimensional theory. Undoubtedly, there are many ways to perceive security assurance and countermeasures for business risk. The principal objective is to determine the relevant factors for the information security assurance program. All factors must be identified on the basis of their expected components. The cybersecurity assurance framework is one of the latest ideas to manage and mitigate the pros and cons of the cyber world.

Key Terms

Security assurance, Information security, Information security assurance framework, Risk management, resource management, incident management, performance management, cybersecurity assurance framework

Points to Remember

1. 100% security is impossible. Absolute security is nothing but finding out the comfort level. This comfort level is experienced based on realizing the effectiveness and limitation imposed on the system.
2. With the increase in the use of information technology, cybersecurity has assumed great importance, as IT resources can be targets, sources, and means of trouble.

Objective-Type Questions

1. Which of the following is not a typical component of a security program?
   a)   The consequences for the person breaking the security policies
   b)   The policies and protective measures that will be used
   c)   The responsibilities of individuals involved in maintaining security
   d)   The responsibilities of those who abide by established security policies
2. Which of the following is a layer of protection for Security?
   a)   Platform-level protection
   b)   Application-level protection
   c)   Record-level protection
   d)   All of the mentioned

3. An assessment of the worst possible damage that could result from a particular hazard is known as
   a) Risk
   b) Hazard probability
   c) Hazard severity
   d) Mishap

4. The basic goals of software security assurance are to ensure that software is designed and developed to_____risks to an organization.

5. Risk can be calculated in terms of ....

6. Which of the following words best describes the possibilities that would pose a threat to an information system?
   a) Threat
   b) Vulnerability
   c) Weakest link
   d) Risk

Short-Answer Type Questions

1. What are the different data sources used in data collection?
2. What do you mean by security assurance?
3. What do you understand by cybersecurity?
4. What are the components of cybersecurity assurance framework?
5. What are the major components of information security assurance framework?
6. Define goals and objectives of security assurance.
7. Define the role and responsibilities of information security assurance framework.
8. What are the major advantages and disadvantages of security assurance process?
9. Highlights the key features of performance management.
10. What do you mean by risk? How risk can be calculated.

Descriptive Questions

1. How do you classify information security risks across an organization?
2. When does a person become an information security risk?
3. What do you mean by operational and communicational risk?
4. What is the difference between information security and cybersecurity?
5. Is information assurance is same as cybersecurity?

References

1. https://www.controlscan.com/blog/right-information-security-assurance-framework/. Last Visited 10 March 2019.
2. B. Alshammari, C. Fridge, and D. Corney, "Developing Secure System: A Comparative Study of Existing Methodologies", *Lecture Notes on Software Engineering*, 2 (2), May 2016, pp. 139–146, doi: 10.7763/LNSE.2016.V4.239.
3. https://resources.sei.cmu.edu/asset_files/certresearchreport/2011_013_001_50359.pdf, Last Access: 01 January 2022.
4. https://owasp.org/www-pdf-archive//SAMM_How_To_V1-1-Final-1page.pdf, Last Access: 01 January 2022.
5. A. Agarwal and R. A. Khan, "Role of Coupling in Vulnerability Propagation Object-Oriented Design Perspective," *Software Engineering: An International Journal (SEIJ)*, 2 (1), 2012, pp. 60–68.
6. R. A. Khan and S. U. Khan,"A Preliminary Structure of Software Security Assurance Model," In *Proceedings of the13th International Conference on Global Software Engineering (ICGSE '18)*. Association for Computing Machinery, New York, NY, USA, 2018, pp. 137–140, doi: 10.1145/3196369.3196385.
7. R. Ng, "A Holistic Approach to Information Security Assurance and Risk Management in an Enterprise", In *Handbook of Research on Information Security and Assurance*, 2009, p.13, IGI Global, Roy Ng (Ryerson University, Canada). doi: 10.4018/978-1-59904-855-0.ch005.
8. M. Wong, "Challenges of Security Assurance Standardization in ICT," *Journal of ICT Standardization*, 6, 2014, pp. 187–200, doi: 10.13052/jicts2245-800X.226.
9. https://www.opentext.com/file_source/OpenText/en_US/PDF/opentext-product-security-assurance-program.pdf, Last Access: 05 March 2022.
10. https://centva.issa.org/wp-content/uploads/2012/10/Software_Security-Cigital-Sept.2012.pdf, Last Access: 10 December 2021.
11. https://www2.deloitte.com/content/dam/Deloitte/ca/Documents/risk/risk-en-cybersecurity-the-role-of-internal-audit-updated.pdf, Last Access: 20 July 2022.
12. https://www2.deloitte.com/content/dam/Deloitte/de/Documents/risk/Risk-Cyber-Intelligence-Center-A-new-approach-to-Cyber-Security-Juni-2017.pdf, Last Access: 20 July 2022.
13. https://www.researchgate.net/publication/331518888_An_Assurance_Framework_for_Independent_Co-assurance_of_Safety_and_Security, Last Access: 20 November 2021.
14. https://www.secura.com/uploads/factsheets/Cybersecurity-Assurance-Services.pdf, Last Access: 20 November 2021.
15. https://safecode.org/publication/SAFECode_Principles_for_Software_Assurance_Assessment.pdf, Last Access: 15 March 2022.

Useful Links

https://www.threatanalysis.com/2010/05/03/threat-vulnerability-risk-commonly-mixed-up-terms/

https://community.synopsys.com/s/article/Software-Security-Metrics-Development

https://www.ahia.org/assets/Uploads/pdfUpload/WhitePapers/CyberAssuranceWhitePaper.pdf.

https://www.isaca.org/Journal/archives/2012/Volume-2/Pages/Fundamental-Concepts-of-IT-Security-Assurance.aspx

http://assets1.dxc.technology/security/downloads/DXC-Security-Threat_and_Vulnerability_Management_Offering_Overview.pdf

https://www.qgcio.qld.gov.au/documents/information-security-assurance-and-classification-guideline

8

Secure Software Development Process

Engineering or technology is all about using the power of science to make life better for people, to reduce cost, to improve comfort, to improve productivity, etc.

N. R. Narayana Murthy

Due to the complexity of the software development process, security issues can greatly affect the quality of the software. Unsafe software can damage an organization's image and sever ties with its customers, partners, and investors. Due to the flaws of human designers and the inherent complexities, software development must be accompanied by quality assurance activities. But this is easier said than done. Software testing can be very tedious and costly. Testing can be time consuming, costly, and provide little or no information on the quality of the testing process. This requires careful planning, preparation, execution, and analysis of the difference between the real and the required situation. Software testing involves checking and confirming a software application or program that congregates the business and technical requirements that lead to its design and development. Planning and preparation for testing emphasizes that testing should not be delayed until delivery, but rather should be done before the product is delivered. From the customer's point of view, testing planning can review requirements and design documentation to significantly address an availability or application functionality issue that could be affected by a defect. Any testing process requires precise planning and preparation steps before performing any measurement operation. [1]

Test objectives include the following:

- Identifying software deficiencies.
- Execution of the program to search for errors at detected weak spots.
- Establishing a good test case with a high probability of finding a hitherto undiscovered bug.
- Running a successful test that detects an uncertain error.
- Ensuring confidence in the system.
- Determining the degree of quality and degree of fulfillment of requirements.
- Ensuring understanding of the entire system and confirming its suitability and functionality.

A good test should be able to identify different error categories in a minimum period of time and effort. Software testing proves that the software works as specified in the technical specifications. The data collected during testing shows the reliability and quality of the software. Software testing reveals flaws in the application code. However, the test can only measure quality, not improve it. However, it is also true that developing test formulations before coding initiates can enhance quality because coders can employ this information when coding and debugging. Consequently, it can be assumed that strengthening security

DOI: 10.1201/9781003330516-8

practices during the entire software development life cycle leads to reliable secure software design. Based on the statements above, this chapter attempts to estimate guidelines for safe software development [1, 2].

8.1 Objectives

This section specifically focuses on:

- Understanding and describing the test in general.
- Understanding the requirements and significance of software testing.
- Demonstrating the role of software testing in improving software quality.
- Confirming the relationship between software testing and software reliability assessment.
- Getting the facts about various problems with software testing?
- Saving the different software test types.
- Ensuring the importance of effective testing.

8.2 Secure Development

Security flaw is the integral component of the security design. Secure development includes a software development process that is reliable, stable, error-free and free from vulnerabilities. The software is now more susceptible to attacks due to its increased complexity, connectivity, and extensibility. Unintentional and deliberate choices made by internal and external parties threaten the security of software at different stages of its development phase. Including safety and further non-functional requirements at various stages of the development life cycle is the best way to protect software against defects. Much research has been done over the years to create 'high-integrity software', and practitioners and researchers have put in enough effort to create secure software. However, despite all efforts, only a few programs were actually designed with a high level of security. Wherever, security is an established criterion and security planning guidelines is supplied as input to implementation team, there is no assurance about the final outcome will meet the safety standards [2, 3].

The development life cycle for secure software consists of composite procedures that involve the early participation of business clients, application developers and project managers, and information security professionals to effectively build safe and reliable products. Research has shown that the cost of correcting a defect or defect is much lower when it is discovered early than later or after the software goes into production. Flaws related to security in a design cannot be diagnosed in code and must be verified through threat modeling and design-time abuse simulations. If a defect is found in later stages, all actions from previous stages must be changed to correct the problem. This provides more effort and time than identifying and fixing vulnerabilities at early stage of the development life cycle [4–6]. Therefore, incorporating security functionalities early into the life cycle helps reduce the cost of software development. Keeping in mind the importance of developing secure software, it highlights the need for changes to create a system that takes software security into account by default from the start. The goal of developing secure software is to identify, implement, align, and maintain software systems where security is critical throughout the system life cycle. The most efficient approach to create secure software is to align the development life cycle progressions with the principles and practices that can help secure design, positioning, and protection. A lack of clear understanding of the technology involved in creating the software can serve as a guide for unsafe use of the software [7–10].

8.3 Microsoft Secure Development Life Cycle

It is a process that is originally developed and tested by Microsoft for the secure development of their products. In 2008, the company decided to publicly share their process and review about this method of secure development. The significance of this model is that it gives an ideal work step to achieve better and effective product security. This secure development model is tested and verified by various companies and organizations. The complimentary part of this model is that it covers approximately every portion of security and provides data retention and disposal. A stepwise work process is described in Figure 8.1. The figure illustrates the predefined seven steps that are executed by software developers to produce secure products based on Microsoft secure development life process [11–12].

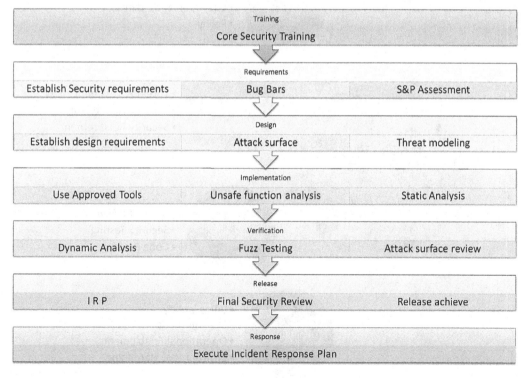

FIGURE 8.1
Microsoft Secure Development Life Cycle.

8.4 OWASP Software Assurance Maturity Model

This is an open-source model managed and developed by OWASP. Due to its open-source nature, the model has a contribution from large and vast companies as well as individual developers. This situation opens a door for better and bigger development associating timely updates based on situation needs. As same to Microsoft secure development process, this model also delivers a stepwise secure development process that can be adopted by companies to produce an effective and secure product. This methodology associates various security aspects and gives three achievements for every step associated with the method [11–13]. A brief display of the method is portrayed in Figure 8.2.

These are two popular and most effective secure development approaches that have effective outcomes through adoption. Further, to identify more about secure development authors categories some of its benefits that are written below.

- High Security: In SDL, constant observing for weaknesses brings about better application quality and relief of business dangers.
- Low Cost: In SDL, early thoughtfulness regarding imperfections altogether lessens the exertion required to identify and fix them.
- Improvement groups get nonstop preparing in secure coding rehearses.

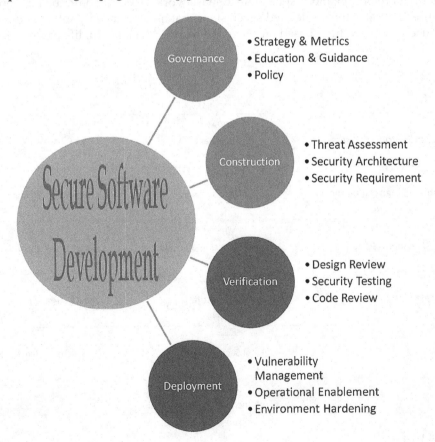

FIGURE 8.2
OWASP Software Assurance Maturity Model.

- Security approaches become more predictable across groups.
- Clients trust you more since they see that extraordinary consideration is paid to their security.
- Inside security improves when SDL is applied to in-house programming apparatuses.

8.5 An Integrated Secure Development Framework

The development practices for software are not usually designed to test a vulnerability that could be exploited by an attacker. In fact, developing a secure software process requires careful consideration of security issues at each phase of the security development cycle. It is well known that security should be part of the system, not an add-on that can be added to the system at a later stage. Adding adequate protection later is pretty tedious since the blueprint can be primarily unsafe. Additional security measures can also provide backward compatibility by affecting unwanted changes in application functionality and interfaces. Moreover, providing additional security requires significant resources and time. Therefore, security is unlikely to be added to the system at a later stage. Given the importance of security in the software development process, it is very imperative to develop techniques that consider security throughout the entire life cycle. The objective is to offer a set of guiding principles for building safer and more reliable software. The proposed build is specific and provides software developers with simple security guidance at every step in depicted in Figure 8.9. It covers a six-step development process and discusses the steps required at each step to create more secure software. Development stages consist of requirements, design, coding, testing, deployment, and maintenance. All actions in the respective stages are discussed in the following sections [14–19].

8.5.1 Securing Requirement Phase

Achieving security requirements becomes more important in networked environments. Various researchers and industry practitioners have been expressing their views on the importance of paying attention to security requirements early in the software development process. However, the recipe with a safe requirement has proven to be quite demanding over the years. Figure 8.3 graphically shows the steps in the security requirements specification phase. Each step consists of specific actions as shown in Table 8.1. The description of steps is defined here as follows:

Identification: This step defines the security requirements that include the security and resilience needs of stakeholders and meet their resilience and survival needs. Several software security issues arise from insufficient or incorrect definition of security requirements. Security targets are designed to meet specified needs. In fact, security objectives are primary aim and limitations that can influence the privacy, truthfulness, and accessibility of a requirement. Security requirements are defined as appropriate to meet security goals. More emphasis should be placed on identifying non-functional security requirements as it facilitates to reduce or eliminate weaknesses in software.

Analysis: Once safety goals have been set and the safety requirements for achieving those goals have been determined, the next step focuses on analyzing them, not including

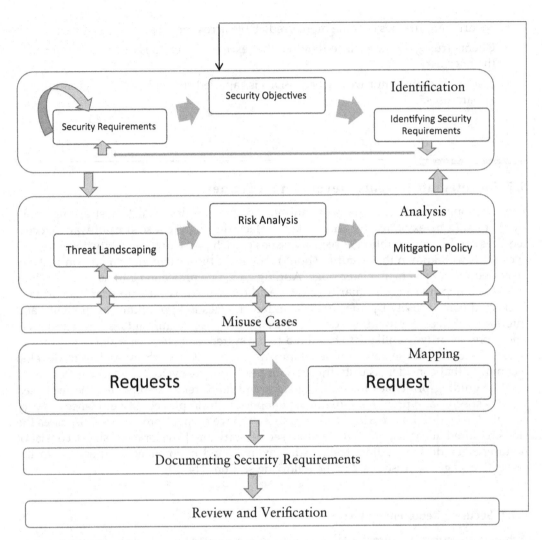

FIGURE 8.3
Steps Involved for Security Requirement Phase.

into their structural and performance facts. Security goals are typical threats in nature to a particular security environment. Threats during detection should be carefully analyzed. The changing nature of requirements specifications causes higher severity proportions and less predictable environment against the threat landscape design. It is necessary to analyze the risks associated with various security issues. Determining what the system should not do is often more difficult than it should. In this context, relevant responses come very similar to the so-called misuse cases, which are responsible for what the system should not do and are therefore very valuable in meeting security requirements.

   Mapping: Non-functional security requirements are often confined and described as software functions at the identification stage. Non-functional security requirements are often captured and illustrate as software functions at the identification stage. These non-functional security requirements must be functionally defined to be included in the software and tested accordingly. Mapping non-functional security requirements make security requirements an integral part of the analysis process.

TABLE 8.1

Prescriptive Actions at All Stages of the Secure Requirements Specification

Steps	Regulatory Procedures to Be Performed
Identification	• Demonstrating security requirements from various point of view, analyze, prioritize, and state • Outline safety objectives to meet identified needs • With the support of functional and non-functional requirements, determination of security requirements to fulfill all security objectives • Featuring software's non-functional security requirements
Analysis	• Threat analysis during design time • Arranging dangerous landscaping • Recording abuse cases for each identified security requirements • Measuring the strength of abuse cases for possible attacks • Risking evaluation to deal with security problems as you develop requirements
Mapping	• Comparing all non-functional security requirements defined with functional requirements • Mapping with exploitable use cases • Transforming all negative and ineffective requests into positive and demanding ones
Documentation	• Including needs, goals, and security requirements in concluding records • Exemplifying the threat landscape, possibility of risk, and mitigation policy
Review & Verification	• Checking documentation for compliance with specified goals and needs • Reviewing all documentation parameters of the acceptance test of security requirements documentation

Documentation: This section is responsible for delivering output. Proper documentation is done by clarifying the required description together with the security objectives. This specification document contains the specified requirements with security threats and associated risks must be identified and listed through specific plans to mitigate them.

Review and verification: The main purpose of drafting specification documents on safety requirements is to confirm the stated objectives with safety requirements, if they require further revision. The acceptability of secure documents should be verified using a variety of parameters, including accuracy, feasibility, sustainability, prioritization, transparency, and verifiability. Based on the evaluations, it is determined whether to recognize the same or to revise it.

8.5.2 Securing Design Phase

Security patterns are often chosen based on the nature of security requirements and potential threats. However, not all safety models are acceptable at this stage. Maximum safety models are recognized at the design stage. The design phase is the most innovative part of the development life cycle. Thus, the design phase has many safety implications. The outline given below corresponds to an observation that explains the relevant steps in the secure design phase. Each step includes a certain action as shown in Figure 8.4. These activities are described in Table 8.2 [20].

Securing Design Architecture: It explains the software architecture from security purview. This step involves designing the design architecture by identifying the key components needed for proper function for security. The security design architecture is a style that proposes the use of strong written language, privileges, and minimal attack areas. Early integration is included as documenting security requirements, along with security

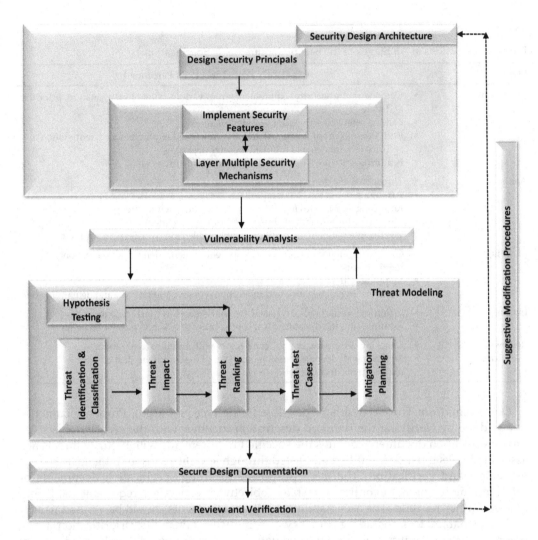

FIGURE 8.4
Steps Involved in Security Design.

design principles and the need for technical and non-technical security audits to create security design architectures.

Threat Modeling: Threat modeling is a common method that facilitates the identification of threats to applications being developed. The software starts with classifying and setting security goals. It transforms applications into physical and logical structures. Threat modeling is done to extend the security management that is indispensable in the design phase. Threat-considered procedures enhance potential design problems that are not commonly observed using other techniques. Software designers and architects try to minimize any security issues that are identified before going beyond design whenever possible. Detailed threat modeling is the best way to design the technical security behavior of design architecture. It contains four major steps, including functional transformation, classification and threat ranking, and plan to mitigate.

Secure design documentation: This step includes documenting a secure design with identified threats and presenting them, including risks, prevention methods, and threat

TABLE 8.2

Involved Actions for Each Step of Secure Designing

Steps	Action Required to Be Performed
Securing Design Architecture	• Determining security prospects of software architecture • Recognition of critical components which are most feasible for security enhancement • Need to discuss the most relevant procedure, languages with strong functionality in nature, Deploy the mechanism of least privilege and identification of attack surface; • Realization of the reflection on security design architecture based on identified latest threats, their priorities
Threat Modeling	• To resolve the risk based on unwanted software functionalities for security design architecture • Recognize the vulnerable portion of design which has less secure environment • Threat enumeration and its prioritization • Plan for threat mitigation through appropriate security mechanism • Recognition of software weaknesses where attacker can easily breach • Need to document to build historical set of information that must include the type, description, target, defensive strategies, and risk-management plan based on identified lasted threats • Proper evaluation required to set priorities and respective impact analysis based on threats • Execute analysis based on attack surface
Documenting artifacts	• Urgent requirement of proper documentation for security design • Perform defensive strategies against 'threat identification, risk description and risk mitigation' • Document the impact analysis and prioritization of threats on their severity
Review & Revise	• Design documents must be reviewed to verify all security issues that must be negotiated as per the expected requirements • Check weather revision is required, perform revision as per need

management plans. The document also contains information about the threats that are prioritized according to the impact they may have.

Review and Verification: This step checks the security design document. Secure design documents are reviewed from the beginning to ensure the safety of the design. These reviews often occur and start with an advanced design review and eventually dive deep into all elements of the program.

8.5.3 Securing Coding Phase

Coding mistakes result in 80% of system infiltration. Definitely, this can be classified as security issue. Improper coding can lead to security issues and unnecessary long-term costs. Software developers are propelled to complete their work before deadlines due to enormous market pressure. Due to lack of security awareness, they are unable to include proper instructions for secure coding. Figure 8.5 illustrates the steps involved during the secure coding phase. Every step involves some specific activity as shown in Table 8.3. These activities are explained in the following section [21].

Secure coding: The programmer should recognize the implementation level defects while writing security code. Artifacts developed during the early phase lead programmers in formulating security code. The programmer must follow the security guideline while writing the code to address the implementation level errors.

Static Analysis: It is primarily responsible for monitoring the general vulnerabilities of software using the most popular tools, including binary code or binary analysis tools. Static analysis tools provide maximum support during the integration phase to monitor the functional weaknesses of the completed software module. Immediate attention must

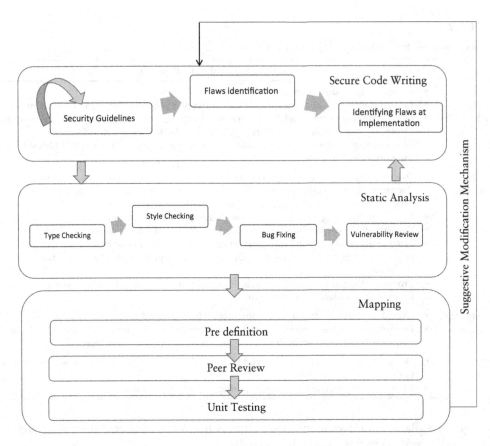

FIGURE 8.5
Steps Involved in Security Coding Phase.

be paid to the occurrence of errors and corrections with error tracking systems. The state-of-art of these tools necessitates the need for developers to analyze voluminous consequences that might hold false positives.

Code review: The decisive opinion of software security must be established through security code reviews. It is necessary to examine the behavior of functionalities based on written codes under security code reviews in manual or automated manner. Automated review tools are helpful for detecting common vulnerabilities in application software with higher percentage of false positives. However, they can be useful in aiding some parts of the code that is being handled at a security level. To reduce the false positives and negative rates, tools often ignore some vulnerability. For this reason, automatic code checking tools should not be considered rather than manual review.

8.5.4 Securing Testing Phase

Security testing is far different from functional testing, but both are equally important. Security testing requires the system to look for vulnerabilities as an attacker would. It does not occur under normal conditions. For this reason, it is important that test plans, along with security testing, be an important element of system development. The figure provided illustrates the relevant steps in the testing phase. Each step includes explicit measures as revealed in the illustration in Figure 8.6. These actions are portrayed in more detail in Table 8.4.

TABLE 8.3

Involved Actions for Each Step of Secure Coding

Steps	Action Required to Be Performed
Secure Coding	• For proper identification of security flaws at the implementation level • It requires the impact analysis on software applications through various security flaws at implementation level • Identification of programming errors rates dependable to security • Role of security guidelines to recognize flaws in applications
Static Analysis	• Highly required automated tools for security to obtain higher ratio of false positive • Use of such mechanism or tools to capture the common vulnerabilities that plague many software programs • Automated tools should work as supportive mechanism for manual code not as replacement security flaws
Code Reviews	• It verifies the fundamentals of software security by checking the codes • To perform security checks while the code is functionally monitored • Review and provide feedback with respect to identifying security flaws in applications and their mechanism to correct them • Determination of the scope for review, coverage, standards, secure requirements, and review process

Organize Secure Test Activities: Security testing should support accessible functional testing. At the very least, testing for software flaws and software testing of programs against unexpected input formats should be done in a test environment similar to understanding the developing environment. Software penetration testing is sometimes also known as security testing. Security testing is responsible to perform such task that was not being performed as per their expectations rather than verifying the functionality of the program. Security testing is the process where design document and threat modeling are being used by testers to analyze the impact of potential attacks and their possessions for the successful attack on the applicability of application.

Prepare Security Test Cases: This step includes the formulation of test cases to attack software. Formulation of test cases is developed through proper consideration of all the assumptions to capture business processes. Security test cases are being used by security testers for active analysis of software programs. For each designed test cases software is managed through assured test environment. Priorities of each test case are also determined.

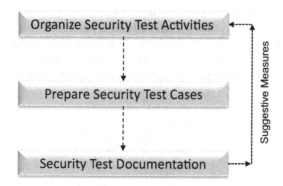

FIGURE 8.6
Steps Involved in Security Testing.

TABLE 8.4

Involved Actions for Each Step of Secure Testing

Steps	Action Required to Be Performed
Secure Test Activities	• Primary responsibility to know the possible attack and their respective impact by using design document, misuse cases and threat modeling • Discover and rank the code region with possible exploits • Categorize the region contiguous to attack surface • Recognize the vulnerable piece of codes where unknown entity can attack • Prioritize and rank according to the severity of impact
Security Test Cases	• Preparation of test cases for successful software attacks • Requires prioritization of test cases • Need to analyze all hypothesis and models for business process • Employ test cases at dynamic level • Perform test against each designed test cases on various issues for the software in test environment
Security Test Documentation	• Need proper documentation for each security test case • Discussion regarding prioritization and ranking for security test cases. • Mention those prioritized list for all vulnerabilities through dynamic analysis and proper documentation required for analysis purpose.

Security Testing Documentation: It is necessary to prepare test case documentation after successful compilation of security test cases and to discuss the prioritized investigation for security flaws and related issues through computerized or manual analytical process.

8.5.5 Securing Deployment Phase

It is crucial to keep a tab on the reaction to the defects and susceptibilities of the system to ensure for latest developed model once the software is installed into its operational environment. After the identification of newly developed prototype, they must be incorporated in requirement phase for additional security enhancement in the successive release. During the installation or the deployment stage, application security supervision, and reaction mechanism is formulated. There are two successive methods, including static analysis and peer-review focused to alleviate or diminish the recently acknowledged security flaws. Figure 8.7 presents an illustrative view of the steps involved during the secure deployment phase. Every step includes certain activities which are specific as mentioned in Table 8.5. These activities are explained in Table 8.5 [22].

Final security review and audit: This step includes the execution of the ultimate security evaluation to make certain that the security risk patterned out through all the preceding stages has been either fixed or there is an improvement mechanism to combat these risks. The security subject-matter experts also try to weed out any remaining security weakness. Security checks make sure whether security best practices have been taken care of throughout the development stage.

FIGURE 8.7

Steps Involved in Security Review and Audit.

TABLE 8.5

Involved Actions for Each Step of Secure Deployment

Steps	Action Required to Be Performed
Final Security Review and audits	• Code review to track any unidentified security flaws • Review analysis to reduce resources and time for deployment • Examine state of software in general • To verify the involvement of software security practices throughout the whole development process

8.5.6 Secure Maintenance

It is imperative for the software administrators to first fully comprehend the security stance of the software. After installation, any flaw that might have skipped previous tests will be appearing for another time and set in a prioritized manner. Novel risk is detected in this phase. Figure 8.8 presents an illustrative view of the steps involved during the security maintenance stage. Each step in this phase includes certain activities which are shown in Figure 8.8. These activities are described in detail in the Table 8.6 [23].

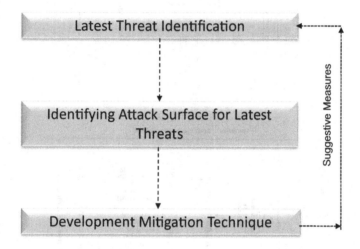

FIGURE 8.8
Steps Involved in Security Maintenance Phase.

TABLE 8.6

Involved Actions for Each Step of Secure Maintenance

Steps	Action Required to Be Performed
New Threats	• To discover latest threats encountering the system • Prioritization of latest threats and perform their impact analysis • Need to address latest threats for updated records • Prepare mitigation plan for latest identified threats
Attack Surface Area	• Recognition of latest threats and region for attack surface • Review the weaknesses at the particular region where threats are identified
Mitigation Techniques	• Expand security areas to discover latest threats • Protection plan for software to avoid security breaches

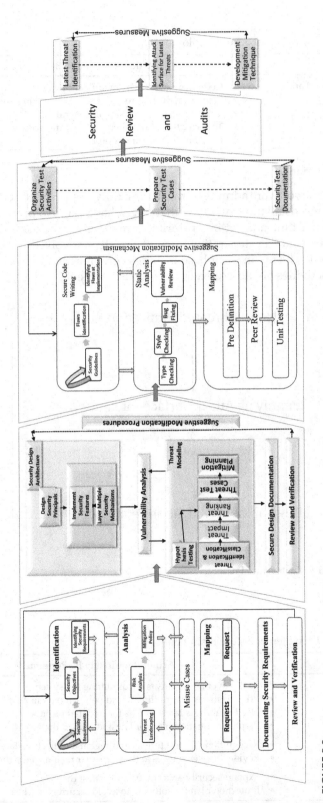

FIGURE 8.9
Secure Software Development Process.

New threats identification: The software cannot be completely secure and new threats remain pouring in time and again. Therefore, it requires some effort to keep the software safe from such security risks. The maintenance team should maintain a tab on new threats which the system encounters after installation so that they are addressed timely and any security breach is shunned and is dealt with properly.

Attack surface area: After installation, it is necessary to be aware of the fragile areas of the application software which are prone to attacks. These areas require extra precautions in deploying security mechanism to evade exploitation.

Developing a mitigation technique: Addressing the security flaws after the installation of the software can be a Herculean task since writing patches is the only way to counter threats. Therefore, security patches are released to fortify the software against new threats and flaws.

8.6 Conclusion

Enhancement of security-aligned efforts throughout the software development cycle is the only way to design robust and secure software. An early amalgamation of security activities into the development process results in cheaper software development. Due to the fundamentally insecure design of the software, updating appropriate security later is very complicated if not impossible. Moreover, it can also alter the attributes and application interfaces, thereby affecting the backward compatibility. The framework proposed in this chapter is an endeavor in this course. The proposed framework is very specific in nature and mandates observing the key activities during the development life cycle to create secure software. A successful assimilation of the mentioned activities in each phase lessens both the effort and time, simultaneously delivering secure software.

Key Terms

Secure Development, Secure Software Development Framework, Securing Requirement Phase, Design Phase Security, Securing Design Architecture, Coding Phase Security, Security Testing Phase, Security Deployment Phase, Secure Maintenance

Points to Ponder

- The primary observation based on secure software development emphasizing continuous concern of security is able to frame secure mechanism through discovering and reducing vulnerabilities in early stage.

- It must be required to include the security assurance mechanism at the primary stage of software development because security considerations must be shared to all stakeholders.
- It must be helpful to minimize the overall intrinsic risk for businesses and development.
- Execution of gap analysis is highly needful to trace the effective activities and policies, which are most feasible for organization or business.
- Assuming best practices for security and ensuring the security of software developed internally before they are deployed can reduce risks from internal and external sources through the software development phase.

Objective-Type Questions

1 Due to the complexity of the software development process, security issues can greatly affect the _____ of the software.
   a) Security
   b) Safety
   c) Quality
   d) Usability

2 Software testing involves checking and confirming a software application or program that congregates the _____requirements that led to its design and development.
   a) Business and technical
   b) Only business
   c) Only technical
   d) None of above

3 Security flaw is the integral component of the _____.
   a) Security requirement
   b) Security design
   c) Security testing
   d) Security maintenance

4 _____ includes a software development process that is reliable, stable, error-free, and free from vulnerabilities.
   a) Security planning
   b) Software development
   c) Secure development
   d) Software assurance

5 The software is now more susceptible to attacks due to its increased _____, connectivity, and extensibility.
   a) Governance
   b) Testability
   c) Usability
   d) Complexity

6 Software specification document contains the specified requirements with _____and associated _____.
   a) Vulnerability and response
   b) Authentication and authorization
   c) Defects and flaws
   d) Security threats and risk

7 Detailed threat modeling is the best way to design the technical security behavior of _____.
   a) Safety feature
   b) Design architecture
   c) Defects
   d) Security analysis

8 Detailed threat modeling contains four major steps, including functional transformation, _____ and threat ranking, and plan to mitigate.
   a) Classification
   b) Association
   c) Coupling
   d) Cohesion

9 Security code review must be performed while the code is examined for _____
   a) Planning
   b) Design
   c) Coding
   d) Functionality

10 During the installation or deployment stage, application security monitoring and response plan is formulated.
   a) Planning and execution
   b) Monitoring and response
   c) Designing and Coding
   d) Efficiency and functionality

Short-Answer Type Questions

1 What do you mean by secure software development process?
2 How security flaws are responsible for unreliable software development.
3 Write down the regulatory procedures for identification process for security requirement phase?
4 What action should be taken for threat modeling for secure designing?
5 What actions should performed for securing design phase?
6 What steps are needed for security coding phase?
7 What do you know by static analysis?
8 What do you know about code reviews?
9 Describe secure code writing through appropriate example.
10 What do you know about security testing?

Descriptive Questions

1 What do you know about the secure maintenance? Discuss the perspective activities in each step during secure maintenance.

2 What do you know about the secure deployment? Discuss the perspective activities in each step during secure deployment.

3 What do you know about the security testing? Discuss the perspective activities in each step during security testing.

4 What do mean by securing coding phase? Discuss the perspective activities in each step during secure coding.

5 What do mean by securing design phase? Discuss the perspective activities in each step during security design.

6 Discuss the perspective framework for secure software development process in details.

7 What are the major components associated with secure development. Highlight each component with their specific functionality.

8 Write down the major objectives for secure development process.

9 How early design approach is much better response that late development approach. Provide specific reasons for that.

10 What do mean by securing requirement phase? Discuss the perspective actions for the each step during secure requirement phase.

References

1. J. Du, Y. Yang and Q. Wang, "An Analysis for Understanding Software Security Requirement Methodologies", *Third IEEE International Conference on Secure Software Integration and Reliability Improvement*, 2009, pp. 141–149.

2. M. Paul, "The Ten Best Practices for Secure Software Development", (ISC)2. https://www.isc2. org/uploadedFiles/%28ISC%292_Public_Content/Certification_Programs/CSSLP/ISC2_WPIV.pdf

3. C. Wysopal. "Building Security into Your software Development Lifecycle", *SC Magazine*, 30 January, 2008. http://www.scmagazineus.com/building-security-into-yoursoftware-development-lifecycle/article/104705/

4. C. Perrin, "Design Simplicity is an Important Element of Open Source Security", *IT Security*, 10 January 2011.

5. J. Allen, "Measuring Software Security", Extracted from the 2009 CERT Research Annual Report, Carnegie Mellon University, pp. 64–65, 2010. www.cert.org/archive/pdf/research-rpt-2009/allen-meassoft-sec.pdf

6. B. Whyte and J. Harrison, "Secure Software Development", *Software Security Failures: who should correct them and how*, Issue V1.0 June 2008.

7. M. S. Merkow and L. Raghavan, "Software Security for Developers", 27 September 2010. http://www.csoonline.com/article/618463/software-security-fordevelopers

8. "Agile Software Development Doesn't Create Secure Software", View Point, 4 March 2011. http://agilescout.com/agile-software-development-doesn't-create-secure-software/

9. "How a Process Model Can Help Bring Security into Software Development", (ISC)2 Government Advisory Board Executive Writers Bureau, 4 Mar 2010.
10. K. M. Goertze, "Introduction to Software Security", *US CERT*, 2009. https://buildsecurityin. us-cert.gov/bsi/547-BSI.html
11. [Online], https://www.veracode.com/security/secure-development
12. [Online], https://www.inforisktoday.com/blogs/security-risks-in-software-development-p-871
13. [Online], https://www.ptsecurity.com/ww-en/analytics/knowledge-base/how-to-approach-secure-software-development/
14. A. Alkussayer and W. H. Allen, "The ISDF Framework: Towards Secure Software Development", *Journal of Information Processing Systems*, 6(1), March 2010, pp. 91–106.
15. J. Viega and G. McGraw, *Building Secure Software*, Addision-Wesley, 2002.
16. M. Howard. "Building More Secure Software with Improved Development Process", *IEEE Security & Privacy*, 2(6), 2004, pp. 63–65.
17. J. K. R. Mathur and A. Mathur, "Software Engineering for Secure Software", Technical Report, Purdue University, 2005.
18. M. Howard and S. Lipner, *The Security Development Lifecycle: A Process for Developing Demonstrably More Secure Software*, Microsoft Press, 2006.
19. J. Viega and G. McGraw, *Building Secure Software*, Addision-Wesley, 2006.
20. J. Viega, "Understanding Software Security", Online link: http://proceedings.ndia.org/3690/ Tuesday_Breakout_RoomB/SecurSoftware.pdf, Last Access: 10 June 2022
21. T. Demopoulos, "Worst Practices in Developing Secure Software", http://www.infosecwriters. com/text_resources/pdf/Worst_Practices_in_App_Sec.pdf
22. M. Schumacher, E. Frenandez-Buglioni, D. Hybertson, F. Buschmann and P. Sommerland, *Security Patterns: Integrating Security and Systems Engineering.* John Wiley & Sons, 2006.
23. S. Simpson, "Fundamental Practices for Secure Software Development, A Guide to the Most Effective Secure Development Practices in use Today", 8 October 2008. www.safecode.org/ publications/SAFECode_Dev_Practices1108.pdf

Useful Links

https://www.microsoft.com/en-us/securityengineering/sdl
https://www.veracode.com/security/secure-development
https://safecode.org/
https://us-cert.cisa.gov/bsi/articles/knowledge/sdlc-process/secure-software-development-life-cycle-processes
https://cyberforces.com/en/services/secure-software-development
https://resources.github.com/whitepapers/Secure-software-development-strategy-essentials/
https://www2.deloitte.com/hu/en/pages/risk/solutions/biztonsagos-szoftverfejlesztes.html

9

Software Security Testing

Program testing can be a very effective way to show the presence of bugs, but is hopelessly inadequate for showing their absence.

Edsger Dijkstra

The growing security incidents and emergent acquaintance among business owners regarding invalidated applications are being rejected due to security problems detected in software. These growing issues are responsible for being emerging consequences on the realm of security testing, which plays a key role on software tester's world. Security testing is responsible to identify the probable weaknesses of applications. These loopholes may be responsible for unintended functionality and having probability of theft or destruction for critical or sensitive information. It may facilitate intruders to access into the system through compromising vulnerabilities of applications. Traditional approaches for security testing do not efficiently confine vulnerabilities and logical errors at early stage. Moreover, it directs to the elevated expenditure for fixing issues acknowledged at later phase. Traditional practices for software testing have insufficient time for developers to fix raising issues [1].

Tensile nature of design is responsible for the occurrences of potential attacks. The designing phase of software development life cycle is being compromised through the various issues, including cryptographic misuses, broken access control, and API for privileged block. Numerous common security issues, including buffer overflow problem, cross site scripting, SQL injection attack, failure to handle missing parameter and improper handling of undefined parameters are the significant issues at the implementation level. The development level can be capable to deal with security issues like insecure configuration management, improper inclusion of source code, and brute force attacks for undue authentication effort. It is highly required to address all security issues at various levels of software development, and these issues must be resolved strategically. Incorporating security testing parallel to software development process is having significant responses against security issues. Therefore, it is an urgent requirement to develop an integrated security testing framework focused on the development life cycle. Another issue is industrialization of security which is a major distress for security experts and academicians working in this area. It's an era where industry needs the industrialization of security. This will contribute to the improvement of security in terms of security measure improvements, product improvements, and policy improvements for security management [1, 2].

9.1 Objectives

It has become necessary and even difficult to examine what is concerned in security testing activities that make it expensive and imperative. What are the requirements to be prepared for each action; how to increase the time; and lastly how to illuminate the area that can be used to save time so that itis clearly visible. Significant time can be saved by using innovative testing techniques if the best activities are identified and implemented in the testing process. The following prioritized activities which are most advantageous for the process of security testing on different perspectives with set objectives are discussed here:

- To reviewing security rules, guideline, and regulations.
- To analyze the security best practices available for implementing security.
- To create security request and attack scenarios.
- To review the process of integrating security within the test life cycle.
- To develop phased security test process.
- To design a guideline to adopt the level of security test process.
- To propose a guideline for the accomplishment of logical tests to verify the appropriate functioning of the implemented security actions.
- To identify deviation from the allowed services defined in the organizations security policy.

9.2 Software Testing

Software testing is a process to appraise the functionality of a software application with an objective to uncover whether the developed software met the particular requirements. It is an effort to recognize the defects for the production of quality product through proper validation of defect free environment. It verifies the expected behavior of functionality meets actual requirements. In software testing process, the purpose for the identification of errors or missing requirements are verified against the actual requisite which must be validated for gap analysis. Generally, software testing is broadly categorized into functional and non-functional testing.

Risk-based approach works as basis to estimate the actual posture of software architecture reality for system and also provides a standard of measurement of attacker's motive – how to breach software security to gain financial benefits. The primary task of testers is strongly motivated to expose the chance of loss or damage by compulsive tests on risk. This will facilitate to gauge the severity of risk and possible attack centric regions which can be easily violated by intruders. As per security concern, it's a phase-wise process under system testing where the Target of Evaluation (TOE) is tested. This demonstration assists an important step toward secure software [2, 3].

9.3 Security Testing

Security vulnerabilities in software systems that vary from local implementation errors to much higher design-level mistakes are the hardest imperfection class to handle, and these kinds of flaws almost always lead to security risk. The goal of security testing is to detect vulnerabilities earlier and ensure security and trustiness of final product. Vulnerability assessment/detection technique provides a valuable methodology for security testing. This chapter provides a detailed survey and analysis of different security-testing tools for comprehensive investigation for vulnerability scanning and detection.

With the technological advancement, security testing is relatively a new concept that ensures the software operations are under control on hostile condition. Within the security realm, security testing is still a relatively new theme. This chapter discusses the types, issues, and support of different security testing tools. It provides a comprehensive investigation of security testing tools for security vulnerability testing at different categories like source code and byte code analysis, web application and web service analysis, network-based analysis, etc.

The identification and prevention of weaknesses and vulnerabilities at early stage are ensuring software security and trustiness and achieving assertion that system manages within the constraint of known set of policies and mechanism. Software security testing, code reviews, and risk analysis are some of the most effective methods for identifying software weaknesses and vulnerabilities. The purpose of software security is to discover vulnerabilities and prevent them from the finished product by implementing security vulnerability detection techniques or security testing tools. This effort is acceptable when it confirms that final software product hold all expected security applicable exceptions and malfunction. There are four key points to consider in a security test that are as follows [3–6].

1. **Network Security**: It includes detecting vulnerabilities in network infrastructure, including resources and policies.
2. **System Software Security**: It focuses on detecting weaknesses in the software that the application is dependent on for its operations.
3. **Client-side Application Security**: It focuses on shielding the client or the browser from any possible manipulations.
4. **Server-side Application Security**: It focuses on the strengthening of the server code and its technologies to thwart any intrusion.

Security testing often involves carrying out complicated steps. But, a simple test like the one mentioned above can also lay bare the vulnerabilities and the most severe security risks.

9.4 Software Security Testing Process

Security testing is considered as an essential resource to develop security of software. Software security testing confirms the secure development and execution of software product, consequently minimizing the probability of security errors being unconfined and revealed by customers or malicious users. Validation of robustness and prevention from security weaknesses for not allowing in the application are the primary responsibility of security testing. It has been recognized as an essential mechanism to ensure trustworthiness and software security. Under any hostile condition, the functionality must be operational verifying the functioning of software security testing after recognition of anticipated security-related anomalies, errors, exceptions, and failures. It works in two-fold manner for any organizational practice environment. The primary layer is responsible, including compliance to withstand the use, and the other layer ensures that the security policy is well understood and implemented by the organization. As per the above discussion, some pertinent observations are highlighted to incorporate security testing on higher priority [7–10].

- To recognize loopholes within applications responsible for loosing data
- To allow protective environment to block intruders for breaching applicability
- To verify the trustworthiness of software for preserving safe behaviors and state change
- Responsible for identifying exploitable flaws and weaknesses within applications
- Responsible for improving the system for distinct services
- Elimination of security flaws at design phase of software development
- Build mechanism for cost reduction and prevention for potential security risk

Determining system's behavior as per intended functionality is the key challenge for security testing process. Operation-ability within the constraints of given set of policies and procedures for preserving security assurance is the common approach for security testing. Security expert Guru Gary McGraw's research article entitled 'Risk-based security testing' provides a clear understanding and simulated approach for attacker's behavior by recognizing system's risk. Acknowledging risk and performing respective software security test on the focused area of codes in which an attack is expected to success.

9.5 An Integrated Approach

Security testing remains incomplete without the addressing the issue of how the system under design defends against attacks during the initial phases of the design stage. An adequate security testing requires testing all the aspects, and not merely the implementation. Test process is responsible for providing protection of the intended system from attack. Strong mitigation procedures play a vital role to ensure security. Security testing with an integrated mechanism throughout the development cycle proposes a comprehensive perspective of the software quality and defends against identified security threats as mentioned in Figure 9.1. The tester must use his knowledge early in security analysis during the prerequisite elicitation phase. The necessary changes can be introduced earlier than the coders begin their process. If security testing is ignored throughout the development stage, the application can develop menacing vulnerabilities, and much vulnerability dissemination will arise during the development phase, putting the organization into enormous risk. Therefore, to extend the perspective on software quality, adopting an integrated security testing approach is critical to identifying vulnerabilities at each stage of development progress and minimizing them at the same time. Integrating software testing into the development process will decrease the cost of damage and potential risks. Therefore, security testing strategies for software products must be developed for each phase as depicted in Figure 9.2.

It has become both crucial as well as challenging to scrutinize what makes the security testing activities so exclusive and significant. It is extremely advisable to search for what must be done at every event to optimize the time and illustrate the fields where it can be

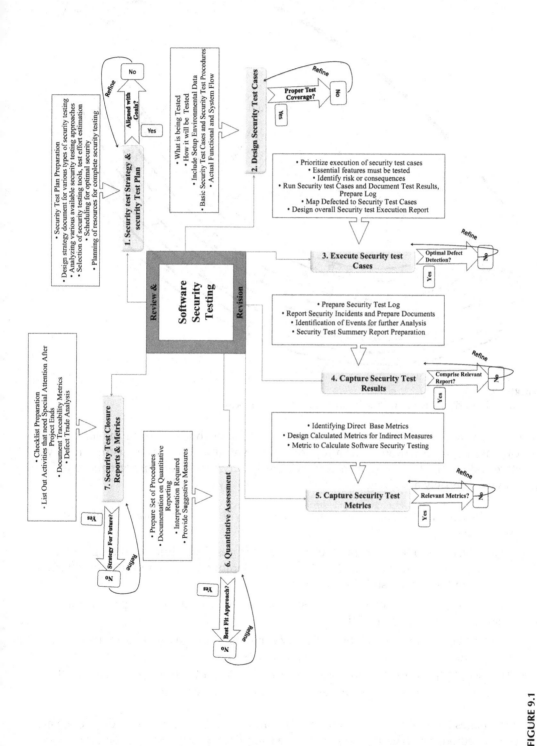

FIGURE 9.1

An Integrated Framework for Software Security Testing.

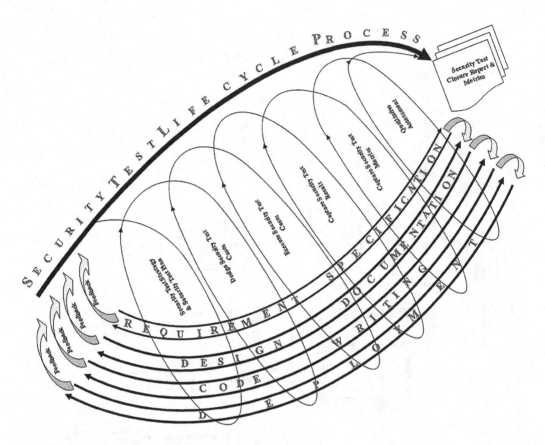

FIGURE 9.2
Incorporated Security Activities with Software Security Testing Process.

employed to save time. The implementation of optimal activities during the testing process can save significant time by the adoption of innovating testing mechanisms. Moreover, an active and insistent method of security testing specifying the most prioritized activities can prove immensely advantageous in the following ways [10–13].

- A well-structured security testing mechanism will direct to more credible tested software.
- The implementation of an apt security testing process, scheduled in the right manner and applied smartly, will result in a considerable decrease in time and effort, enhancing the quality simultaneously.
- Developing prescriptive security test processes will result in the production of quality product in minimal time.
- The automation process can be positively exploited through dynamic security testing actions.
- The possibility of profits through the software significantly increases due to the implementation of an appropriate and accurate security test activity.

The advantages listed above stress upon the requirement to shift from an undeveloped and makeshift method of operation, to incorporate a complete security testing process. An active security testing process involves an extensive range of skills and actions, which includes classification, compilation, and documentation, along with the supporting resources. Within such perspective, test behavior must be prioritized with the definitive intention of delivering ultimate profit of security, to the final users. Therefore, it underlines the urgency for the need to have a generally acknowledged procedure of software security testing that can be incorporated with each stage of the software development life cycle to develop security software. Figure 9.2 proposes a prescriptive framework to meet the demands of the software users. The proposed process is divided into seven phases, which are as follows.

- Security test strategies and test plan
- Designing security test cases
- Executing security test cases
- Capturing security test results
- Capturing security test metrics
- Qualitative assessment
- Closure reports for security test

The figure given below shows the security test life cycle process stating as a separate process that is firmly connected to the development activities. Each of the seven phases mentioned above has been described below.

9.5.1 Security Test Strategy and Test Plan

This phase needs the preparation of a suitable security testing plan to allow security testing to be associated with security requirements and to declare entry and exit criteria for each phase of testing. The test plan supposed to distinguish between the items and features that need to be tested, the type of test that needs to be achieved, the personnel to perform the test, the resources and schedule essential to perform the analysis, and the risks surrounding to plan. The involved steps involved for preparing security test strategy and policy are mentioned in Figure 9.3.

9.5.2 Designing Security Test Cases

This phase is responsible for conception, corroboration, and modification of security test cases and test scripts. Positive, negative, real-world scenario, and boundary conditions are the four major aspects to perform test cases. It is highly required to configure the actual prerequisites to conduct security test cases under predefined criteria for test cases. The involved steps for preparing security test design are mentioned in Figure 9.4.

9.5.3 Executing Security Test Cases

This phase requires the execution of security test scripts in a coherent ordering with explicit input data. The outcome should be scrutinized, and output should be documented in test sheets. Out of the massive compilation of test cases, their priorities of implementation should be determined based on numerous justifications and non-arbitrary criteria. The test results must be recorded, and the failed instances with their defects should be documented. After that, the security test plan and test cases should be evaluated and improved. The proposed steps in executing security test cases are depicted in Figure 9.5.

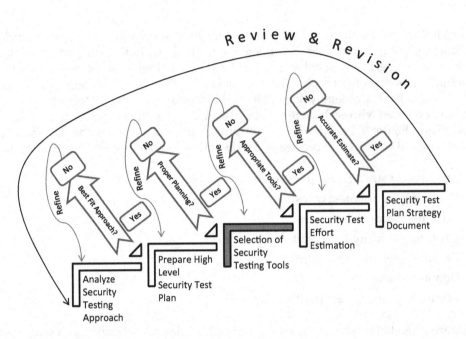

FIGURE 9.3
Perspective Activities for Security Test Strategy and Test Plan.

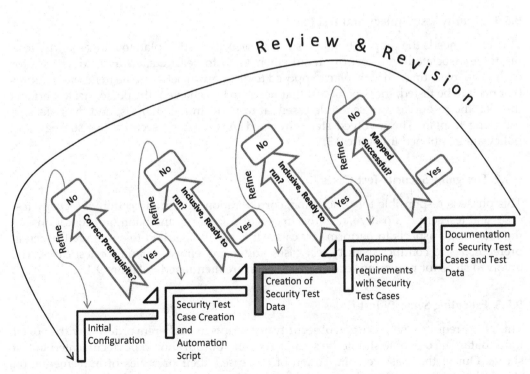

FIGURE 9.4
Perspective Activities for Design Security Test Cases.

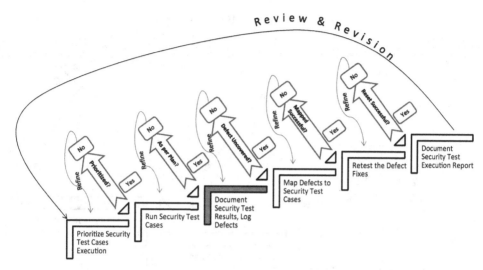

FIGURE 9.5
Prescriptive Step in Executing Security Test Cases.

9.5.4 Capturing Security Test Result

After successfully executing the security test case, the recognized defects must be fixed and re-tested. The results can thereupon be declared to pass or not succeed. The test observations should be well acknowledged. Moreover, a test log must be created to consist of historical remarks of significant facts regarding the execution of tests. Finally, a test synopsis should be organized with an abbreviation of the outcome of test activities connected with one or more test design requirements, and an estimation supported by such findings. The details regarding execution of test cases are mentioned in Figure 9.6.

9.5.5 Capturing Security Test Metrics

The security test metric must be recognized to support in specifically evaluating the project endeavor, addressing the interest of metric group and software managers. These are responsible for the improvement of software security testing efforts at development and testing processes. These security test metrics are capable to offer precise information to project managers and test team lead on the basis of project status reports. Most of the fundamental parameters are easy reckoning that mainly test analysts keep track of, in some or the other form. Measured security test metric transforms the primary metric data into more functional information. The involved steps for capturing the test metrics are depicted in Figure 9.7.

9.5.6 Qualitative Assessment

Product quality measurement parameters to evaluate product quality are summarized at this stage. A number of generally accepted parameters are selected for which the evaluation will be performed. From these quantitative outcomes, a report on the quality of the work is created which is later made available to the final user. Interpretations and suggestive measures, which are based on the qualitative assessment, are proposed. Figure 9.8 depicts the prescriptive step in qualitative evaluations.

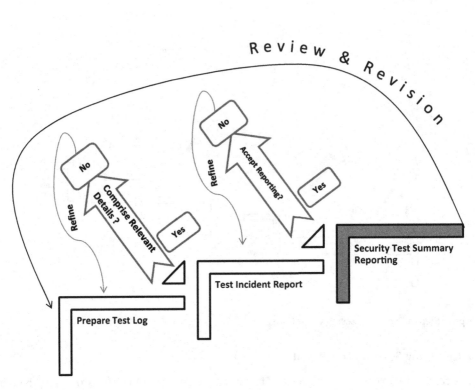

FIGURE 9.6
Perspective Steps Involved for Capturing Security Test Result

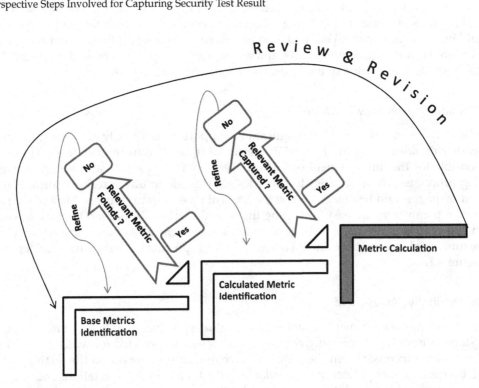

FIGURE 9.7
Perspective Steps Involved for Capturing Security Test Matrices

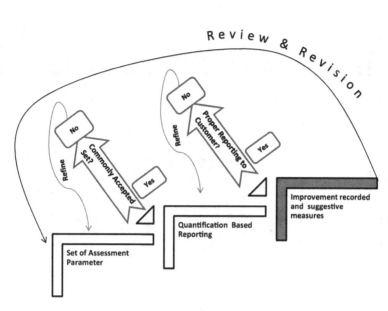

FIGURE 9.8
Perspective Steps Involved for Qualitative Assessment

9.5.7 Security Test Closure Reports

The expected security outcome successfully achieved the desired goals are being well documented and archived. This project-related knowledge is used as a reference for project planning on the basis of test meets and exit criteria. Time, test exposures, budget, software applications, decisive business objectives, quality, steps involved for preserving outcome, results and observations are the exit criteria. It is demanding for test closure document to prepare a checklist of activities that must be carried out upon the closure of project.

9.6 Software Security Testing Tools

The exponential increase in the use of software applications, internet services, where all information is available in a single click needs an effective security mechanism with automated or semi-automated way to test and validate correct functions. They are transferring their sensitive information to servers which can be used through web application with the help of internet or intranet. In most of the scenario, the strong security testing mechanism needs to require handling malicious intruders and finding potential vulnerabilities. It facilitates to confirm software dependability in terms of inconsistently safe behaviors and state changes. It also explores exploitable flaws and vulnerabilities to reduce software security risk for improved efficiency of security testing. Various types of security testing tools are available to help security professionals to assess the possible vulnerabilities in software services. This means that the presence of vulnerabilities in the application reflects that the application may be compromised at any time. The more vulnerability a program has, the easier it is to attack. Table 9.1, entitled Security Testing Tools, analyzes the types, nature of tools, security issues, and language supports, source and phase where it works. Different types of testing tools are available to discover vulnerabilities in each phase of development process. These security testing tools detect or scan vulnerabilities on source code, network, web services, web applications, software, and its design validation phase.

TABLE 9.1

Security Testing Tools: A Revisit [14–54]

Tool Name	Type of Tools	Support to Language/ Based Upon	Security Issues	Phase Analysis/ Mode of Use	Source
RATS	Scanning tool	Languages like C,C++,Perl, php& python	BOF,TOCTOU,RC	At source code level	Secure software/ fortify software/ HP
beSTROM	Fuzzing tool	In house software application & devices	Application anomalies	NA	Beyond security
Zed Attack Proxy	Automated scanning/ penetration testing tool	JAVA &web-based applications	Security vulnerabilities	Source code	Open source
nCircle Certified PCI Scan Services	Scanning	Network-based software applications	PCI data security standard relevant conditions	NA	nCircle
Fortify360	Scanning/detection	Software application level	Vulnerability disclosure	Static code analysis/ dynamic run time observation	Fortify software/ HP
Perimeter Check	Vulnerability assessment	Languages which provides services for Servers/website/ firewalls/routers	Security vulnerabilities: interrupt services/data theft/system destruction	External network devices	Security Metrics Inc.
Core Impact Pro	Vulnerability assessment/scanner and penetration testing software	Software application/ web-based applications/servers & devices	Confirm exploitable vulnerabilities/metrics for efficacy of layered defenses/ validate compliance	Security testing best practices into a six-step process	Core Security Technologies
C5 Compliance Platform	Identification/ evaluation/ summarization	Heterogeneous System	Security Vulnerabilities	XML Specification Languages	Secure Elements Inc
Security Metrics Appliances	Detection/prevention	Integrated software & hardware devices	Vulnerability assessment	By entering IP and DNS, network check list is being created for testing	Security metrics
SARA	Remote self-scan, API facilities security analysis tool	Unix based	API & Plug-in facilities for third party application	API, plug in facility	Advance Research Corp.

Found Stone	Vulnerability management software tool/vulnerability assessment	Software application level	Hardware appliance, software product/managed services	NA	McAfee
NetIQ security analyzer	Vulnerabilities scanning/assessment product	Windows/solaris/Linux	Multi-platform vulnerabilities scanning/assessment within schedule interval	NA	NA
Seeker	Vulnerability detection	AJAX/adobe flex & Air/RIA/.Net/J2EE/HTTPS	Web security testing to pinpoints and reveal risk areas of source code and code correlation	Source code	Quotium technologies
Zero day scan	Security scanning services	Web-based applications	Web-based XSS, SQL injection vulnerabilities	NA	Kyplex Cloud Security
App Scan source edition	Identification software security vulnerabilities	C/C++/.NET/Java/JSP/Java Script/ColdFusion/ASP/PHP/Perl/VB/PL/SQL/T-SQL/COBOL	Recognition of security weaknesses the time of integrating security testing with software development process	Source code/commercial	IBM rational
Klocwork insight	Defect detection/security vulnerabilities	C,C++,C#, JAVA	Defect detection, architectural and build over build analysis	Source code	Klocwork Insigh
Astree	Runtime errors	Astrée analyzes structured C programs, with complex memory usages, but without dynamic memory allocation and recursion.	Runtime error and assertion violations by abstract interpretations	Code Level	NA
Find Bugs	Bug scan	Java	Open source byte code analyzer	Code level	BCEL Jakarta, University of Maryland
BOON	Buffer overrun vulnerabilities/error scan	Programming language support like C & Unix SML/NJ in BOON	Integer range analysis	Code level	David Wagner, in collaboration with Jeff Foster,

(Continued)

TABLE 9.1 (*Continued*)

Security Testing Tools: A Revisit [14–54]

Tool Name	Type of Tools	Support to Language/ Based Upon	Security Issues	Phase Analysis/ Mode of Use	Source
CQual	Format string vulnerabilities	CQUAL Java-based support. C, C++ is supported by Oink.	Perform a taint analysis and then uses type inference rules to propagates the qualifiers to detect format string vulnerabilities by type checking	NA	Ashcraft and Engler 2002
Eau Claire	Identification of security breaches in C programs	C	Eau Claire automatically checks for array bounds errors and null pointer dereferences	Code Level	B.V. Chess, Improving Corp.
Splint	Security vulnerabilities and coding error	C Unix command-line program,	Checking code specifications by proper observation of source codes	C Source code including headed header	David Evans, David Larochelle
SecureCFM	Source code	Linux & windows environment	Responsible for audit of ColdFusion source code (CFML), Recognize Cross Site Scripting vulnerabilities	Source code	Secure CFM is copyright © 2002 Dimitri Muringer
ITS4	Scanning security vulnerabilities	C,C++ software written in C	ITS 4 scans source code for calls with malicious functions stored in the database. Buffer Overflow, FSP, SE, TOCTOU, Usage Weak random no generation User Interface	Open source code	John Viega, J.T. Bloch, Yoshi Kohno, Gary McGraw Reliable Software Technologies Dulles, Virginia
AcunetixWVS	Vulnerabilities scanner/ detection	Windows	NA	Commercial / limited capability	Acunetix
Burp Suite	Security vulnerabilities scanner	HTML document	Analyze the degree of uncertainty in the application, tokens, or other items for which the application relies on unpredictability for security.	Commercial/free (limited capability)	PortSwiger

Name	Category	Platform	Description	License	Vendor
GamaScan	Security vulnerabilities scanner	Windows	It is complex web application security service examine regular dynamic tests associated with simulated web-application attacks during the scanning process.	Commercial	GamaSec
Grabber	Web application scanner	Windows, Linux, Unix Python, Beautiful Soup and PyXML	Automatics verification on websites/scripts, only tell you what vulnerability it is... not how to solve it.	Open source	Romain Gaucher
Grendel-Scan	Security testing tool for web application in Open source environment	Windows, Linux and Macintosh	To detect common web application vulnerabilities, and features geared at aiding manual penetration tests through automated testing modules.	Open Source	David Byrne
Hailstorm	Security assessments on Cloud and Web applications	Windows	Cloud and Web security, risk management at SDLC level.	Commercial	Cenzic
N-Stealth	Web application security scanner, auditing, network, web	Windows, Linux	Web Server security check Backup security check Cross-site Scripting	Commercial	N-Stalker
Netsparker	Web application vulnerability scanner	Windows	SQL Injection, Cross-Site Scripting, Netsparker identifies: Error-based SQL Injections Boolean SQL Injections Blind (Time-based) SQL Injections	Commercial	Mavituna Security
Nikto	Web server scanner	Unix/Linux	Web server scanner, execute standard and server type explicit checks. captures cookies	Open Source	CIRT
ParosPro	Web security auditor	Windows	Allow companies to perform assessment based on plug-ins designed to target various security vulnerability	Commercial	MileSCAN/Chinotec

(Continued)

TABLE 9.1 (*Continued*)

Security Testing Tools: A Revisit [14–54]

Tool Name	Type of Tools	Support to Language/ Based Upon	Security Issues	Phase Analysis/ Mode of Use	Source
QualysGuard	NA	N/A	NA	Commercial	Qualys
Retina	Network security scanner	Windows/Unix	Widespread vulnerability Database mainly for Unix, Good reporting module	Commercial	eEye Digital Security
ScanDo	Web application scanner, Scan all types web application including Flash, Java Script, ASP, XML, & web services	Windows	Automatically identifying vulnerability at all stages of software life cycle. Assess risk level as application evolved.	Commercial	KaVaDoInc
Securityk.QA Toolbar	Web application security	Windows	During QA phase of the SDLC, QA graph can base the toolbar to perform security/regression testing. Tools bar can execute several application security testes per page, resulting in HTML report with identified issues and mitigation strategies.	Commercial	iSec Partners
Sentinel	NA	N/A	NA	Commercial	White Hat Security
Wapiti	Web application vulnerability scanner/ security auditor	Windows, Unix/Linux and Macintosh	File handling errors, database injection (PHP/JSP/ASP SQL Injections and XPathInjections), XSS (Cross Site Scripting) Injection, LDAP Injection, Command Execution detection (HTTP Response Splitting, session fixation…)	Open source	Informática Gesfor/ MicolasSurribas
WebApp360	Web application vulnerabilities such as (XSS) and SQL Injection	Windows	NA	Commercial	nCircle

Tool	Function	Platform/Language	Description	License	Vendor
WebInspect	Automated vulnerability scanning	Windows	Dynamically a black box testing tool which detect vulnerability by actually performing attack	Commercial	HP
Wikto	Wikto is a web server assessment tool. It is used for Web server fingerprinting, directory and link extraction	Windows	For SQL injections, looking for vulnerabilities in their Internet-facing Web servers.	Open Source	Sensepost
NTOSpider	Security scanner	Evaluate site exposure risk, Position threat priorities, Generate high quality graphical HTML reports, and security posture through vulnerabilities and threat exposure	Windows/forms, cookies, scripts, SQL strings and ODBC connectors, authentication, applets/objects, hidden fields, etc.	Commercial	NT Objectives
Vega	Web security scanner	Attack modules are written in JavaScript	Instances of SQL injection, cross-site scripting (XSS), and other vulnerabilities in your web applications. It includes an intercepting proxy for interactive web application debugging	Free & open source	SubgraphInc
MileScanParosPro	Vulnerability scanning /security auditing platform	Web-based applications languages	Site's hierarchy is collected via network spider. Vulnerability scanning based on plug-ins	NA	Milescan Technologies
Aribisec Web Analyzer	Security scanner	HTML code	Scanning for potentially malicious links	Analyzes site structure, content and configuration	Free & paid version
Skipfish	Security scanner	NA	NA	NA	Michal Zalewski/ Google

(Continued)

TABLE 9.1 (*Continued*)

Security Testing Tools: A Revisit [14–54]

Tool Name	Type of Tools	Support to Language/ Based Upon	Security Issues	Phase Analysis/ Mode of Use	Source
Websecurify	Vulnerability detector	Windows, Mac OS, Linux and others	Identification of web vulnerability as well as OWSAP Top 10 by using advance browser automation, discovering and fuzzing technologies.	Commercial/free	GNUCITIZEN/ web securify
Samurai Web Testing Framework	Web pen testing framework	Linux	NA	Open source/free	Inguardians Inc.
Arachni	Scanner	HTTP responses	Can detect changes during scanning through dynamic nature of web application	Open source/free	TasosLaskos
Sparse	Was initially built to find coding faults in kernel Code.	C	NA	NA	NA
Flawfinder	Security Weakness (Flaws) Identification	Python support (Unix, Windows, OS/2, Mac, Amiga Supported Languages: C, C++	Buffer overflow, format string problem, shell execution, insecure temp files, race condition, access violations	Source code	David A. Wheeler
MOPS	Identifying security issues that be able to modeled by a finite state automation (FSA)	Unix program platform Languages: C	Object files are embedded with control flow graph and executable by also wrapping the linker.	MOPS workings on basic C source, but can also ensure source RPMs static (compile-time) analysis tool	Hao Chen, David Wagner
WebKing	NA	Windows/Linux/ Solaris	NA	Commercial	Parasoft
WebScanService	NA	N/A	NA	Commercial	German Web Security
Websecurify	NA	Windows, Mac OS, Linux, and others	NA	Commercial/Free	GNUCITIZEN/ Web securify

Web Scarab	Vulnerability scanner (web-based applications)	XML format	Sql injection, CSS, cookie poisoning, parameter tampering	Open Source	GNU
W3af	Framework for web application security	Python	Vulnerability due to blind SQL injection, vulnerability raises due to buffer overflow, Multiple CORS misconfigurations, Insecure DAV configurations, CSRF vulnerability	Open Source, GPLv2	Andres Riancho
Ratproxy	Used for web application security	Testing software in semi-automatic nature supported by Linux, FreeBSD, MacOS X, and Windows (Cygwin) systems	Differentiateamong CSS style sheets and JavaScript codes	Open Source	NA

9.7 Conclusion

Combining the phased security testing process with the development life cycle has become quintessentially significant, to meet the objective of detecting faults at every phase well in advance, to minimize developmental cost, delivery time, and rework efforts. To accomplish this goal, a binding framework constituting of seven steps is proposed, which will prove crucial in identifying threats and preventing migration. The projected work can assist the testers to comprehend healthier and implement security test efficiently and effectively, thereby delivering secure software.

Key Terms

Software Testing, Security Testing, Software Security Testing Process, Security Test Strategy and Test Plan, Designing Security Test Cases, Executing Security Test Cases, Capturing Security Test Result, Capturing Security Test Metrics, Qualitative Assessment, Security Test Closure Report, Software Security Testing Tools

Point to Remember

- •. Security testing is accountable for recognizing the possible vulnerabilities among software applications.
- •. The proclaimed ambiguity may be responsible for inadvertent behavior and having likelihood of theft or destruction for critical or sensitive information.
- •. Software testing activities have major responsibility in the production of trustworthy systems and account for a considerable quantity of resources, including time, money, and personnel.
- •. Software security testing is responsible for discovering vulnerabilities through proper implementation of security vulnerability detection mechanism at early stage of development life cycle.
- •. Test process is accountable to offer protection of the intended system from attack.

Objective-Type Questions

1. Security testing is responsible to identify the probable _____ of applications.
   a)   Weaknesses
   b)   Strength
   c)   Document
   d)   Parameter

2. Tensile nature of _____ is responsible for the occurrences of potential attacks.
   a)   Requirement
   b)   Code
   c)   Design
   d)   Deployment

3. _____ is a process to appraise the functionality of a software application with an objective to uncover whether the developed software met the particular requirements.
   a)   Software design
   b)   Software testing
   c)   Software coding
   d)   Software maintenance

4. It verifies the expected behavior of functionality meets actual requirements. Is it true or false?
   a)   True
   b)   False

5. The goal of security testing is to detect _____ earlier and ensures security and trustiness of final product.
   a)   Vulnerabilities
   b)   Debugging
   c)   Testing
   d)   Error

6. Vulnerability assessment/detection technique provides a valuable methodology for _____ .
   a)   Software testing
   b)   Security testing
   c)   Software design
   d)   Security design

7. Software security testing, code reviews and _____ are some most effective methods for identifying software weaknesses and vulnerabilities.
   a)   Risk analysis
   b)   Vulnerability assessment
   c)   Risk mitigation
   d)   Risk exposure

8. Software security testing confirms the secure development and execution of software product consequently minimizing the probability of _____ being unconfined and revealed by customers or malicious users.
   a)   Security errors
   b)   Security risk
   c)   Software risk
   d)   Software errors

9. Validation of robustness and prevention from security weaknesses for not allowing in the application are the primary responsibilities of _____ .
   a)   Security testing
   b)   Software testing
   c)   Software reliability
   d)   Software dependability

10. Security expert Guru Gary McGraw's research article entitled 'Risk-based security testing' provides a clear understanding and simulated approach for attacker's behavior by recognizing system's risk.
    a)   Risk-based security testing
    b)   Security testing with risk
    c)   Risk analysis and software testing
    d)   Risk analysis and security testing

Short-Answer Type Questions

1. What do you understand by software testing?
2. Why software testing is the most important activity for software development?
3. Why security testing is needed for software development?
4. What do you understand by security vulnerabilities?
5. What are the other four key points to consider in a security test?
6. Explain about risk-based security testing in detail.
7. Discuss the pertinent observations to incorporate security testing on higher priority.
8. What do you understand by test case and test process?
9. Describe security test case and security test plan in brief.
10. What do you mean by software security testing tools? Explain few of them.

Descriptive Questions

1. How software testing is related with software quality assurance? How much software testing contributes in improving software quality?
2. Suggest a guideline to select a minimum set of test cases sufficiently effective for revealing potential faults in a program.
3. How poor planning of testing effort affects overall security testing. Suggests guidelines to improve the planning of security testing effort?
4. Prepare a guideline to select the appropriate methodology for testing software.
5. How security testing is related with software security assurance? How much security testing contributes in improving software security?
6. Discuss the proposed framework for software security testing process in detail.
7. Write down the perspective phases for software security testing that can be incorporated with software development life cycle to develop security software.
8. Discuss the mechanism for Security Test Strategy and Test Plan.

9. Discuss the mechanism for Designing Security Test Cases and Executing Security Test Cases.

10. Describe various software security testing tools in detail and categorize them according to their respective usability at different level.

References

1 G. Kavitha Jayaraman, *Incorporating Security in Software Testing Life Cycle*, Cognizant Technology Solutions, 2009.

2 Risk-Based Software Security Testing, Software Assurance Pocket Guide Series: Development, Volume III, Version 0.5 September 1, 2009.

3 B. Potter and G. McGraw, "Software Security Testing, *IEEE Security & Privacy*, 2004, pp. 32–36.

4 S. Turpe, "Security Testing: Turning Practice into Theory," *IEEE International Conference on Software Testing, Verification and Validation Workshop (ICSTW08)*, IEEE Computer Society, 2008.

5 H. Song, W. Liang, Z. Changyou and Y. Hong, "A Software Security Testing Method Based on Typical Defects,"*2010 International Conference on Computer Application and System Modelling (ICCASM 2010)*, IEEE Computer Society, 2010, pp. V5-150–153.

6 SOA Test Methodology, Torry Harris Business Solution, www.thbs.com/soa.

7 A. Marback, H. Do, K. He, S. Kondamarri and D. Xu, "A Threat Model based Approach to Security Testing," *Software: Practice and Experience*, 2012, Published Online in Wiley Online Library, doi: 10.1002/spe.2111.

8 T.-Y. Gu, Y.-S. Shi and Y.-U. Fang, *Research on Software Security Testing*. World Academy of Science, Engineering and Technology,2010, pp. 647–651.

9 Available at: www.cert.org

10 S. Paithis, "The Future of Software Security," pp. 61–62, www.testingexperience.com.

11 Software Security Testing, Software Assurance Pocket Guide Series: Development, Volume III, Version 1.0 (May 21, 2012).

12 L. Lazic and N. Mastorakis, "Cost Effective Software Test Metrics," *WSEAS Transactions on Computers*, 7(6), June 2008, pp. 599–619.

13 S. A. Khan, R. A. Khan and R. Choudhary "Software Security Testing Process", *6th International Conference on Software, Knowledge, Information Management and Applications*, Chengdu University, China, 9–11September.

14 http://www.securesoftware.com/resources/download_rats.html

15 https://www.fortify.com/ssa-elements/threat-intelligence/rats.html

16 https://www.owasp.org/index.../OWASP_Zed_Attack_Proxy_Project

17 http://www.ncircle.com/pdf/resources/nCircle-DS-PCIScanSvc-1001-06.pdf

18 S. Balasubramanium, "Stride Towards Better Application Security", Utah State University, Master Thesis, All graduate Thesis and Dissertation Paper 210, 2008.

19 https://www.securitymetrics.com/networkcheckinfo.adp

20 www.coresecurity.com

21 http://h21007.www2.hp.com/portal/download/product/16344/C5%20Compliance%20Platform%20Datasheet%20FINAL%2003%2007%2007_1181914942029.pdf

22 https://www.securitymetrics.com/appliance_features.adp

23 http://www-arc.com/sara/

24 http://www.foundstone.com/

25 https://www.netiq.com/

26 http://www.acwgroup.com/acw/aca_pacific/phil/Web_Catalogues/ESN/NetIQ_Security_Analyzer.pdf

27 www.quotium.com/prod/security.php

28 http://www.kyplex.com/website-security-scanner.html
29 L. Aurones, "Tools Based Approach to Assessing Web Application Security", Helsinki University of Technology, Telecommunication Software and Multimedia Laboratory, T-110.501, Seminar on Network Security, HUT TMZ, November 4, 2002, pp.1–20.
30 http://www.klocwork.com/products/insight/index.php
31 http://www.astree.ens.fr/
32 J. Wilander, "Modeling and Visualizing Security Properties of Code Using Dependence Graphs", Dept. of Computer & Information Science, Linkoping's University.
33 M. Jones, "A Practice Guide to Vulnerability Checkers", Secologic Project, University of Hamburg/Security in Distributed System, 2006.
34 http://scfm.sourceforge.net/Auditing,
35 http://www.acunetix.com/vulnerability-scanner/
36 http://portswigger.net/burp/
37 www.gamasec.com/gamascan.aspx
38 http://rgaucher.info/beta/grabber/
39 http://securitytube-tools.net/index.php?title=Grendel_Scan
40 http://www.cenzic.com/index.html
41 http://www.nstalker.com/products/nstealth/download.php
42 http://www.mavitunasecurity.com/
43 http://cirt.net/nikto2/
44 www.milescan.com/
45 www.qualys.com/
46 www.eeye.com/-
47 Retina Enterprise Suite Security Target Version 1.0, "Science Applications International Corporation Common Criteria Laboratory," Columbia, 25 May 2007.
48 https://www.whitehatsec.com/assets/DS/DS_4pgSentinel020311.pdf
49 J. Grossman, "The Top Five Myths of Website Security", A White Hat Security White Paper, February 2007.
50 http://www.ict-romulus.eu/web/wapiti
51 http://samate.nist.gov/index.php/Web_Application_Vulnerability_Scanners.html
52 http://www.sensepost.com/cms/resources/labs/tools/pentest/wikto/using_wikto.pdf
53 http://www.ntobjectives.com/security-software/ntospider-application-security-scanner/
54 S. A. Khan, R. A. Khan, Software Security Testing Tools: A Revisit, International Conference on Emerging Trends in Electrical, Communication and Information Technologies, ICECIT 2012, Proceeding Published by Elsevier, ISBN: 978-81-312-3411-2, pp: 321–333

Useful Links

http://scfm.sourceforge.net/auditing
http://www.acunetix.com/vulnerability-scanner/
http://portswigger.net/burp/
www.gamasec.com/gamascan.aspx
http://rgaucher.info/beta/grabber/
http://securitytube-tools.net/index.php?title=Grendel_Scan
http://www.cenzic.com/index.html
http://www.nstalker.com/products/nstealth/download.php
http://www.mavitunasecurity.com/
http://cirt.net/nikto2/
www.milescan.com/
www.qualys.com/
www.eeye.com/-

10

Implementing Security Testing: A Case Study

There's no silver bullet solution with cyber security, a layered defense is the only viable defense.

James Scott

10.1 Objectives

Investigating what goes into security testing operations that make them so expensive and vital has become mandatory, if not difficult. It is incredibly desirable to look up what needs to be done for each operation, optimize time, and ultimately determine where it might be used to save time. Significant time may be saved with innovative testing approaches if ideal activities are discovered and executed during the testing process. The study's goal is to detect security flaws and vulnerabilities early in the software development life cycle so that a successful security test plan may be implemented.

The specifications for the security test plan will be determined based on the correct and appropriate usage of their characteristics. The activities linked to optimizing vulnerabilities that occur during security testing are included in the test case assessment process, which employs a specific set of security attributes to mitigate vulnerabilities in a test suite. Furthermore, an effective and prescriptive security testing method that specifies alleged and prioritized actions may be helpful in various aspects and articulated with the following set of objectives:

- To investigate the security best practices that can be used to implement security.
- To build attack scenarios and security requests.
- To investigate potential threats to the software in development and the importance of detecting security flaws and vulnerabilities early in the SDLC.
- To create a step-by-step security testing procedure.
- To create a framework for implementing the security test process at a higher level.
- To develop a workable security test plan definition and the factors that influence it.
- To develop a procedure for conducting acceptance testing to ensure that the security measures are functioning correctly.
- To detect deviations from the organization's security policy's approved services.
- To use quantitative assessment to determine the value of security qualities.
- To create a hybrid approach for improved security testing using test plan specifications that are based on their performance and success.
- To theoretically and practically validate the suggested paradigm.

DOI: 10.1201/9781003330516-10

10.2 Planning for Security Testing

Security testing aims to uncover security flaws before making them available to end-users. One of the primary goals of security testing is to determine whether the software implementation's security features are compatible with the design [1]. This is a time when the industrialization of security is required. This is the case in terms of security measures, product upgrades, and security management policy improvements [2]. The study's significance is to establish a viable method for measuring software security, as most parts are challenging to quantify. Research on software measurement has become increasingly vital for software developers and consumers. As a result, the overall impact of such a study, with its direct contributions to the area of knowledge, could be significant, either directly or indirectly, in terms of the following:

- To see if software behaves in a predictable and secure manner.
- To ensure that software does not have any vulnerabilities or flaws.
- To determine whether any of the system's intended functions are unlawful or unwanted.
- To ensure the software's long-term viability.
- To determine the software's reliability.
- It could serve as a platform for choosing a sufficient minimal collection of test cases.
- It may aid in a better understanding of the software system's design and architecture information, allowing you to comprehend the development and maintenance process.
- It may aid in identifying system/software design flaws early in the software development life cycle, resulting in less effort spent on security assurance and the avoidance of unnecessary operating expenditures.
- It may also detect flaws during the design phase, allowing us to pinpoint vulnerabilities.
- It can be used to assess software security and generate a cost estimate for a software project, making it easier to estimate and plan new operations.
- It could aid in determining the effectiveness of software development based on quantitative criteria such as productivity, quality, lead time, maintainability, etc.

10.3 Security Test Case Optimization Framework

Assessing whether an information system secures data and functions as intended is known as security testing. It is the most popular method for ensuring that a system operates within the restrictions of a set of policies and processes. Gary McGraw's risk-based security testing is motivated to comprehend and simulate the attacker's strategy. A software security tester can correctly focus on parts of code where an attack is likely to succeed by identifying risks in the system and generating tests based on those risks [1, 3, 4]. Security testing aids in detecting flaws that could result in the loss of sensitive data or the entry of attackers into a system.

Security testing has moved into the world of software testers due to an increase in the number of security incidents and a growing awareness among business owners about apps that have been invalidated due to security vulnerabilities. Security testing is all about identifying all of the program's potential flaws and vulnerabilities that could lead to the loss or theft of extremely sensitive data, the intruder's destruction of the application, or allowing any intruder access to the system [5]. Traditional security testing methods fail to detect vulnerabilities and logical problems early on. It also leads to high costs for resolving concerns discovered later. Developers are given extremely little time to remedy bugs in traditional testing. Because security is an essential aspect of the entire life cycle of a software product, it cannot be overlooked. Any vulnerability, design defect, or lack of design principles or metrics can jeopardize the software's overall security. The following are some of the most crucial points:

- Developing secure software requires more than simply securing sensitive and secret data; it also necessitates the development of a scheme of events that can resist the benchmark standards set for a secure software system.
- This will aid in the development of a roadmap for creating impregnable and efficient software.
- To achieve this criterion, the test case structure must be upgraded, allowing for the detection of more flaws and reducing software failures.
- There are already several sophisticated software applications, and by utilizing an optimized security testing framework, software systems with even greater complexity and maximum security can be produced in the future.
- This optimized framework allows for early identification and quick reaction to a security issue. As a result, a security test case optimization framework is critical for maximizing and maintaining a software system's defenses while also keeping development costs low.
- The test case optimization framework for software security is new ground, and much more progress can be made in this area in the future, assisting in the development of resilient software applications.

Test case optimization is critical within the complete range of actions for security testing of software in development [6]. The methods and attributes required to test a given layer of software code are crucial in the overall process, as is optimizing a test suite to satisfy the requirements of a testing region and piece of code under test. Nonetheless, the research on test case optimization has uncovered two critical difficulties. The first is that present test case prioritization algorithms neglect the potential of prioritizing many test suites at once. Second, current test case prioritization systems prioritize all test cases with identical weight components, ignoring the optimal relevance of attribute weightage to a specific group of vulnerabilities to be targeted. Thus, no systematic algorithm is applied. Industrial software systems are notoriously tricky for testers and developers to test since they are massive and evaluating them in a short period is nearly impossible.

These systems are frequently more prominent than a single test suite, particularly software integration testing [7], necessitating careful attention to the nuances of the prioritization methods used. Because the complexity and size of the software systems used in businesses are so immense, the priority is to identify the vulnerabilities and weigh the qualities to improve the fault detection rate. Fixing threats and vulnerabilities, reducing irregularities and non-conformance to standards, and cutting unnecessary complexity

FIGURE 10.1
Security Test Case Optimization Framework.

early in the development life cycle all lead to the development of highly secure end products, as shown in the following discussion. Under the auspices of the 'Design and Development of Security Test Case Optimization Framework,' depicted in Figure 10.1, the research's primary goal is to devise a mechanism to anticipate software security early in the design phase of the SDLC.

In light of the security mentioned in earlier threats, it is reasonable to conclude that efforts should be made to address these difficulties to manage efficient and secure software development. A suitable testing framework is offered for assessing software security vulnerabilities, which necessitates the urgent need to handle security testing at the design stage and investigate program complexity [7–11]. Organizations that build software have seen tremendous growth in developing more secure software. Still, today's critical requirement is to uncover vulnerabilities early in the design phase by using a security testing framework. Early detection of vulnerabilities may be accomplished by implementing the proposed framework, which would save a significant amount of time and money in the production process. The security testing methodology is based on seven principles: Security Test Plan Specification, Security Attribute Identification, Security Attribute Evaluation, Test Case Execution, and Results Capture, Optimization, and Validation. As and when necessary, review and revision will be carried out.

10.3.1 Security Test Plan Specification

It's an integral part of the security testing framework's development. The system initially detects the weakest area, after which it creates a security test plan that ensures role-based authorization, password control, access level management, and other functions [7, 8]. The goal is to create a test strategy that combines the mapping of security attributes and offers better results based on the demands of the enterprise. The security test plan specification's environmental, strategic, technological, and operational components are separated into four sections. The physical characteristics of the facilities, such as hardware, communications and system software, mode of use or interface, and other software or supplies, are included in the environmental specification. Because the strategic specification is the foundation of the test plan, it should include a description of how software security testing should be done and highlight topics that have a significant impact on the testing's performance and, as a result, on the project's overall success.

The proper selection of relevant tools and automation for specific difficulties to alleviate the task of testing staff is a big issue in the case of technical specifications. Because different potential tool users may have other demands, the same tool may be chosen more than once. The outcome of all the selected test cases that are conducted is observed and recorded during the operational specification process. Both the input and the results will be recorded in automated testing. The characteristics to be tested, objects to be tested, type of testing to be undertaken, resources and timeline to imperforate testing, as well as associated risks, should all be identified in the above-mentioned high-level test plan. As a result, implementing this technique will assist save time spent manually searching for test data that meets consumers' expectations [9]. The use of an early detection technique also considerably minimizes the danger of data breaches and contributes to improving security testing quality.

10.3.2 Identification of Security Attributes

During security testing, identifying security aspects is crucial. For software developers and testers, these characteristics serve as a road map. An attempt has been made to identify security attributes useful in software design quantification. The goal of identifying security attributes is to target critical features connected to a particular type of vulnerability issue discovered during software testing. This can be accomplished through the quantification of security properties, which will allow engineers to spot software system flaws early and keep track of the number of vulnerabilities at any point during the testing process. When establishing a test plan, all of the factors connected to security should be considered.

10.3.3 Evaluation of Security Attributes

During this procedure, soft computing techniques are used to identify the correlations between each characteristic. This can be accomplished by doing a thorough literature review and consulting an expert. Security qualities will be prioritized and ranked according to their weights to conduct case-by-case testing and identify gaps and other vulnerabilities in the software. It's critical to analyze security qualities based on the vulnerability they target while creating a comprehensive and foolproof security testing framework. If and when the vulnerability is discovered, a combination of security traits can be used to create a viable and practical framework for addressing a security issue at any point of testing.

10.3.4 Test Case Execution & Capturing the Results

Vulnerability detection aims to locate the crack in the armor or a vulnerable part or weak spot in the plan. A thorough security feature design has been built at this point. This will be accomplished by completing both the use case and an alternate case scenario to comprehend and develop a plan to counter and protect the software structure from threats and vulnerabilities. By conducting thorough testing, these hazards can be identified in a methodical manner. As the program is being developed; this will also aid the designer in developing mitigation measures for potential risks and directing them to focus on the sections of the software system that are susceptible to attack. Test cases are run to improve security testing, and vulnerabilities are discovered across all modules by running tests on them. Using testing to identify or capture the risk or repercussions will lead to developing a secure design. Localization of faults, categorization of software failures, and the distribution of various defects are all advantages of this cognitive process. The findings will be recorded to be processed further.

10.3.5 Optimization

Cases can be prioritized in this process by examining the many domains for which software is being produced and performing optimal security tests and validating the final program, which should meet the user's expectations and be applicable. The initial step toward optimization is to eliminate redundancy caused by defects in all modules, develop metrics, and finally use prioritization approaches to discover the shortest way to decrease the security risk. In addition, the test case prioritization is optimized using a hybrid technique. The main goal is to bring together all of the best security testing and validation activities and processes to develop an integrated best path to reduce faults based on priority and execute them to create a better user-specific and safe software system. In addition, it will identify vulnerabilities in the essential data and lower the system's infrastructure costs. This will also assist the designer in devising strategies to safeguard the system from potential threats and help them concentrate on the areas of the system that could be hacked.

10.3.6 Validation

To validate the results here, the researcher has used both the main methods, including theoretical and empirical methods. The theoretical validation is done based on critical examine and expert opinions. On other hand, empirical validation is done based on a hypothesis test.

10.3.7 Review and Revision

The review & revision may be done if required; at all stages to bring forth more refined structural guidelines.

10.4 Test Case Evaluation

The increasing complexity and extensibility of software applications have hampered the security structure and related security testing operations, posing a unique challenge to developers and researchers to develop better software application security testing methodologies. Through the optimal usage of the security testing optimization procedure, the relevant test suites of all modules where the problem of recurring failures in fault discovery arises can be healed. This will save time and money during the software application development process and eliminate the need for rework on a specific development activity [10, 11].

Researchers have utilized the ACO technique to target various subsystems/areas of software development. However, it has yet to be employed in security testing. As a result, this suggested topic considers using the ACO technique to tackle challenges connected to optimizing the security testing of a software program after a complete investigation. The ACO-based algorithm gives the proposed testing procedures an advantage over standard testing techniques since they are more result-oriented and time-consuming, which reduces the software system's development cost. As a result of the ACO-based method, the security attributes are used to detect faults and give the shortest path to mitigate those errors based on their weightage.

10.4.1 Case Study: Mobile Payment Wallet

These days, device-based mobile wallets are widely used. These can use a variety of technologies to send payment information from a device (such as a mobile phone) to a merchant's point of sale (POS). Magnetic Secure Transmission (MST), Near Field Communication (NFC), Quick Recognition Code (QR), Bluetooth Low Energy (BLE), SMS, and the Internet are all examples of mobile communication technologies that can be used to send payment data from a mobile device to a POS. Sign In, Profile Update, Bill Payments & Recharges, Add Money, mPIN Change, Funds Transfer, and Transaction Details are the seven modules of the proposed case study on Mobile Payment Wallet, as illustrated in Figure 10.2. To use the program, the user will enter his or her login credentials, which include a username and a four-digit mPIN that is unique to that user, into the Sign-In module (M1).

The second module (M2) is Pro File Update, which allows the authenticated user to make changes to their account, such as updating their address, bank account, and Aadhaar seeding, among other things. This data is extremely important and cannot be modified or accessed by anyone else. The customer can utilize the extra money from their online wallet in the third module (M3) to pay their bills, such as energy bills, credit card bills, tax payments, gas bills, cellphone recharges, and DTH recharges, and online retail transactions, among other things. If the user's wallet balance is low, they can add money to it using the

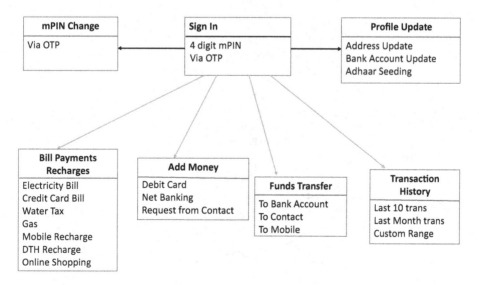

FIGURE 10.2
Pictorial Representation of the Mobile Payment Wallet Application.

fourth method of component (M4). Debit or credit cards, net banking, or a contact request can all be used. The way these payments are processed isn't changed by credit/debit card networks' mobile payments; they're still generally based on standard card-based card payment systems.

The user can modify the four-digit mPIN in the fifth module (M5). The update request is validated by sending an OTP (One Time Password) to the user's registered mobile number, authenticating the transaction. The funds can be transmitted to a specified bank account, a contact, or a mobile phone associated with the user's profile in the sixth module (M6). Module seven (M7) will provide full details of individual online transactions; these details may include the most recent transaction details, transaction details from the previous month, or transaction details for a specific period defined by the user.

10.4.2 Test Case Sampling and its Execution

Software security test cases are scenarios where use cases and alternate cases are drawn, as shown in Figure 10.3. These test cases are drawn to study the faults in the system, to do an in-depth analysis of the types of security threats or breaches a software system can go through, analyze the reliability and dependability of the software system, whether it can withstand the faults occurring in various environments, etc.

To study the behavior of a software system in alternate test case scenarios, the tester must consider all the possible energy sources that challenge the security of the software system in all possible ways to find the weak link or loopholes in the software structure. Seven test cases will be developed for each module concerning security attributes. Thus, we get a total of 49 test cases. In Table 10.1, 10 faults are shown that may occur during the use of the application concerning the seven security attributes, i.e., authentication, authorization, confidentiality, availability, integrity, non-repudiation, and resilience.

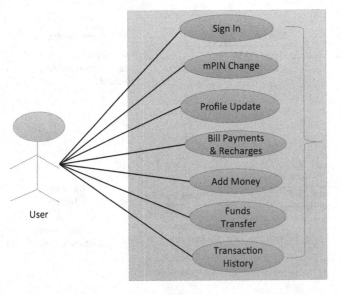

FIGURE 10.3
A Use Case Diagram of Mobile Payment Wallet System.

TABLE 10.1

Description of the Faults

Faults	Description
Flt1	RNG (Random Number Generation) Failure
Flt2	Network Error
Flt3	Segmentation Fault
Flt4	File/Data not Found
Flt5	Data Loss
Flt6	Infinite Loop
Flt7	Communication Error
Flt8	Configuration Error
Flt9	Service Fault
Flt10	Coupling Fault

10.4.2.1 Module-1: Sign In

The user uses this module for signing into the system. It will authenticate the user by accepting the user name and mPIN as login credentials and raises an error if wrong credentials are entered. Sign-In's alternate use case scenario that includes test cases 1–7 can be studied in this module. In test case 1, if the system tries to read data from a wrong segment from memory, then flt3 is raised. In test case-2, the authentication may fail due to the wrong mPIN entered, or the file may not be found to match entered mPIN, thus raising flt2, and flt4, or the poor connectivity will raise flt7, similarly when the service is not available flt9 will occur. During the application startup phase, when the user enters the wrong parameter, the configuration error is raised as per flt8 in test case-3. For test case-4, a break in the network or file read could lead to flt2, flt4, and flt9. After the successful startup of the application, if the information could not be passed to the next module, then flt10 may occur in test case-5.

Further, if the user could not authenticate his digital signature to the server, flt1 will occur, leading to a communication gap. Hence flt7 will occur in test case-6. Finally, in test case -7, the application may fail to start because of flt8 or halt due to flt6. Table 10.2 shows the faults covered by each test case.

The result obtained from these seven modules of the different test cases is mapped to remove redundancy that may exist in the output of the result. Thus, a combined sample test case is obtained regarding each security attribute, as shown in Table 10.3. Moreover, these samples of combined test cases concerning each security attribute are determined based on fault cover and its execution time.

TABLE 10.2

Sample Test Cases w. r. t. to each Attribute of Security and Faults Identified for Module-1

Test Case w.r.t each Security Attributes/Faults	Flt1	Flt2	Flt3	Flt4	Flt5	Flt6	Flt7	Flt8	Flt9	Flt10
TC 1 (Authorization)	–	–	✓	–	–	–	–	–	–	–
TC 2 (Authentication)	–	✓	–	✓	–	–	✓	–	✓	–
TC 3 (Confidentiality)	–	–	–	–	–	–	–	✓	–	–
TC 4 (Availability)	–	✓	–	✓	–	–	–	–	✓	–
TC 5 (Integrity)	–	–	–	–	–	–	–	–	–	✓
TC 6 (Non-repudiation)	✓	–	–	–	–	–	–	✓	–	–
TC 7 (Resilience)	–	–	–	–	–	–	–	✓	–	–

TABLE 10.3

Combined Sample Test Cases w. r. t. to each Attribute of Security, Faults Identified, and Execution Time

S. No	Combined Test Cases	Total Number of Faults Covered during Security Test	Respective Module in which Faults are found	Total Execution Time Per Unit
1	CTC1 (Authorization)	Flt1, Flt3	Mi, i = 1, 2.......7	7
2	CTC2 (Authentication)	Flt2, Flt4, Flt7, Flt9	Mi, i = 1, 2.......7	4
3	CTC3 (Confidentiality)	Flt1, Flt5, Flt7, Flt8	Mi, i = 1, 3, 4, 5, 6, 7	5
4	CTC4 (Availability)	Flt2, Flt4, Flt9	Mi, i = 1, 2.......7	4
5	CTC5 (Integrity)	Flt3, Flt6, Flt10	Mi, i = 1, 2.......7	4
6	CTC6 (Non-repudiation)	Flt1, Flt7	Mi, i = 1, 2.......7	5
7	CTC7 (Resilience)	Flt3, Flt6, Flt8	Mi, i = 1, 2, 3, 7	4

Where CTC: Combined Test Cases, Flt: Faults, M1, M2 ...M7 are modules.

To find optimized prioritization order for fault coverage is the utmost requirement for industry/organization. We now apply the ACO technique to resolve such problems that occurred during test case optimization. Reordering test suites can be more effective at finding faults if testing can be terminated earlier [11, 12]. In this section, we present the execution of this algorithm in time-based prioritization.

The security regression test suite CTC contains seven combined test cases with the elementary order {CTC1, CTC2, CTC3, CTC4, CTC5, CTC6, CTC7} along with their execution time as shown in Table 10.9. In this procedure, combined test case CTC1 can obtain two faults, {flt1, flt3} in seven minutes, CTC2, finds four faults, {flt2,flt4,flt7,flt9} in four minutes, and CTC3 obtain four faults, {flt1, flt5, flt7, flt8} in five minutes. Combined test case CTC4 and CTC5 obtain three faults in fourminutes, {flt2, flt4, flt9} and {flt3, flt6, flt10} respectively. Combined test case CTC6, finds two faults in five minutes, {flt1, flt7} and CTC7 finds three faults in four minutes, {flt3, flt6, flt8}.

The combined test suite is obtained from all seven test case scenarios after removing redundancy. The problem of selection of optimized security test case prioritization based on maximum fault analytical capacity of the test cases obtained from set 'T' (Test Suite) of 'n' combined test cases, find subset 'S', which consists of 'm' test cases (m<n), where the test cases are selected and optimized. The problem can be depicted as an undirected graph G (V,E), where V is the set of nodes and E is the set of edges in the graph. 'WTi' is the weight of 'it h' edge. It describes the pheromone trail deposited on the edge ei ∈ E, reflecting the amount of fault coverage 'Flti' on the chosen path within a time constraint, 'MAX_TIME'. Initially, all edges are set to zero.

10.4.2.2 Assumptions for ACO based Algorithm

The assumptions for applying ACO based algorithm for optimizing the security test cases are given below:

- Original test suite, T = {t1, t2...... t49}
- Combined Test Suite, CTC = {CTC1, CTC2,........., CTC7}
- Set of all faults, F = {flt1, flt2......flt10 }

- Each of the combined test case CTCi; i = 1, 2,...7 from CTC covers some or all the faults from Flt.

- After every iteration, the minimum execution time of ant is added to current execution time. Once the current execution exceeds MAX_TIME, the algorithm terminates a constant to constrain the algorithm (MAX_TIME = 84 minutes).

- A number of artificial ants to search through the test case space is 7, i.e., An1 to An7 (which is equal to the number of combined test cases).

- WTi, is the weight of each edge 'i', which is assumed to be the amount of pheromone deposited on edge.

- The pheromone deposition rate is assumed to be +1 or 100% for each ant that has crossed the edge on the best path.

- The pheromone evaporation rate is assumed to be k% of WTi (k = 10) to be reduced for each edge after each loop iteration.

10.5 Optimization of Security Test Cases

Figure 10.4 shows the flow graph used to optimize security test cases based on an iterative manner.

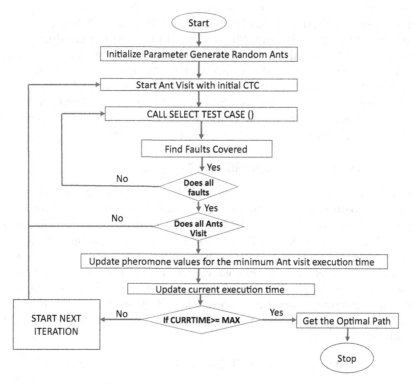

FIGURE 10.4
Flowchart of ACO based Proposed Approach.

10.5.1 ACO based Algorithm for Optimized Security Test Case

Prioritization

Step 1: Initialize the parameters and generate the colony of ants.

Step 2: Place the ant at the starting node i.e. the initial CTC.

Step 3: Find all the faults covered by the initial CTC.

Step 4: Select a test case using the procedure SELECT_TEST_CASE() and find the faults covered.

Step 5: Repeat step4 until all the faults are covered.

Step 6: If all the faults have been covered, send the next ant. Repeat this step until all the ants have once visited.

Step 7: Update pheromone values corresponding to the ant having minimum execution time.

Step 8: Update the current execution time.

Step 9: Repeat step 2 to step 8 for next iteration if current execution time is less than MAX_TIME.

Step 10: If the current execution time exceeds the MAX_TIME then get the optimal path and terminate the algorithm.

The execution of ACO-based algorithm at each iteration is shown in Tables 10.5–10.8. The maximum time limit is set to be 84 minutes, after which the algorithm will terminate, and the iteration will end. In all four iterations, each ant will chose random paths and stopped till the fault coverage criterion is absolutely met. All the ants will select the best possible path through which they could cover the distance in minimum total time. The best optimum path through which all the faults will be covered is obtained through this technique. The ACO-based algorithm's output after the first iteration is shown in Table 10.5. It shows the faults covered by each of the ants and the time is taken. The adjacency matrix of the graph corresponding to the path covered by each ant is shown in Table 10.6.

After the second iteration, the output of the ACO-based algorithm is shown in Table 10.7, and the corresponding adjacency matrix is shown in Table 10.8.

10.5.2 Obtaining the Results through Different Techniques

The proposed framework based on ACO technique has been compared to traditional methods such as no ordering, reverse ordering, random ordering and optimal ordering of the combined test cases are shown in Table 10.8. A metric proposed by Elbaum known as Average Percentage of Fault Detected (APFD) has been used to quantify the test suite's rate of fault detection that is instrumental in measuring the rate of fault detection per percentage of test suite execution [13, 14]. For validation, multifarious optimized prioritization criteria may be applied to a test suite with the aim of meeting the objective, i.e., to detect the fault in minimum time using the best possible and shortest path [15–18]. All the results obtained from various methods are calculated and compared with the help of APFD metric as shown below:

$$APFD = 1 - \left\{ (Tf1 + Tf2 + ... + Tfm) / mn \right\} + (1 / 2n)$$

where n is the no. of test cases and m is the no. of faults. (Tf1,....,Tfm) are the position of first test T that exhibit the fault.

TABLE 10.5

Execution of Algorithm (1st Iteration)

ACO	An1			An2			An3			An4			An5			An6			An7		
	P C	E T	Flt.C	P C	E T	Flt.C	P C	E T	Flt.C	P C	E T	Flt.C	P C	E T	Flt.C	P C	E T	Flt.C	P C	E T	Flt.C
FIRST ITERATION OBSERVATION	CT C1	7	1,3	CT C2	4	2,4,7,9	CT C3	5	1,5,7,8	CT C4	4	2,4,9	CT C5	4	3,6,10	CT C6	5	1,7	CT C7	4	3,6,8
	CT C5	4	3,6,10	CT C6	5	1,7	CT C4	4	2,4,9	CT C1	7	1,3	CT C7	4	3,6,8	CT C1	7	1,3	CT C2	4	2,4,7,9
	CT C2	4	2,4,7,9	CT C4	4	2,4,9	CT C5	4	3,6,10	CT C3	5	1,5,7,8	CT C1	7	1,3	CT C5	4	3,6,10	CT C6	5	1,7
	CT C3	5	1,5,7,8	CT C1	7	1,3				CT C2	4	2,4,7,9	CT C6	5	1,7	CT C3	5	1,5,7,8	CT C1	7	1,3
				CT C5	4	3,6,10				CT C7	4	3,6,8	CT C3	5	1,5,7,8	CT C2	4	2,4,7,9	CT C5	4	3,6,10
				CT C7	4	3,6,8				CT C6	5	1,7	CT C2	4	2,4,7,9				CT C4	4	2,4,9
				CT C3	5	1,5,7,8				CT C5	4	3,6,10							CT C3	5	1,5,7,8
Total Execution time (Units)	20			33			13			33			29			25			33		

Where PC: Path Covered, ET: Execution Time, Flt.C: Faults Covered.

TABLE 10.6

Adjacency Matrix of Pheromone Deposited after First Iteration

	An1	An2	An3	An4	An5	An6	An7
An1	0.0	0.0	0.0	0.0	0.0	0.0	0.0
An2	0.0	0.0	0.0	0.0	0.0	0.0	0.0
An3	0.0	0.0	0.0	0.9	0.0	0.0	0.0
An4	0.0	0.0	0.0	0.0	0.9	0.0	0.0
An5	0.0	0.0	0.0	0.0	0.0	0.0	0.0
An6	0.0	0.0	0.0	0.0	0.0	0.0	0.0
An7	0.0	0.0	0.0	0.0	0.0	0.0	0.0

TABLE 10.7

Ordering of Test Cases through Different Techniques

S. No.	No Ordering	Reverse Ordering	Random Ordering	Optimal Ordering	ACO based Ordering
1.	CTC1	CTC7	CTC5	CTC2	CTC2
2.	CTC2	CTC6	CTC7	CTC3	CTC5
3.	CTC3	CTC5	CTC2	CTC5	CTC1
4.	CTC4	CTC4	CTC3	CTC7	CTC3
5.	CTC5	CTC3	CTC4	CTC4	CTC7
6.	CTC6	CTC2	CTC1	CTC6	CTC4
7.	CTC7	CTC1	CTC 6	CTC1	CTC6

TABLE 10.8

Results of Test Case Optimization through Different Techniques

	No Ordering	Reverse Ordering	Random Ordering	Optimal Ordering	ACO based Ordering
APFD Metric Results	0.700	0.685	0.585	0.742	0.757
	70.00 %	68.50 %	58.50 %	74.20 %	75.70 %

10.6 Contextual Interpretation

Table 10.9 shows the optimized ordering of test cases from a security testing perspective. Further, many techniques are used to optimize the test cases, including no ordering, reverse ordering, random ordering, optimal ordering, and ACO-based ordering. Table 10.8 shows the overall improvements in their results. The results obtained through APFD metrics show that the ACO-based ordering is better than the traditional ordering techniques. The comparison made above and the results obtained through the APFD metric have demonstrated that the ACO technique provides the best result in terms of early fault detection. Hence, it is clear that the ACO technique is superior to other approaches.

TABLE 10.9

Overall Improvements

		Improvements	Percentage
No Ordering Vs ACO based Ordering	**0.757–0.700**	**0.057**	**7.53 %**
Reverse Ordering Vs ACO based Ordering	0.757–0.685	0.072	9.51 %
Random Ordering Vs ACO based Ordering	0.757–0.585	0.172	22.72 %
Optimal Ordering Vs ACO based Ordering	0.757–0.742	0.015	2.00 %

10.7 Automated Security Testing

Automated testing is responsible for finding any defects or weaknesses in software programs during software development. Automated testing can be performed during the development process, reducing development time. This is in charge of discovering vulnerabilities in programs utilizing automated techniques and adequate scanning. This will defend against intruders using automated scripts to exploit specific vulnerabilities. These automated scripts find and patch gaps in the apps automatically. These automated security testing programs can operate in any environment, including online applications, and generate reports on the list of vulnerabilities found in those applications. These automated security testing methods are more useful for penetration testers and security auditors to find vulnerabilities, and developers and administrators frequently utilize them before software releases. The differences between automated testing and manual testing are discussed in Table 10.10 [19, 20].

Best Practices for Automated Security Testing

- Requirement of complete security audits to determine significant risks from the product.
- The straightforward task of initiating process slowly from simple to complex process coverage.

TABLE 10.10

Differences between Automated Testing and Manual Testing

Manual Testing	Automated Testing
In-depth penetration testing	Regular security testing using a fully automated and up-to-date service or performed using special automated testing software tools to execute a test case suite.
Performed by security experts often working as external consultants	Increases knowledge across the organization
Not integrated into the development process and capable of finding visible and hidden defects	Easy to understand reports; some tools are Ranorex Studio, Kobiton, ZAPTEST, LambdaTest, Avo Assure
Test case execution is done manually.	Complements compliance and support team's security efforts
manual testing, different types of testing like unit, integration, security, performance, and bug tracking	modern agile and DevOps software projects now include automated testing from inception
Tools like Jira, Bugzilla, Mantis, Zap, NUnit, Tessy, LoadRunner, Citrus, SonarQube	Parts are a selection of test tools, the scope of automation, planning, design, test execution, and maintenance

- Best feasible for repetitive and real-world entity task
- Voluminous data

Specific areas of software testing where automation testing performs

- Tools for code analysis
- Scanning for appropriate configuration
- Application-level testing

10.7.1 List of Automation Testing Tools

Various automation testing tools are commercially accessible as well as open source. Although open-source software is more stable and has a more advanced architecture, it often falls short of commercial alternatives for customer support and technological improvements. The following is a list of tools:

- Contrast Security: Contract Security is a runtime application security tool that runs inside applications to identify potential faults.
- Burp Intruder: Burp Intruder is an infrastructure scanner used to ensure that applications interact correctly with the environment.
- OWASP ZAP: OWASP ZAP is an infrastructure scanner that is open-source in nature. It functions similarly to Burp Intruder.
- Veracode: Veracode refers to a code analysis tool to find vulnerabilities within an application structure.
- BDD Security: BDD Security is a test automation framework where users can employ natural language syntax to describe security functions as features.
- Mitten: Mitten is an open-source test automation framework that uses the Python programming language.
- Microsoft Azure Advisor: Microsoft Azure advisor is a cloud-based consultant service that provides recommendations according to an individual's requirements.
- GauntIT: GauntIT is a test automation framework ideal for those accustomed to Ruby development.

There are several best practices for securing the goods. An iterative approach is one of the most acceptable ways to integrate automated testing techniques into the product pipeline. Significant security-related testing is necessary at the last minute, causing a production delay. The following are a few suggestions for increasing productivity:

- Integrating automated testing processes to deal with potential vulnerabilities
- Break large projects into smaller parts
- Code dependencies analysis
- Test for malicious attacks
- Training for the best practices required for the development

10.8 Impact and Importance

Security testing is a technique for integrating optimal security testing into software applications to identify vulnerabilities or flaws. The goal is to identify vulnerable sites and document the mitigating work that has been done. As a result, the higher the accuracy of security testing, the lower the risk of vulnerabilities. Maintaining software security and client confidentiality helps maintain reasonable confidence between businesses and consumers. A robust security testing framework can aid in the discovery of complete security and privacy issues, as well as the protection of software against unauthorized access, malicious attacks, and other sorts of harmful vulnerabilities. Open Web Application Security Project is committed to dispersal of information on application security. It identifies the top ten most critical application security risks at interval of two to three year.Their efforts are to make security risk more visible to society that each stakeholders can be aware about the negative impact and develop concrete mechanism for protection. It demands more contribution to application development society to update themselves for deeper impact analysis and solution. It gives the basic information about likelihood and technical impact about the risk using the ratings used by OWASP Risk Rating Methodology. According to OWASP, the following are some of the most severe security concerns are mentioned in Table 10.11.

TABLE 10.11

The Top 10 OWASP Vulnerabilities

Top 10	2017–2018	2013	2007	2004
A1	Injection	Injection	Cross Site Scripting (XSS) Flaws	Unvalidated Input
A2	Broken Authentication and Session Management	Broken Authentication and Session Management	Injection Flaws	Broken Access Control
A3	Sensitive Data Exposure	Cross Site Scripting (XSS)	Malicious File Execution	Broken Authentication and Session Management
A4	XML External Entities (XXE)	Insecure Direct Object References	Insecure Direct Object References	Cross Site Scripting (XSS) Flaws
A5	Broken Access control	Security misconfigurations	Cross Site Request Forgery	Buffer Overflows
A6	Security misconfigurations	Sensitive Data Exposure	Information Leakage and Improper Error FI and ling	Injection Flaws
A7	Cross Site Scripting (XSS)	Missing Function Level Access Control	Broken Authentication and Session Management	Improper Error Handling
A8	Insecure Deserialization	Cross Site Request Forgery	Insecure Cryptographic Storage	Insecure Storage
A9	Using Components with known vulnerabilities	Using Components with known vulnerabilities	Insecure Communication	Denial of Service
A10	Insufficient logging and monitoring	Unvalidated Redirects and Forwards	Failure to Restrict URL Access	Insecure Configuration Management

10.9 Conclusion

The requirements for safety testing and case optimization in the development of secure software are growing by the day. Furthermore, defects cost money and cause production delays, which can also put people's lives in danger. When current software systems are employed, they must ensure that the functioning is dependable and secure. In today's world of digital services, improved software security is an essential factor that distinguishes products. If you want your business to succeed, you must ensure that your items are safe. This is not a benefit but rather a must for the company's success. Researchers and business insiders agree that secure software is critical, but the topic of how, when, and where to quantify security is still a work in progress.

This document covered all of the strategies for optimizing test suites for software security. We used the ACO technique to prioritize test cases more effectively. We employed the ACO technique for early defect identification in security test suites and remediated the issues because it delivers the best possible order. Only when research is validated and accomplishes the objectives intended for it will a new approach be embraced by society or industry. In other words, the success of a software application's validation proves its flawless performance. A systematic validation is required to verify the usability and profitability of the framework for security test case optimization of an application and develop an entirely safe software architecture.

Pre-tryouts are part of the framework's empirical validation. Pre-trials are conducted via a mobile payment wallet application. Various graphs and tables are created to explain the security functions of the mobile payment wallet application. According to both pre-ACO and post-ACO metrics, the framework for security test case optimization is good at eliminating errors and determining the best way to avoid vulnerability propagation in the design.

Key Terms

Software testing; security testing; security design; optimizing test suites.

Point to Remember

- •. Security testing is a sort of software testing that identifies system vulnerabilities and ensures that the system's data and resources are safe from potential invaders.
- •. Security testing assures that the software system and application are free of dangers and risks that could result in a data breach.
- •. Any system's security testing aims to uncover all possible flaws and weaknesses in the system that could lead to the loss of data or the organization's reputation.

Objective-Type Questions

1. In which of the following, a person is constantly followed/chased by another person or a group of several people?
   a) Phishing
   b) Bulling
   c) Stalking
   d) Identity theft

2. Which one of the following can be considered as the class of computer threats?
   a) Dos Attack
   b) Phishing
   c) Soliciting
   d) Both A and C

3. Which of the following is not an ACID property?
   a) Consistency
   b) Isolation
   c) Durability
   d) Availability

4. Which of the following are possible vulnerabilities in a database?
   a) Using DELETE to delete table data
   b) Using the DROP command
   c) SQL injection
   d) All of the above

5. Which of the following should be included in the scope of penetration testing?
   a) DNS server
   b) Mail server
   c) Communication links
   d) All of the above

Short-Answer Type Questions

- What is security testing?
- List the attributes of security testing?
- What is 'penetration testing'?
- Name the two common techniques used to protect a password file?
- What is the full form of ACO?

Descriptive Questions

- Define and discuss the list of some factors that can cause vulnerabilities.
- Discuss in detail about test optimization of security testing.
- What are the phases of the security testing framework? Discuss in detail.

References

1   G. McGraw, "Software Security," *IEEE Security & Privacy*, 2(2), pp. 80–83, 2004.

2   Available at: https://www.veracode.com/state-of-software-securityreport

3   J. Alsalam, S. Banerjee, G. Musick and R. Saftoiu, "Computer Security and Rootkits", *White Paper*. http://.cs.washington.edu/courses/csep590/05au/whitepaper_turnin/whitep aper_rev12_final.pdf

4   G. D. Everett and R. McLeod, *Software Testing- Testing Across the Entire Development Life Cycle*, Hoboken, New Jersey: John Wiley & Sons, Inc., IEEE Press, 2007.

5   E. E. Ogheneovo, "Software Dysfunction: Why Do Software Fail", *Journal of Computer and Communications*, 2, pp. 25–35, 2014.

6   Available at: http://outfresh.com/knowledge-base/6-famoussoftware-disasters-due -lack-testing/

7   R. A. Khan, "From Threat to Security Indexing: A Casual Chain", *Computer Fraud and Security*, 2009, pp. 9–12, 2009.

8   I. Schie Ferdecker, J. Grossmann and M. Schneider "Model-Based Security Testing", *Workshop on Model-Based Testing (EPTCS 80)*, 80, pp. 1–12, 2012.

9   Gu Tian-yang, Shi Yin-Sheng and Fang You-Yuan, "Research on Software Security Testing", *International Journal of Computer, Electrical, Automation, Control and Information Engineering*, 4, pp. 1446–1450, 2010.

10 G. Rothermel, R. J. Untch and C. Chu, "Prioritizing Test Cases for Regression Testing", *IEEE Transactions on Software Engineering*, 27(10), pp. 929–948, 2001.

11 T. L. Graves, M. J. Harrold, M. J. Kim, A. Porter and G. Rothermel, "An Empirical Study of Regression Test Selection Techniques", *ACM Transactions on Software Engineering and Methodology*, 10(2), pp: 184–208, 2001.

12 U. Waheed, "Security Regression Testing Framework for Web Application Development", Thesis, University of Oslo, pp. 1–106, 2014.

13 S. Elbaum, A. G. Malishevsky and G. Rothermel, "Prioritizing Test Cases for Regression Testing", *International Symposium of Software Testing and Analysis*, pp. 102–112, August 2000.

14 S. Elbaum, G. Rothermel, S. Kanduri, A. G. Malishevsky, "Selecting a Cost-effective Test Case Prioritization Technique", *Software Quality Journal*, 12(3), pp. 185–210, 2004.

15 G. Rothermel, R. H. Untch, C. Chu and M. J. Harrold, "Test Case Prioritization: An Empirical Study", *Proceedings of the International Conference on Software Maintenance*, Oxford, UK, pp. 179–188, 1999.

16 K. R. Walcott, M. L. Soffa, G. M. Kapfhammer and R. S. Robert, "Time Aware Test Suite Prioritization" In Proceedings of the 2006 international symposium on Software testing and analysis (ISSTA '06). Association for Computing Machinery, New York, NY, USA, 1–12. https:// doi.org/10.1145/1146238.1146240, 2006.

17 J. Ning, C. Zhang, P. Sun and Y. Feng, "Comparative Study of Ant Colony Algorithms for Multi-Objective Optimization", *MDPI Information*, December 2018, 1–19.

18 L. Li, S. Ju and Y. Zhang, "Improved Ant Colony Optimization for the Travelling Salesman Problem", 2008 International Conference on Intelligent Computation Technology and Automation (ICICTA), 2008, pp. 76–80, doi: 10.1109/ICICTA.2008.265.

19 R. Kumar, S. A. Khan and R. A. Khan, "Software Security Testing: A Pertinent Framework", *Journal of Global Research in Computer Science (JGRCS)*, 5(3), pp: 23–27, March 2014.

20 B. D. R. Marino, H. M. Haddad, "Security Vulnerabilities and Mitigation Strategies for Application Development", *Proc. IEEE Conference on Information Technology: New Generations (ITNG'09)*, IEEE, pp. 235–240, 2009.

Useful Links

https://www.wisdomjobs.com/e-university/security-testing-interview-questions.html
https://www.educba.com/security-testing-interview-questions/
https://www.geeksforgeeks.org/software-testing-security-testing/

11

Implementing Security: A Case Study

Security used to be an inconvenience sometimes, but now it's a necessity all the time.

Martina Navratilova

No matter to which part of the globe it belongs, information is available with a mouse click. Intensive security-oriented services ranging from internet banking, trading, online buying, selling, etc., are carried out unhesitatingly. These services require the privacy of the information and assets. When security-intensive information is floating everywhere, anyone with malicious intent can misuse this information. Software security expert Guru Garry McGraw states about software security as follows: Software security is about building secure software, i.e., designing software to be secure, making sure that the software is secure and educating software developers, architects, and users about how to build secure software.

Software security is the idea of engineering software to function correctly despite malicious attacks. This approach tends to make software proactive. Security modeling is a method when integrated with the software development life cycle. It entails identifying and addressing security flaws in developing software. It is widely accepted and acknowledged that software security must be quantified, commencing with the design phase of the development life cycle. Incorporating security into the software development life cycle reduces the development cost and effort.

11.1 Objectives

Upon successful completion of this chapter, the students would be proficient to accomplish the following:

- Understanding and defining the concept of security estimation through a case study on vulnerability identification and mitigation
- Discussion on a perspective framework for security quantification through design complexity
- Realization of the importance of software security and design complexity for object-oriented software
- Realization of security and design complexity factors for object-oriented perspective
- Realization of the correlation between security and complexity attributes
- Realization of the need of software security metrics and models and further model development for analysis and estimation purpose

DOI: 10.1201/9781003330516-11

- Contextual interpretation of security estimation
- Another case study of quantification based on software analyzability using quality metrics and their contextual interpretations
- Impact analysis

11.2 The Concept

Perceived complexity in any application is directly related to the lines of code of the software. This is one of the primary metrics used to measure software applications [1, 2]. As lines of code increase at the code level, things become harder to understand. At the design level of software development, enough complexity is also responsible for making things harder to understand and less analyzable. Complexity must be kept within their limits, and it must not exceed a specific limit determined in detailed design. It is a well-established concept that producing software products with higher security requires an optimized level of design complexity that should never go beyond the average acceptance level.

11.3 Implementations Perspective

The optimization is achieved by adequately altering design properties and their relations with security factors. There is always a balance between design complexities and security concerns [3]. Perceived design complexity extends beyond the commonly accepted level, resulting in a loss of model effectiveness in terms of financial viability, product usability, and overall market values. Therefore, it is highly desirable to consider complexity as a significant factor in design security, with the extended level of design complexity having a negative impact on security attributes. The following observations from the case study are as follows:

- It will help identify underlying vulnerabilities of the applications and critical minimization vulnerabilities at an early stage of the development life cycle, leading to a secure end product.
- Security quantification will be helpful for accurate planning of software projects to facilitate cost, time, and resource estimation, including planning for new activities.
- Another advantage of quantification is determining the impact and trying to build such a mechanism to minimize vulnerabilities and be capable of introducing design alternatives in the development of object-oriented software.
- Literature reveals the facts about quantification that it will be helpful to provide a comparison among various versions of designs and choose the most secure based on observation and assessment.
- It shows which design has more vulnerability among different versions of object-oriented software.

The outcome of the study will facilitate researchers in various ways as follows:

- The proposed case study will encourage the development of a perspective framework for security quantification using various methodologies, including regression approach, Markov chain analysis, fuzzy estimation techniques, predictive analysis using ML, automated security estimation, and others with better acceptability for good security and better security vulnerability detection models.
- To explore metric-based approaches for formulating appropriate metrics that provide the basis for building modified or refined principles.
- Helpful for security rating and ranking using fuzzy techniques to determine the threshold values of available metrics and plan for updated ones for accurate quantitative interpretations.
- These approaches are welcome for setting security benchmark values to standardize procedures for organizations.

11.4 An Integrated Approach

Two case studies are discussed addressing security quantification with respect to vulnerability identification and mitigation and CIA evaluation through complexity in an object-oriented design perspective [4, 5]. They are as follows:

i) A case study for estimating security concerning software vulnerability detection and analysis framework (SVDA) has different layered skeletons. It can play a vital role anywhere in the software design phase. Frameworks may include actual programs, specific programming interfaces, and block diagrams or basic skeletons and programming tool flow diagrams. A framework is generally more comprehensive than a protocol and more prescriptive than a structure. Vulnerability is a concept of rapport people have with their surroundings' social services, institutions, and the cultural values that maintain and challenge them. In other words, the concept of vulnerability expresses the multidimensionality of disaster by focusing attention on the totality of relationships in a given social situation. It will be in a state of amalgamation with environmental forces. Uninterrupted augmentation of vulnerability may cause a higher rate of exploitation. Both tangible and intangible costs can be reduced by putting preventive methodology into operation to build safe and sound software. The proposed framework detects and analyzes vulnerabilities in the design phase.
ii) Another case study is being used to measure the security values of object-oriented software from a complexity perspective. This study is more beneficial for both design and architectural information from an object-oriented software perspective, facilitating comprehensive development and avoidable maintenance.

11.4.1 Case Study on Vulnerability Perspective

It is evident from the literature that due to security holes left during the development of the software, it becomes more vulnerable and is a threat to security. The term 'venerability' expresses itself as a weakness in the design phase that can be exploited and lead

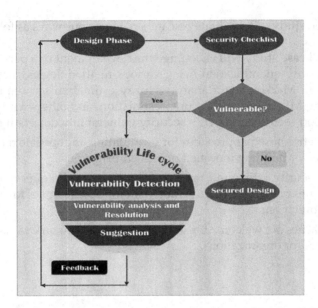

FIGURE 11.1
Software Vulnerability Detection and Analysis Framework (SVDA).

to undesired consequences for software applications. One of the most challenging tasks for secure software development is the prevention of vulnerabilities at each phase of the SDLC. Multiple processes must be performed to produce secure software, and each phase's reflections must be investigated to estimate the security ramifications appropriately. It is a continuous process at all stages of the development life cycle. A framework is proposed to estimate vulnerability in the design phase in Figure 11.1.

11.4.2 The Process

The proposed framework detects and analyzes vulnerabilities in the design phase. Each time, the output of the design phase is verified against the given security checklist, which can be developed by the rigorous analysis of security people to develop secure software. If the output of the phase fulfills the fundamentals of security, the stage is declared secure. If it is not, the outcome is presumed to have a vulnerability life cycle as an input where it is appropriately examined to detect vulnerabilities. In the form of feedback, the documented suggestions are sent as input to the design phase, from which the vulnerable output is received as input. The exact process is repeated until the outcome of that particular phase becomes secure. The objective of the proposed framework is designed to prevent vulnerabilities in software development. The proposed framework SVDA is divided into three broad categories to meet the stated objectives at the design phase, including vulnerability detection, vulnerability analysis and resolution, and documentation on suggestive measures.

Phase I: Vulnerability Detection: It is an apparent matter to first identify and detect the vulnerabilities in the development process of software. Vulnerable inputs are analyzed, and vulnerabilities are detected in the primary phase. There are various steps involved in vulnerability detection, as follows:

Research: Depending on the nature of the product, it is necessary to examine all possibilities for identifying threats and attacks on an ad hoc basis, based on past experiences.

Verification: This phase is responsible for accessing damages due to vulnerabilities in the applications. This assessment will evaluate the potential for damage after the exploitation of a vulnerability and is helpful in figuring out the actual impact of the environment through analysis.

Report: This phase will report the anomalies, and further investigation for the next phase of the development life cycle will proceed.

Phase-II: Vulnerability Analysis and Resolution: This phase is responsible for vulnerability analysis, its origin, and associated causes for mitigation. The steps involved in this phase are as follows:

Vulnerability Classification: Classification explores the analysis and origin: when was the vulnerability introduced and when was it first detected? It will make it easier and cheaper to deal with problems caused by the same type of vulnerability, which means less work and money.

Vulnerability Prioritization: Prioritization of vulnerabilities will help determine the order or rank based on specific criteria. It will help diagnose the maximum and minimum impact of the vulnerability on software, and it should be resolved accordingly. These are the few examples that will support prioritization on the following basis:

- Experienced damage, if it is exploited.
- Severity and cost of mitigation.
- Efforts to detection

Extracting Direct and Indirect Causes: After completion of classification, similar types of vulnerabilities are grouped together, and the focus of analysis for each vulnerability will help to determine its direct and indirect causes. This analysis will be helpful to resolve vulnerabilities and determine some actions based on their cause.

Identifying Security Activities: It will make it easier to figure out which security activities are best for dealing with a certain vulnerability.

Choosing Appropriate Security Activity: Various factors influence security activities, including application cost, effect on SDLC, and the number of vulnerabilities mitigated.

Phase-III: Documentation on Suggestive Measures: The above phase is responsible for delivering suggestions extracted from the study of the above stage. The systematic collection of responses will reveal why and how the development process can resolve vulnerabilities within an application by minimizing their causes.

11.4.3 Framework Implementation

The proposed framework [6] is implemented exclusively in the design phase, keeping the propagation of vulnerabilities in mind. The idea is to investigate the contribution of object-oriented design properties, including inheritance, coupling, encapsulation, and cohesion, to vulnerability propagation. Initially, at the vulnerability detection phase, the design phase vulnerabilities or their causes are identified. In the Vulnerability Analysis and Resolution phase, various metrics related to object-oriented design properties are computed. Based on the analysis of these metrics' values, the suggestion is made for the design property to be further manipulated to improve security. The suggestive instructions are generated according to the Vulnerability Analysis and Resolution Phase results.

Phase-I: Vulnerability/Causes Detection: Vulnerabilities are system flaws that can be exploited at any moment and tend to breach security regulations. A software vulnerability is described as' vulnerability to attack', meaning that every entity in the software that is subject to attacks is deemed vulnerable. From the point of view of object-oriented design, an attribute is vulnerable if it has one or more of the following characteristics:

- To Provide access points for external applications,
- To process confidential data,
- To require internal network connectivity,
- To allow user authentication and control.

The aforementioned features are the primary sources of an object-oriented design's vulnerability.

Phase-II: Vulnerability Analysis and Resolution: The object-oriented design has vital entities, including classes, objects, methods, and attributes. These basic entities are responsible for organizing to form the software design using the essential design characteristics like encapsulation, polymorphism, coupling, cohesion, abstraction, and inheritance. It is clear from the literature that measuring their values is essential for minimizing vulnerability and its propagation or controlling vulnerability propagation. You can reduce vulnerabilities by getting rid of features that make adware vulnerabilities and using more functions that stop vulnerabilities from spreading.

The Vulnerability Analysis and Resolution phase derives metrics and algorithms for computing these metrics (for each design property, i.e., inheritance, coupling, cohesion, and encapsulation). The metrics Attribute Vulnerability Ratio (AVR) [7], Coupling Induced Vulnerability Propagation Factor (CIVPF) [8], Vulnerability Confinement Capacity (VCC) [9], and Vulnerable Association (VA) [10] are proposed for inheritance, coupling, encapsulation, and cohesion respectively. The definition of each metric is given as follows:

11.4.3.1 Metric-1: Attribute Vulnerability Ratio (AVR)

A class will be vulnerable in object-oriented design if it consists of one or more vulnerable attributes (see definition-1 and definition-2) [11]. Due to the transitive nature of inheritance, a vulnerable class will propagate vulnerability to its descendants. Mathematically, Vulnerability Propagation (VP) of class C, denoted by VP(C), contains classes in the hierarchy that directly or indirectly inherit class C, i.e., descendants of class C. Therefore,

$$VP(C) = \{C_i : C_i \in \text{set of classes in hierarchy}\}$$

Set VP (C) cardinality reflects the number of classes that have been vulnerable as a result of class C. Therefore,

$$\text{The number of classes that are vulnerable due to class } C = |VP(C)|$$

In addition, the Vulnerability propagation of Class C is the total number of classes that directly or indirectly inherit class C.

If M is the number of vulnerable classes in a design and VP (1), VP (2)....VP (M) is the corresponding Vulnerability Propagation of these classes, then VPF may be defined mathematically as follows:

$$VPF = |VP(1) \cup VP(2)....\cup VP(M)| / M \qquad (11.1)$$

Attribute Vulnerability Ratio (AVR) of an object-oriented design is the total number of elements in vulnerable set divided by the number of classes in the design.

$$AVR = \frac{\text{Number of Elements in Vulnerable Set}}{\text{Number of Classes in OOD}}$$

11.4.3.2 Algorithm Development for Computation of VPF Metric

There are some possibilities that inheritance hierarchy comprehended with no class or one or more vulnerable classes. First, it is required to calculate the Vulnerability Propagation Factor (VPF) values by estimating vulnerability propagation due to each vulnerable class Ci due to the inheritance hierarchy of the design class. Combining all vulnerability propagation that occurred due to each vulnerable class will provide the overall responsibility for the design. An algorithm is being produced to calculate the vulnerability propagation factor for the design is mentioned in Figure 11.2.

It uses the Breadth-First Search (BFS) algorithms to calculate the vulnerability propagation factor. First, it collects identified vulnerable class VUL {1.... N} in a queue and an array H [M] of inheritance graphs as input. Where N is defined as the total number of classified vulnerable classes and M is as design inheritance hierarchies.

Progress is demonstrated through algorithms by classifying vertex states into different sections, including unknown, known, or traversed. Initially, the vertex is unknown and then discovered after it becomes known. Later, it becomes traversed when all of its adjacent vertices become known. The approach implies that adjacency lists represent inheritance graphs H = (V, E). It keeps various extra data structures with each vertex in Inheritance graphs. The state of each vertex u € V is recorded in the variable status [u], and the

VPF (VUL [1...M], H [N])
1. vp = 0
2. for [i =1; i≤ M; i++]
3.   *status* [VUL[i]] = *known*
4. for [i =1; i≤ M; i++]
5.   *vul* ← Head (VUL)
6.   *count* = 0
7.   for [j=1; j≤ N; j++]
8.   if *vul* € H[j]
9.   Call VP (H[j], *vul*)
10.   Exit
11.   dequeue (VUL)
12.   vp = vp + (*count*-1)
13. vpf_design = vp/ M

FIGURE 11.2
Algorithm-1: Algorithm for Computing VPF.

VP (H[j], *vul*)

1. for each vertex u $\in$ V (H[j]) – *vul*

2. if *status* [u] = Nil

3.   then do *status*[u] ← *unknown*

4.   p[u] ← Nil

5. p[*vul*] ← Nil

6. Q ← *vul*

7. While Q $\neq$ $\emptyset$

8.   do u ← head (Q)

9.   for each v $\in$ adj [u]

10.   do if *status*[v] ← *unknown*

11.   then status[v] ← known

12.   p [v] ← u

13.   enqueue (Q, v)

14.   dequeue (Q)

15.   status [u] ← traversed

16.   count ← count + 1

FIGURE 11.3
Algorithm for Computing VP Due to Inheritance.

predecessor of u is saved in the variable p [u]. The program employs two FIFO queues, VUL storing all susceptible vertices and Q maintaining a collection of all known vertices. Figure 11.3 describes the algorithm for computing VP due to inheritance.

11.4.3.3 Analysis of AVR

The metric value of AVR generated suggestions to build guidelines to minimize vulner-abilities. If n ($\geq$0) is the total number of vulnerable attributes in a design, then the numera-tor in Equation (4.1) would lie between 0 and M (total number of classes in the design),i.e.

$$0 \leq |V\,P1\,U\,VP2....U\,VPn| \leq M$$

Using the above inequality, the value of AVR of a design will always be greater than 0 and less than or equal to 1,i.e.

$$0 < AVR \leq 1$$

Considering the values of AVR mentioned above states that the higher values belong to more vulnerability in the design. It will help achieve higher security in design by lowering the value of AVR for a lesser number of vulnerabilities. The range of AVR from 0 to 1 signi-fies the minimum limit; i.e. zero will provide a more secure design with less vulnerability.

11.4.3.4 Metric-2: Coupling Induced Vulnerability Propagation Factor (CIVPF)

Another metric development is to evaluate the vulnerability propagation factor induced by coupling. In this case study, two classes are defined such as Class A is Root Vulnerable Class, and Class B isvariously associated with class A as mentioned below:

- Class B can inherit vulnerable attributes from Class A
- Some methods of Class B can call Vulnerable methods of Class A
- Some methods of B can be passed as a parameter to vulnerable attributes of A
- Vulnerable class A is the type of an attribute of class B.

As per the above assumption, Class A and B would be recognized as Coupling Induced Vulnerability Propagation, and Class B will be addressed as an Induced Vulnerable Class.

Based on the above observation, different conditions arise in the first case where one of the attributes of Class B has type A, where Class is an induced vulnerable class. Coupling Induced Vulnerability Propagation is defined as weak vulnerability propagation due to its type of propagation.

'Coupling Induced Vulnerability Propagation Factor (CIVPF) of an object-oriented design is the ratio of total induced vulnerability propagation through all root vulnerable classes to the number of classes in the design'.

$$CIVPF = \frac{\text{Total induced vulnerability propagation}}{\text{No.of classes in OOD}}$$

11.4.3.5 Algorithm Development for Computing CIVPF Metric

The aim of the work is to investigate how vulnerabilities are propagated from root vulner-able classes to others. All the classes communicating with the root vulnerable class through its vulnerable attribute will be strong vulnerable. The other classes in design communicat-ing with strong vulnerable classes are weak vulnerable and the vulnerability propagation becomes weaker and weaker for the next levels of communication. If there are n vulner-able attributes in the design and M classes are root vulnerable due to n attributes such that (n≥ M, where class having more than one attributes), Coupling Induced Vulnerability Propagation Factor may be evaluated as mentioned below.

The overall Coupling Induced Vulnerability Propagation (CIVP) values are denoted by P for object-oriented design due to n vulnerable attributes, from the root vulnerable class C_i is as follows:

$$CIVP = P1 + P2 + \dots Pn$$

Hence, $CIVP = \sum_{i=1}^{n} Pi$

So, Coupling Induced Vulnerability Propagation Factor comes out as:

$CIVPF = CIVP / N = \sum_{i=1}^{n} Pi / N$, Where, N is the total number of classes in OOD.

11.4.3.6 *Working of an Algorithm to Compute CIVPF*

The case study based on object-oriented design shows that the total number of classes N has M root, vulnerable class. Class_list [1…N] is taken for the input that holds the design classes, and a queue VUL [1…M] contains the vulnerable root class. Based on vulnerable attributes in the design, the algorithm generates an Induced Vulnerable graph. The vulnerable root class may have more than one vulnerable attribute, so there is a chance for more than one induced vulnerable graph as a distinguished vertex because generated vulnerable graphs are famed as root vulnerable classes.

The algorithm maintains several additional data structures, including three lists, namely, parent_list, atr_list, atr_type, and a queue IVC.

The parent_list contains all the parent classes of an induced vulnerable class. atr_list is the list of all attributes (own, inherited, and imported) corresponding to a class. The list atr_type of class C consists of all the types class C declares to its attributes. The queue IVC contains all induced vulnerable classes.

11.4.3.7 *Analysis of CIVPF*

Analysis of CIVPF metric is highly required to explore two more suitable cases.

Let Li represents the total Coupling Induced Vulnerability Propagation from a root vulnerable class Ci to the others, then overall Coupling Induced Vulnerability Propagation in an OOD due to p vulnerable attributes may be given as:

$$CIVP_{OOD} = L1 + L2 + ... + Lp$$

Hence,

$$CIVP_{OOD} = \sum\nolimits_{i=1}^{p} Li \qquad (11.2)$$

So, Coupling Induced Vulnerability Propagation Factor comes out as:

$$CIVPF = CIVP_{OOD} / M = \sum\nolimits_{i=1}^{p} Li / M \qquad (11.3)$$

Where, M is the total number of classes in OOD. An algorithm computing CIVPF has been described in the next subsection.

Case 1: The first case deals with when the vulnerable class has established no communication with other classes via their vulnerable attributes. Such a case has the value of Li = 0 for each vulnerable class. The value of CIVP is zero due to no more induced vulnerability propagation. Therefore, the value is as follows:

$$CIVP(min) = \sum\nolimits_{i=1}^{n} Li = 0 \qquad (11.4)$$

Case 2: The second example argues that when a root vulnerable class generates vulnerability in remaining M-1 classes, these classes become vulnerable. These generated vulnerable classes, unlike their parent susceptible classes, may transmit weak vulnerability among themselves.

Therefore, L_i may be calculated as:

$$L_i = M \times (M - 1) / 2, \text{ for each root vulnerable class}$$

In this case, CIVP will be max and numerator of equation will be

$$CIVP(\max) = \sum_{i=1}^{n} Li = n \times M \times (M - 1) / 2 \tag{11.5}$$

Equation (2.5.2-d) and equation (2.5.2-e) are summarized to yield the inequality

$$0 \leq CIVP \leq n \times M \times (M - 1) / 2$$

Using the above inequality, the range of CIVPF of Equation (11.3) comes out to be

$$0 \leq CIVPF \leq n \times (M - 1) / 2 \tag{11.6}$$

Since, it is assumed that $n > 0$, and $M \geq 1$ for any object-oriented design. Hence, the interpretation about CIVPF may be drawn as: 'The higher the CIVPF of a design, the higher vulnerable the design is'.

11.4.3.8 Metric-3: Vulnerability Confinement Capacity (VCC) of a Class

Another metric is required to deal with the complex nature of software by exploring the concept of coupling and inheritance. Identity disclosure will support knowing about other classes' existence in the class. The vulnerable class may have a chance to encapsulate vulnerability more effectively by not learning from other classes in the design.

It will count the less vulnerable confinement capacity by disclosing its identity more times. The formula to estimate the Vulnerability Confinement Capacity (VCC) of a class for object-oriented design is as follows:

Vulnerability Confinement of a class is the ratio of Write Protection and Accessibility Restriction (WPAR) to the number of times a class discloses its identity.

$$VCC\_VulClass = \frac{WPAR}{\text{Total Identity Disclosure Count}}$$

The WPAR can be computed as the ratio of the number of protected (the attributes having accessibility restriction and write protection) vulnerable attributes to the total number of vulnerable attributes of the class.

$$WPAR = \frac{\text{Number of Protected Vulnerable Attributes}}{\text{Total Number of Vulnerable Attributes in the Class}}$$

11.4.3.9 Metric-4: Vulnerability Confinement Capacity of an Object-Oriented Design

The security strength of a system can be estimated by the average security strength of its components. In the case of object-oriented design, security strength or vulnerability confinement capacity is equal to the average of the VCC of all of its vulnerable classes.

$$VCC\_OOD = \frac{\sum_{i=1}^{m} VCC\_Class(i)}{m}$$

Where, m is the number of vulnerable classes.

Algorithm Development for Computing VCC Metric

This case study consists of a total number of classes N out of M as a vulnerable class. An algorithm has been proposed to compute VCC for each vulnerable class using which it calculates Vulnerability Confinement Capacity (VCC).

11.4.3.10 Analysis of VCC

Case-1: A vulnerable class does not disclose its identity at all. (It is assumed that identity disclosure will always be greater than 0 i.e. identity disclosure $\geq$1). In that case, from the definition of metric-4, vulnerability confinement capacity of a class will be given as:

$$VCC\_VulClass = \text{Write Protection and Accessibility Restriction}(WPAR) \quad (11.7)$$

If the class is able to provide write protection and accessibility restriction to all of its vulnerable attributes then,

$$WPAR = 1$$

By putting the value of WAPR, VCC_VulClass can be rewritten as:

$$VCC\_VulClass = 1$$

This shows that if a class is able to protect all of its vulnerable attributes and does not disclose its identity then it will have maximum value of VCC metric i.e. 1.

If all the classes in the design have maximum VCC value then from metric definition-5, VCC_OOD comes out to be maximum, i.e.

$$\max(VCC\_OOD) = 1 \quad (11.8)$$

Case-2: A vulnerable class discloses its identity to all the remaining N-1 classes in the design as many number of times as the total number of attributes and methods in all the design. Also, the class is not able to provide write protection and accessibility restriction to any of its vulnerable attributes (WPAR=0). In that case, the class will have minimum vulnerability confinement capacity, i.e.

$$VCC\_VulClass = 0 \tag{11.9}$$

If there are M venerable classes and all are having minimum VCC i.e. 0, then from metric definition-5, VCC of an object oriented design will be 0, i.e.

$$VCC\_OOD = 0 \tag{11.10}$$

Combining Equations (11.7) and (11.9), the inequality can be obtained as:

$$0 \le VCC\_OOD \le 1$$

On the basis of the above inequality, the interpretation about VCC of an object-oriented design can be drawn as: '*The higher the VCC of an OOD, the more secure the design is*'.

11.4.3.11 Metric-5: Vulnerable Association of a Method

The more vulnerable attributes are associated with a method, the more vulnerable the method will become. The vulnerable method will propagate vulnerability to the other classes while communicating.

Vulnerable Association of a method in a vulnerable class can be defined as the ratio of the number of vulnerable attributes in the method to the total number of vulnerable attributes in the class.

Mathematically, Vulnerable Association of a method (VA_method) may be given as:

$$VA\_Method = \frac{\text{Number of Vulnerable attributes Associated with the Method}}{\text{Total Number of Vulnerable Attributes in the Class}}$$

11.4.3.12 Metric-6: Vulnerable Association of a Class

The vulnerable Association of a class is the indicator of the vulnerability propagation capacity of a class. A class with more high vulnerability dense methods will have more ability to propagate vulnerabilities throughout the design.

Vulnerable Association within a class can be defined as the ratio of summation of the Vulnerable Association of each method in the class with the number of methods in that class.

Mathematically, Vulnerable Association of a class (VA_class) may be given as:

$$VA\_Class = \frac{\Sigma \ \text{Vulnerable Association of Each Method}}{\text{Total Number of Methods in the Class}}$$

11.4.3.13 Developing Algorithm for Computing VA Metric

An algorithm for computing Vulnerable Association (VA) for an object-oriented design is proposed as given in Algorithm-5. The algorithm takes as input a queue VUL of vulnerable classes. Every time a class is fetched from the head of the queue VUL, VA of all of its associated methods is computed and then the same is computed for the class. The process goes on till the end of the queue VUL is reached. Finally, VA of object-oriented design is computed. Algorithm-5: Algorithm for Computing VA

11.4.3.14 Analysis of VA

Case-1: By analyzing the metric-(5), it is found that a method would have maximum VA, if it is associated to all the vulnerable attributes present in the class. Hence,

$$\max\left(\text{VA}\_\text{Method}\right)=1$$

It is also clear from metric-6 that a class will have maximum value of VA if VA of all of its methods is maximum i.e. 1. Hence,

$$\max\left(\text{VA}\_\text{Class}\right)=1$$

In a similar way from definition of metric-7, it is concluded that an object oriented design would have its maximum value if all of its vulnerable classes also have their maximum VA i.e. 1. Hence,

$$\max\left(\text{VA}\_\text{Design}\right)=1$$

Case-2: Analysis of metric-7 reveals that minimum value of VA for a method will exist if it associates none of the vulnerable attributes in the class. Hence,

$$\min\left(\text{VA}\_\text{Method}\right)=0$$

The minimum value of VA for a class is encountered, if all of its methods have the value of VA as 0. Hence,

$$\min\left(\text{VA}\_\text{Class}\right)=0$$

Similarly, Minimum value of VA for a design is encountered, if all of its classes have the value of VA as 0. Hence,

$$\min\left(\text{VA}\_\text{Design}\right)=1$$

From case-1 and case-2, it is clear that the maximum and minimum value of VA for an object oriented design will be 1 and 0 respectively. So, it is concluded that VA for an OOD will lie between 0 and 1, i.e.,

$$0\le\text{VA}\_\text{Design}\le1$$

Hence from the above discussion, it is concluded, 'The greater the VA, the more vulnerable the design'.

11.4.3.15 Metric-7: Vulnerable Association of Design

In a similar way as the vulnerable association of a method (VA_Method) and vulnerable association of a class (VA_Class) are computed, the Vulnerable Association of an object-oriented design is defined and calculated as:

Vulnerable Association of an object-oriented design (VA_OOD) is the ratio of the summation of Vulnerable Association of each class to the number of vulnerable classes in the design.

Mathematically, Vulnerable Association of an object-oriented design (VA_OOD) may be given as:

$$VA\_OOD = \frac{\Sigma\,\text{Vulnerable Association of Each Class}}{\text{Total Number of Vulnerable Classes in the Design}}$$

Phase -III: Suggestions: The analysis of the proposed metrics reveals that in order to come up with a better object-oriented design, one must follow the following suggestions irrespective of the nature of the software.

- The measure Attribute Vulnerability Ratio (AVR) must be minimized i.e., the inheritance of vulnerable classes should be kept as low as possible.
- The measure Coupling Induced Vulnerability Propagation Factor (CIVPF) must be minimized i.e., the coupling of vulnerable classes through its vulnerable attributes must be minimum.
- The measure Vulnerability Confinement Capacity (VCC) must be maximized for each vulnerable class i.e., vulnerable attributes must be encapsulated in the vulnerable classes as tightly as possible.
- The measure Vulnerable Association (VA) must be minimized i.e., cohesion of vulnerable elements of vulnerable classes should be kept as low as possible.

In the light of the above guidelines, the following recommendations are made to the designer in order to minimize vulnerability propagation for developing more secure software.

- Keep the inheritance of vulnerable classes as low as possible.
- If there is inheritance of vulnerable classes, be sure that vulnerable attributes and methods are not used unnecessarily by the descendant classes.
- Try to avoid the coupling of vulnerable classes as much as possible.
- Calling of a vulnerable method by some other method must be avoided until necessary.
- A vulnerable attribute must not pass as parameter to some other method until necessary.
- The type of an attribute in a class should not be declared as a vulnerable class until necessary.
- A vulnerable class should not be passed as parameter to some method of a non-vulnerable class.
- Any method of a non-vulnerable class must not have the return type of a vulnerable class until necessary.

- The privacy of a vulnerable attribute must be maintained, it must not be declared in more than one class. The similar holds for vulnerable methods too.
- A vulnerable attribute must not be given open access. The visibility options of a vulnerable attributes must be as strict as possible.
- A vulnerable attribute must be writing protected until necessary i.e., only the read methods may associate with the vulnerable attributes unless it is required.
- If there is a write method for the vulnerable attributes and if according to design decisions, it is not needed elsewhere then its visibility must be kept private.

11.4.4 Validation of the Framework

Validation of the framework is performed using an object-oriented design of an ATM. The class hierarchy of the design is given in Figure 11.4. Initially, all the proposed metrics, namely AVR, CIVPF, VCC, and VA, are calculated for the design. The design is then refactored using the proposed suggestions. Metrics are recollected and are compared with the previously collected metrics. The comparison shows considerable improvement in the security of the ATM design.

(i) **Identifying Vulnerable Attributes**

From the available design documents, it is found that design contains 22 classes, which are listed as: *'DESIGN = (ATM, CustomerConsole, Receipt, ReceiptPrinter, session, transaction, withdrawal, transfer, enquiry, deposit, status, message, money, balances,*

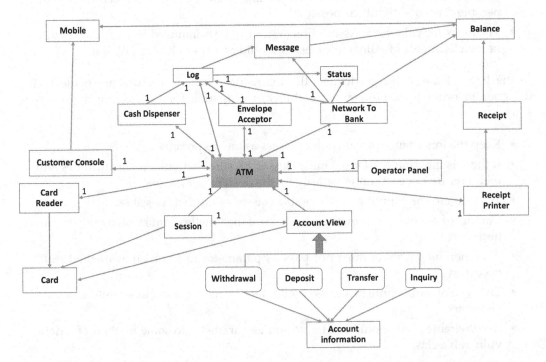

FIGURE 11.4
Class Hierarchy of ATM Software.

log, cashDispensor, NetworkToBank, OperatorPanel, CardReader, card, AccountInformation, Envelopeacceptor)'.

Analysis of the ATM design in Figure 11.4 yields that there are four vulnerable attributes present in the design.

These are *pin, totalBal, availableBal and cents*. These attributes possess one or more of the causes for being vulnerable discussed as:

- To provide an entry point for the user.
- To check authenticity of user.
- To work as a communication interface between user and ATM.
- To attend confidential information.

On the basis of the identified vulnerable attributes, vulnerable classes are identified. These include *transaction, balances and money.* The next step is to collect the metric values for the design.

(ii) **Collection of Metrics Values**

After identification of the vulnerable attributes and vulnerable classes, metric values for the metrics AVR, CIVPF, VCC and VA have been collected for the design. Each metric shows vulnerability propagation/ confinement due to inheritance, coupling, encapsulation and cohesion respectively.

11.4.4.1 Computation of AVR for the Design

While computing value for the metric Attribute Vulnerability Ratio (AVR), vulnerable trees are generated for each vulnerable attribute. Vulnerable trees show the vulnerability propagation due to a vulnerable attribute. Four vulnerable trees are generated corresponding to four identified vulnerable attributes. The vulnerable trees corresponding to *totalBal, availableBal, cents* and *pin* are shown in Figures 11.5–11.7 respectively.

The trees corresponding to vulnerable attributes *totalBal, availableBal,* and *cents* have only one node. This shows that classes with these attributes propagate less vulnerability than the class with *pin* as its vulnerable attribute. The vulnerable tree corresponding to the

FIGURE 11.5
Vulnerable Tree Corresponding to Vulnerable Attribute *totalBal.*

FIGURE 11.6
Vulnerable Tree Corresponding to Vulnerable Attribute *availableBal.*

FIGURE 11.7
Vulnerable Tree Corresponding to Vulnerable Attribute *cents*.

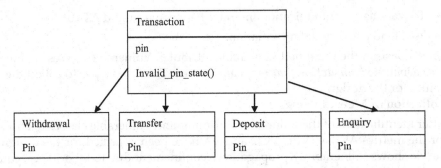

FIGURE 11.8
Vulnerable Tree Corresponding to Vulnerable Attribute *pin*.

TABLE 11.1

Computation and Result of the AVR of the Design

	Vulnerable Set	Union of Vulnerable Set	No. of Classes	AVR
Balances/Total Bal	1	7	22	0.318
Balances/Available Bal	1			
Money/Cents	1			
Transaction/Pin	5			

vulnerable attribute *pin* shown in Figure 11.8 has five nodes while others have only one. To summarize, more nodes in a vulnerable tree show more chances of propagation of vulnerabilities by the corresponding vulnerable attribute. The computation and result of the AVR of the design are shown in Table 11.1.

11.4.4.2 Computation of CIVPF for the Design

While computing the value for the metric Coupling Induced Vulnerability Propagation Factor (CIVPF), vulnerable graphs are generated for each vulnerable attribute. Vulnerable graphs show vulnerability propagation due to vulnerable attributes. The vulnerable graphs provide aid for the minimization of vulnerability propagation. Four vulnerable graphs are generated corresponding to four identified vulnerable attributes. The vulnerable graphs corresponding to totalBal, availableBal, cents, and pin are shown in Figures 11.9–11.11, respectively.

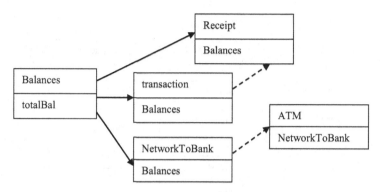

FIGURE 11.9
Vulnerable Graph Corresponding to Vulnerable Attribute *totalBal*.

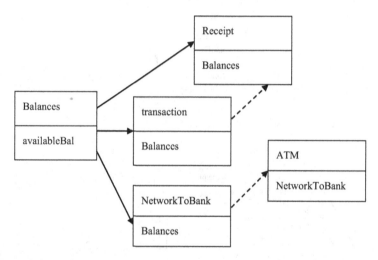

FIGURE 11.10
Vulnerable Graph Corresponding to Vulnerable Attribute *availableBal*.

The graphs corresponding to vulnerable attributes totalBal, availableBal, cents, and pin have 5, 5, 8, and 18 nodes, respectively depicted in Figure 11.12. The number of vulnerable links corresponding to vulnerable attributes totalBal, availableBal, cents, and pin is 5, 5, 7, and 23. More vulnerable links associated with a vulnerable attribute show more vulnerability propagation due to that vulnerable attribute. According to the analysis, the vulnerable attribute pin propagates more vulnerability throughout the design than the other vulnerable attributes. The reason is that the vulnerable graph corresponding to the vulnerable attribute pin has 23 vulnerable links. The number of links associated with each vulnerable attribute and computation of AVR is shown in Table 11.2.

11.4.4.3 Computation of VCC for the Design

While computing the value for the metric Vulnerability Confinement Capacity (VCC), Identity Disclosure count for each vulnerable class is calculated. Identity Disclosure count for the classes *money*, *balances*, and *message* has come out to be 17, 3, and 9, respectively as

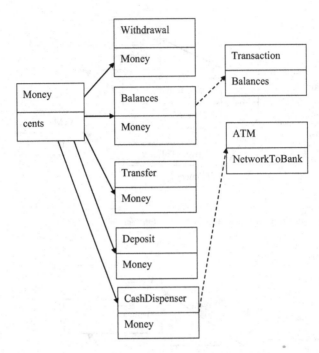

FIGURE 11.11
Vulnerable Graph Corresponding to Vulnerable Attribute *Cents*.

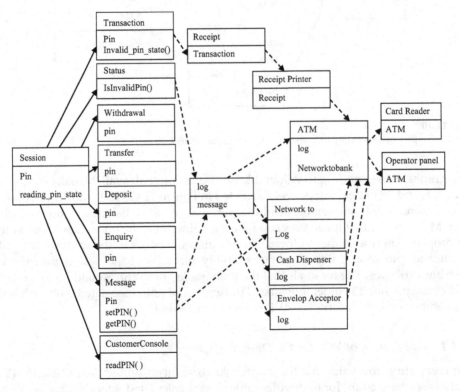

FIGURE 11.12
Vulnerable Graph Corresponding to Vulnerable Attribute *pin*.

TABLE 11.2

Computation of CIVPF

Vulnerable Class/Vulnerable Attributes ↓	Li	∑ Li	No. of Classes	CIVPF
Session/pin	23	40	22	1.818
Balances/Total Bal	5			
Balances/Available Bal	5			
Money/Cents	7			

TABLE 11.3

Computation of VCC for Vulnerable Classes as well as for Design

Classes Involved in Identity Disclosure of Vulnerable Classes		Number of Identity Disclosure Count For Vulnerable Classes		
		Money	Balances	Message
	Transfer	1	0	1
	Deposit	1	0	1
	Withdrawal	1	0	1
	O_panel	1	0	0
	Balances	5	0	0
	Message	2	0	0
	Log	1	0	0
	C_console	1	0	0
	Cash_disp	4	0	0
	Transaction	0	1	3
	Receipt	0	1	0
	Net_bank	0	1	0
	Inquiry	0	0	1
	Session	0	0	2
Total Identity Disclosure Count		17	3	9
Vulnerability Confinement Capacity (VCC)		0.05882	0.0000	0.0000
Vulnerability Confinement Capacity (VCC) of the Design			0.01961	

shown in Table 11.3. The corresponding VCC for each of these classes is 0.05882, 0.0000, and 0.0000 respectively. Finally, VCC of the design is 0.01961.

11.4.4.4 Computation of VA for the Design

While computing the value of the vulnerable metric Association (VA), firstly Vulnerable Association (VA) of vulnerable methods of each class is calculated. With the help of VA of methods, the Vulnerable Association (VA) of each vulnerable class is computed. Finally, the Vulnerable Association (VA) of the design is obtained. Vulnerable Association (VA) of the class balances and its vulnerable methods and after computation of VAs of all the vulnerable classes, the VA of the design is computed in Table 11.4

The metric values for the metrics AVR, CIVPF, VCC and VA are summarized in Table 11.4.

TABLE 11.4

Metric Values for the Design

Vulnerable Classes	VA	ΣVA	VA of the ATM Design
Balances	.75	2.240	.560
Message	.3		
Money	.857		
Session	.333		

(iii) Minimizing Vulnerabilities

Vulnerability minimization of an object-oriented design involves an analysis of the vulnerable classes of the design. Vulnerable classes mean all those classes that are initially identified as vulnerable due to vulnerable attributes and methods and the classes that have now become vulnerable due to vulnerability propagation. The aim is to identify the classes which violate the given guidelines for vulnerability minimization.

The Move Method rule states that move a method m of a class A to another class B that uses the method most. The method m can be removed entirely from class A. The Move Attribute rule states that move an attribute of class A to another class B that uses the attribute most. By following the above two refactoring rules, the attribute pin and setPIN(int pin) are completely removed from the class message without altering the overall behavior of the ATM design.

(iv) Recollection and Comparison of Metric Values

For the purpose of checking whether the new design obtained after implementing vulnerability minimization guidelines is more secure than the old one, the metrics values are again computed for the new object-oriented design received after refactoring. The computed new metric values and the old values are shown in Table 11.5. The values reflect a considerable improvement in the security of the resulting design over the old design. This shows the effectiveness of the proposed vulnerability minimization guidelines. Figure 11.13 graphically shows a comparative analysis of the old and the new values.

11.4.5 Case Study on CIA Perspective

A Security Quantification Framework through Complexity (SQFC) is a case study comprising five phases: Security Design and Conceptualization, Factor Identification, Quantification, Validation, and Review & Revision.

TABLE 11.5

Comparison of Old and New Metric Values for the Design

Metrics→	AVR	CIVPF	VCC	VA
Old Values→	0.318	1.818	0.01961	.564
New Values→	0.318	1.68	0.06723	.539

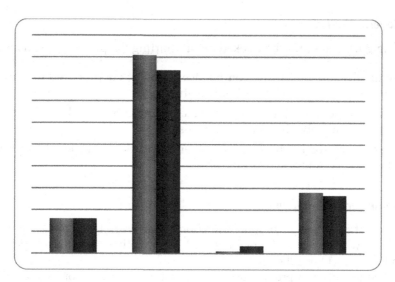

FIGURE 11.13
Graphical Representation of Comparison of Old and new Metric Values.

11.4.5.1 The Framework

The proposed framework is implemented through developing three models for security attributes, including confidentiality, integrity, and availability quantification models (CQM^{OOD}, IQM^{OOD}, AQM^{OOD}). These models are used to develop a single measure of the Security Quantification Model for Object-Oriented Design (SQM^{OOD}) to quantify the security of the object-oriented design. These quantification models are developed using multiple regression techniques on object-oriented design constructs. The framework implementation and model development are described in detail as follows:

11.4.5.2 Premises

While considering complexity as a critical parameter to quantify security for object-oriented software at the design phase, the following premises are taken into account for the framework development:

- The commonly accepted set of software security attributes, including confidentiality, integrity, and availability, must be identified early stage of the development life cycle.
- To recognize complexity factors that impact security attributes and their behavior that have a sound impact and are best implemented for object-oriented software perspective.
- To check the possibilities for evaluating complexity as a key factor based on software security and their integrated approach for the measurement.
- To assess all possibilities for uncovering errors at the design phase.
- Use a common set of desired metrics and their features to support evaluation and further development based on derived values from the metrics.

11.4.5.3 Generic Guidelines

The following guidelines must be tracked before starting the process of evaluation:

- It is highly desirable to ensure compliance to collect the proposed methodology's standard set of essential and desirable features.
- Ensure that all security and complexity factors to be measured for object-oriented design are adequately identified and persisted.
- Need assurance for establishing a proper correlation with identified attributes with their related metrics.

11.4.5.4 Framework Development

The development of the Security Quantification Framework through Complexity (SQF^C) is encompassed with five phases together with prescriptive steps for each and has been depicted in Figure 11.14 as follows:

Security design and conceptualization: This phase is responsible for the possible solutions to related problems, their facts analysis, and possibilities for steady implementation. This phase is responsible for developing secure designs based on a review of security design best practices and their consolidated rules based on design parameters and related metrics. The following activities are done through this phase for security design and conceptualization.

- *Access needs and significance*: This section will recognize the needs and their significance related to preliminary phase for secure design with complexity perspective.
- *Exploring development feasibility*: It is responsible to check and verify the development feasibility on the basis of availability, tools, scope and models that serves the larger interest of the concept.

Identify theoretical basis through best practices: It will set theoretical viability of the proposed framework.

- *Selection of metric attributes*: This portion is responsible for metric selection on relevant attributes for software development. This paradigm emphasizes the role of internal and external structure, focusing on the complexity of individual entities and measuring the interconnectivity among entities. The tangible properties of the design, including structuring internal and external behavior, relationship, and functionalities, are directly associated with design properties like encapsulation, abstraction, inheritance, coupling, cohesion, and inherent hierarchies.

Factor Identification: This phase's focus is responsible for identifying factors for security, complexity, and their contextual relationship. The measurement approach will deliver a conclusive declaration of measures to be taken, cognitive predictions of utilized metrics, and a way for incorporating the properties into metrics computations. This phase is responsible for the following activities including:

- Selection of object-oriented design parameters
- Identification of complexity factors
- Identification of security factors
- Measures and strategy establishment

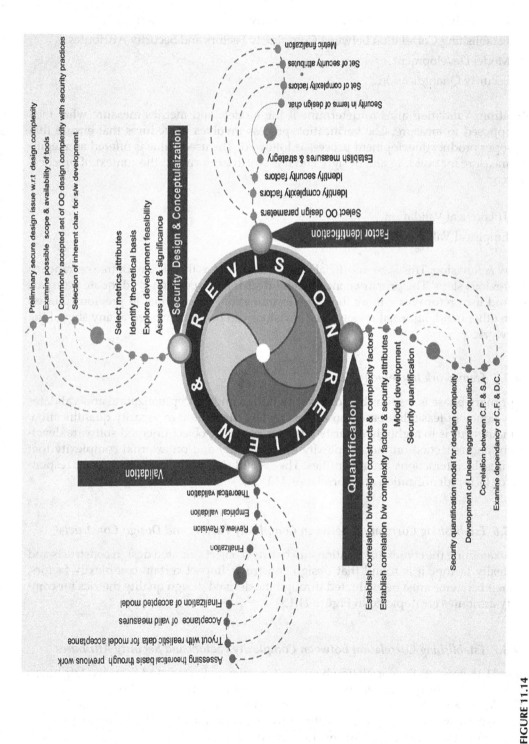

FIGURE 11.14
Security Quantification Framework through Object Oriented Design Complexity (SQF°).

Quantification: The purpose of this phase is to estimate security and bridge the gap to trade of security goals and cost. The following steps will be performed.

- Establishing Correlation between Complexity Factors and Design Constructs
- Establishing Correlation between Complexity Factors and Security Attributes
- Model Development
- Security Quantification

Validation: Validation aims to determine if the models and metrics measure what they are supposed to measure. The verification process involves procedures that ensure that the proper product development process is followed. The used value is offered as a legitimate measure for building and design, and it is worth exploring in the context of practical research.

- Theoretical Validation
- Empirical Validation

Review & Revision: This is an unofficial stage, designated as the fifth, with free entrance to any previous steps. The primary concept behind such a prescription is adequate transparency and then return for a more thorough examination, considering all previous phases. On the other hand, informal reviews and revisions can be implemented at any step of the framework.

11.4.5.5 Framework Implementation

The primary phase is responsible for security design and conceptualization and validates its development feasibility based on regress review carried out in security quantification. The main focus is to highlight security analysis regarding object-oriented software development and reflection on the complexity of each entity and on external complexity that measures the interactions among entities. The second step is the most crucial part responsible for factor identification and correlation [12, 13].

11.4.5.6 Establishing Correlation between Complexity Factors and Design Constructs

After examining the contextual relationship between object-oriented design constructs and complexity factors, it is found that design constructs impact certain complexity factors, and their behavior must be evaluated through the derived design quality metrics for complexity attributes are depicted in Figure 11.15.

11.4.5.7 Establishing Correlation between Complexity Factors and Security Attributes

Figure 11.16 presents the correlation between Complexity Factors and Security Attributes. The details of security attributes which is the part of the study are as follows:

Confidentiality: It ensures that unauthorized persons do not access information.

Integrity: This mechanism ensures that information is not altered by unauthorized persons in a way that is not detectable by authorized users.

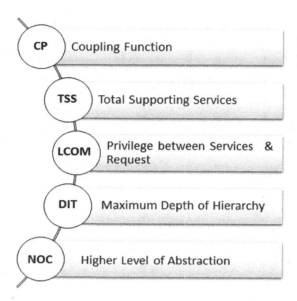

FIGURE 11.15
Derived design metrics for complexity attributes.

Availability: The mechanism of ensuring that a system is operational and functional at a given moment, usually provided through redundancy; loss of availability is often referred to as 'denial-of-service', comes under the realm of availability.

11.4.5.8 Model Development

The generic quality models [14–16] have been considered to develop the Confidentiality Quantification Model for Object-Oriented Design (CQMOOD). The steps involved are as follows:

[1] To identify complexity factors that have an influence on confidentiality at the design phase

[2] To identify object-oriented design characteristics

[3] To establish correlation among them

11.4.5.9 Development of Confidentiality Quantification Model for Object Oriented Design (CQM^{OOD})

Depending on the relationship between confidentiality and complexity, the relative importance of individual factors that significantly affect safety during the design phase is measured proportionally. The multiple linear regression techniques are used to obtain the coefficients. This technology creates relationships between dependent and multiple independent variables, as shown in author's previous work [17–19].

Further, a multiple linear regression model is fitted for the minimal set of confidentiality metric and is shown in Equation (11.3) [11, 20–22].

$$\text{Confidentiality} = \alpha + \beta 1 \times \text{CP} + \beta 2 \times \text{TSS} + \beta 3 \times \text{MDH} \qquad (11.11)$$

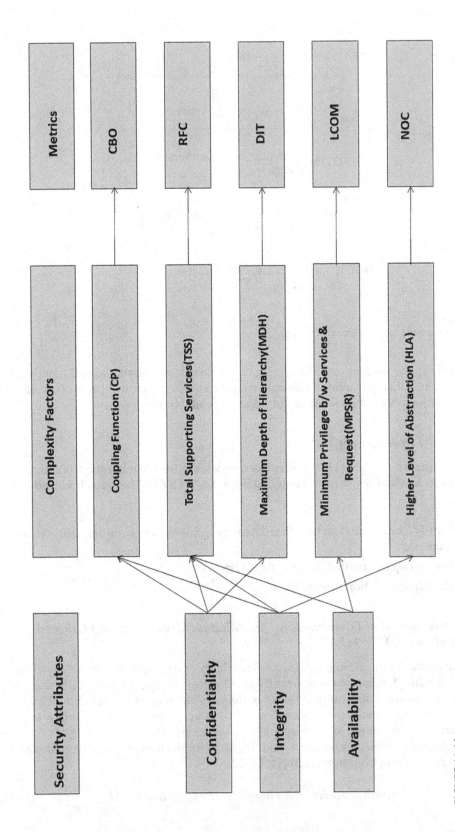

FIGURE 11.16
Correlation between Complexity Factors and Security Attributes.

11.4.5.10 Development of Integrity Quantification Model for Object Oriented Design (IQM^{OOD})

The same procedure will be adopted to quantify integrity using the case mentioned above study of the online shopping management system at the design phase. Model development for integrity quantification is carried out with the help of object-oriented design, and standard values for integrity is evaluated using the formula [13, 23–25].

Further, a multiple linear regression model is fitted for the minimal set of integrity metrics and is shown in Equation (11.6).

$$\text{Integrity} = \alpha + \beta 1 \times CP + \beta 2 \times TSS + \beta 3 \times HLA \qquad (11.12)$$

11.4.5.11 Development of Availability Quantification Model for Object Oriented Design (AQM^{OODC})

The same study takes care of availability quantification, and standard values for availability are taken from the given formula. A multiple linear regression model is fitted for the minimal set of availability metrics [1, 26, 27].

Further, the RC is set of risky classes in class hierarchy. TC is used to count total classes.

$$\text{Availability} = \alpha + \beta 1 \times TSS + \beta 2 \times MPSR \qquad (11.13)$$

11.4.5.12 Development of Security Quantification Model for Object Oriented Design (SQM^{OOD})

Development of security quantification model is also based on multiple linear regression techniques as depicted in Figure 11.17, where an online purchases system class hierarchy is being used to quantify security values. For calculated values of confidentiality, integrity and availability, only five versions of class hierarchy of online purchase system is being used as a case study. The same process is repeated again to find the security values through MR techniques.

$$\text{Security} = \alpha + \beta 1 \times \text{Confidentiality} + \beta 2 \times \text{Integrity} + \beta 3 \times \text{Availability} \qquad (11.14)$$

$$\text{Security} = -0.401 - 0.133 \times \text{Confidentiality} + 0.605 \times \text{Integrity} + 1.172 \times \text{Availability} \qquad (11.15)$$

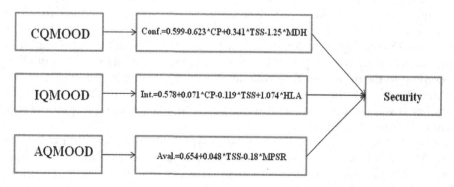

FIGURE 11.17
Security Quantification Modeling.

TABLE 11.6

Metric Calculation for Security

Class Diagram	Conf_Cal	Int_Cal	Aval_Cal
CD1	0.477	0.623	0.542
CD2	0.763	0.354	0.626
CD3	0.533	0.395	0.639
CD4	0.504	0.527	0.590
CD5	0.489	0.604	0.522

TABLE 11.7

SQMOOD Summary

R	R Square	Adjusted R Square	Std. Error of the Estimate
.998	.995	0.982	0.0056

11.4.5.13 Validating SQM^{OOD}

The validation process is necessary to check model effectiveness and efficiency for its practical usefulness. All proposed models are validated using sample try-outs. Tables 11.6 and 11.7 are showing the values related to security metrics and their relative R values based on calculation to check for model effectiveness. For the acceptance of the model, it is highly desirable to check the validity of the proposed model. A 2-sample t-test has been carried out to test the significance of the model. A hypothesis test based on a 2-sample t-test is being performed, and the difference between the two standard means is the observed confidence interval. The results of statistical interpretations will describe model effectiveness and implementation feasibility.

11.5 Analyzability: A Case Study

This case study strongly influences many of its quality aspects by decomposing software systems into various components for designing efficient software architecture. There are numerous ways to deal with the perceived complexity responsible for un-secure product development. Decomposing complex software design will facilitate higher analyzability. The term analyzability is an important term for the maintainability of a high-quality product. According to the definition regarding analyzability, it is responsible for rectifying the defects and diagnosing the cause of failure. Decomposition controlled analyzability, but the question is what should be the level required to achieve optimal point and how to break down and rectify failures.

A case study has been adopted targeting analyzability quantification object-oriented software. Maintainability has many critical components: analyzability, changeability, stability, and testability depicted in Figure 11.18. This essential component has a profound impact on maintainability concerning defect identification and the process of recovering failures of the applications. A contextual relationship between object-oriented design

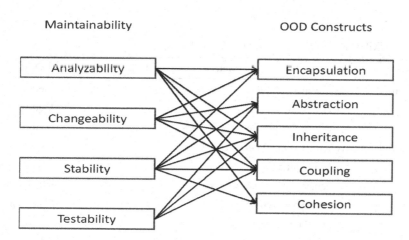

FIGURE 11.18
Correlation Diagram.

constructs and analyzability factors has been established. A metric-based approach is being provided to quantify the analyzability. This case study will provide empirical validation and statistical significance to model validity and effectiveness.

11.5.1 Assessment of Object-Oriented Design

Software design properties are tangible that assessed by their internal and external structure, an association of various functionalities, and their relationship to design components, attributes, methods, and classes.

11.5.2 Assessment of Quality Attributes

The main objective is to adopt an object-oriented design and implement them to develop a reliable, adaptable, and flexible software system. The inclusion of maintainability will justify the quality improvement mechanism for the software products.

11.5.3 Mapping Maintainability Properties with Object-Oriented Design Properties

Systematic Development by relating software maintainability with design properties will provide a sound basis for choosing objective decisions about design trade-offs and provide a platform for predictive analysis to designers based on systems attributes. The ultimate goal is to evaluate various trade-offs and overall system performance through quantitative assessment.

Object-oriented programming metrics are one factor to examine in order to give trustworthy guidance for object-oriented analysis and design across the software development life cycle. Object-oriented metrics can be used to examine source code as a quality indication. A testing engineer may choose from a large set of object-oriented metrics. But the problem a tester has to face is selecting an appropriate set of metrics for his measurement because there is no one metric that may incorporate all the aspects of object-oriented design.

As a result, the issue addressed is not one of a shortage of metrics, but rather of selecting those indicators that match the unique demands of each software project. Several

TABLE 11.8

Metric Suit for UML Class Diagram Structural Complexity

Source Ideas	Metrics	Object-Oriented Structure
Traditional Metrics	Cyclomatic Complexity	Method
	Lines of Codes	Method
	Comment Percentage	Method
Object-Oriented Metrics	Weighted Method per Class	Class/Method
	Response for a Class	Class/Message
	Lack of Cohesion of Methods	Class/Cohesion
	Coupling between Objects	Coupling
	Depth of Inheritance Tree	Inheritance
	Number of Children	Inheritance
UML class diagram structural complexity	Total Number of Associations (NAssou)	Association
	Total Number of Aggregation (NAgg)	Association
	Total Number of Dependencies (NDep)	Inheritance
	Total Number of Generalizations (NGen)	Inheritance
	Total Number of Aggregations Hierarchies (NAggh)	Inheritance
	Total Number of Generalizations Hierarchies (NGenh)	Inheritance
	Maximum DIT (MaxDIT)	Inheritance
	Maximum Hagg (MaxHagg)	Inheritance
	Total Number of Classes (Nc)	Class
	Total Number of Attributes (Na)	Class/Method
	Total Number of Methods (Nm)	Method

object-oriented metrics employ information learned from structured programming metrics to alter such measures to meet the objectives of object-oriented programming.

A comprehensive review of metrics suggested by various researchers and practitioners indicates that the object-oriented metric ultimately relies on *class*. So it appears to be good to develop a suite of class-based metrics that may be used to predict the analyzability that incorporates all aspects of object-oriented design. It takes into account encapsulation, inheritance, coupling, and cohesion. Thereby, it may indicate the analyzability of the entire class based on all these factors and the related metrics are shown in Table 11.8.

11.5.4 Calculation of Metrics Suit on Class Diagram

This case study proposed the following four metrics to calculate the values from the class diagram. The data used in Table 2 is taken from the data set presented by Genero et al. [28]. These values can also be calculated by using simple class diagram in UML notations [29]. The metric proposed for Encapsulation (NM) is counted through identified class operations. Class hierarchies will provide the metric values for Inheritance Metrics (Max DIT). The values of coupling and cohesion are calculated through Coupling Metrics (Assoc) and Cohesion Metrics (NA). The detailed values of the four following metrics are calculated and in Table 11.9.

TABLE 11.9

Metrics Calculation

Class Diagram	NM	Max DIT	N Assoc	NA
C1	26	1	2	18
C2	35	1	3	22
C3	26	2	0	9
C4	38	4	0	17
C5	76	2	10	42
C6	98	4	12	56
C7	79	3	11	44
C8	69	5	1	32
C9	84	3	14	42
C10	47	2	6	34

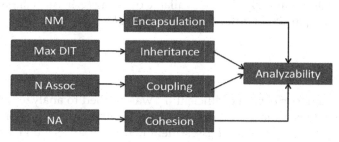

FIGURE 11.19
Analyzability Quantification Model.

The first step is to identify the exact metrics used to establish a link between object-oriented design properties and the analyzability of the software, which is depicted in Figure 11.19. The quantified value of analyzability is having a remarkable significance in achieving maintainability index. The maintainability index of software design is helpful for low cost maintenance estimation. A multiple linear regression technique has been proposed to establish models for analyzability. The following multivariate liner model is proposed in equation 13.

$$Y = \alpha + \beta 1 \times X1 + \beta 2 \times X2 + \beta 3 \times X3 + \dots \beta n \times Xn \qquad (11.16)$$

Where Y is defined for dependent variable, X1, X2…Xn is being used for independent variables and coefficient of the independent variables are defined through $\beta 1$, $\beta 2\dots\beta n$.

A controlled experiment of the 28 class diagrams presented by Genero et al. [26] is being used for model development. Analyzability is taken as an independent variable as per the definition of equation 1. The used data is responsible to calculate the values for encapsulation, inheritance, coupling, and cohesion to show the relationship with design properties. A computational formula is summarized in equation 2 as per their components weights are as follows:

$$\text{Analyzability} = 1.078 - .029\,\text{NM} + .659\max\text{DIT} + .228\,\text{N Assoc} + .064\,\text{NA}$$

$$\text{Analyzability} = 1.078 - .029\,\text{Encapsulation} + .659\,\text{Inheritance} + .228 \qquad (11.17)$$

$$\times\text{Coupling} + .064\,\text{Cohesion}$$

11.5.5 An Experimental Validation

This section evaluates how well the proposed metrics predict the 'analyzability' of object-oriented software. The internal characteristics of a design vary significantly depending on the aim and domain of the design. Empirical studies are required for software engineering practices in order to evaluate proposed techniques for appropriate execution. It examines the model's need for improvement in terms of effectiveness and efficiency. The best approach for claiming model acceptance is empirical validation. In light of this, sample trials were used to perform experimental validation of the suggested model for analyzability evaluation. The value of analyzability is available by using (Genero et al., 2001) data set for specified 10 Projects [26–28] in order to validate the suggested analyzability quantification model.

11.5.6 Statistical Analysis

The Spearman's rank correlation coefficient 'r_s' was applied to analyze the importance of the relationship between the metric design–based Complexity evaluation and the evaluator's project implementation-based assessment [29, 30]. It gives a nonparametric significance test that works well with ranked data without accurate proportional scaling and may be used to find nonlinear correlations. For two separate assessments of n items, X1 and X2, the values of X1 and X2 are rated from 1 to 'n' based on their relative size within the evaluations. Differences in ranks 'd' are determined for each X1 and X2 pair in relative rank. The sum of all d^2 s denoted by $\sum d^2$ is used in computer$_s$ using the formula:

$$1.0 \leq r_s \leq +1.0 \quad r_s = 1 - \frac{6\Sigma d^2}{n(n^2 - 1)} \qquad (11.18)$$

r_s= Coefficient of Rank Correlation
n= No. of Paired Observation
$\sum$= Notations meaning 'the sum'
d= difference between the ranks for each pair of observations.

11.5.7 Contextual Interpretation

Table 11.10 shows how the correlation values between metric suits determined the analyzability rankings of the ten projects based on design and implementation. Table 11.10

TABLE 11.10

Metric Suits and Evaluators Ranking Correlation's of Projects

	P1	P2	P3	P4	P5	P6	P7	P8	P9	P10
Computed	2	3	1	4	5	10	8	6	9	7
Known	3	3	1	4	6	6	6	5	5	4
$\Sigma d2$	1	0	0	0	1	16	4	1	16	9
rs	.99	1	1	1	.99	.90	.97	1	.90	.94
rs> .817	√	√	√	√	√	√	√	√	√	√

examines pairs of Metric Suits – Evaluator with Correlation values 'r_s' greater than (.817). The correlation values in Table 11.10 reveal that the analyzability indicators assessed using the suggested metrics suites are significantly connected.

The recommended metrics for measuring analyzability in object-oriented design were validated using structural and functional data from object-oriented software. Several functionally similar projects have also illustrated the metric suites' capacity to assess overall analyzability from design information. The model's estimate of overall project analyzability demonstrated a statistically significant association with evaluating overall project analyzability features obtained by independent assessors. Metrics may be used efficiently in the design process to check analyzability and overall program quality. However, large-scale experiments may be required to generalize and standardize.

11.6 Assessment Reflection

As the design phase of the software development process produces the skeleton of the software, the phase is most responsible for security-related weaknesses in software. Hence, security improvement in the design phase is important. Without quantification, nothing can be predicted. Therefore, quantification of security and vulnerability has become an urgent way to help predict the immunity and resilience of software. Development of secure software which can withstand attacks is an emergent need for today's environment. Software security can also be addressed by putting a check on complexity. Complexity plays an important role in deciding design security. Therefore, an effort is required to find out the normal acceptance level of design complexity for producing a secure design. Security can be measured by analyzing object-oriented design constructs, computing design complexity factors, and measuring security attributes including confidentiality, integrity, and availability. Minimizing vulnerabilities in the early stages of the software development life cycle has proved one of the best ways to deliver secure software. Unfortunately, little work has been cited in the literature to minimize vulnerability propagation in object-oriented software design. Hence, there appears an urgent need to develop a vulnerability-centric approach to minimize vulnerabilities in the design phase of object-oriented software.

In light of the objectives of the case studies, the three-fold case studies are carried out for the course of study. The *first contribution* is a framework proposed for Software

Vulnerability Detection and Analysis (SVDA), which aims to minimize vulnerabilities in the design phase of software under development. Vulnerabilities are weaknesses in the system that can be exploited at any point of time and lead to undesired consequences. Prevention of vulnerability propagation in the design phase is one of the most effective ways of developing secure software with minimal vulnerability. The proposed framework is used to detect and analyze vulnerabilities in the design phase. Each time the output of the design phase is validated against a given security checklist, which can be developed by rigorous security analysis for the development of secure software. If the output of the phase fulfills fundamentals for security, the phase is declared secure. If it is not, the output is taken to the vulnerability life cycle as input where it is properly analyzed for the detection of vulnerabilities. The documented suggestions, in the form of feedback, are sent as input to the design phase, from where the vulnerable output was received as input. The same process is repeated until the output of that particular phase becomes secure. The framework SVDA comprises of three major phases, including *Vulnerability Detection, Vulnerability Analysis and Resolution*, and *Documentation on Suggestive Measures*. On implementing the framework, metrics and algorithms are derived. The metrics Attribute Vulnerability Ratio (AVR), Coupling Induced Vulnerability Propagation Factor (CIVPF), Vulnerability Confinement Capacity (VCC), and Vulnerable Association (VA) are proposed for inheritance, coupling, encapsulation, and cohesion, respectively. Validation of the framework is performed using an object-oriented design of an ATM. Initially, all the proposed metrics, namely AVR, CIVPF, VCC, and VA, are calculated for the design. The design is then refactored using the proposed suggestions. Metrics are recollected and are compared with the previously collected metrics. The comparison shows considerable improvement in the security of the ATM design.

The *second contribution* is the development of the Security Quantification Framework through Complexity (SQF^C). The framework is prescriptive in nature and comprises of five phases, including *Security Design and Conceptualization, Factor Identification, Quantification, Validation, and Review & Revision*. Confidentiality, Integrity, and Availability have been identified as the key attributes of software security. The framework is implemented to develop the Confidentiality Quantification Model for Object Oriented Design (CQMOOD), the Integrity Quantification Model for Object Oriented Design (IQM^{OOD}) and the Availability Quantification Model for Object Oriented Design (AQM^{OOD}). Further, a Security Quantification Model for Object-Oriented Design (SQM^{OOD}) has been developed using multi-linear regression techniques to quantify object-oriented design security through complexity.

The third case study discusses the model development for analyzability assessment for object-oriented design, which is more feasible to predict the maintainability index for low-cost analysis.

11.7 Experiences

The assessment process was implemented on a given data set, and it was found by the quality executive that the process works properly and the industry is gradually improving its level of security by improving the design properties.

11.8 Societal Impacts

A security breach of software may be a matter of life and death for a human being. A report says that there was a malware, or Trojan, behind the fatal Spanish plane crash in 2008, killing 154 lives. The occurrence of these incidents was simply because of malware. In Jan 2010, login credentials for more than 8,300 customers were stolen from New York's Suffolk County National Bank after breaching its security and accessing a server that hosted its online banking system. The presence of vulnerabilities is at the root of many software failures and causes much loss to the government as well as private organizations in terms of money and reputation. The loss due to Code Red Worm has been estimated at $2.6 billion, and due to NachiWorm, operations at Air Canada and the CSX railroad were affected very badly.

Due to the wide applicability of information systems, software security has become a crucial component of every software engineering process. Software security metrics are measurements to assess security-related imperfections introduced during software development. Most security measurements either quantify security at a system level or code level. This, however, makes it very difficult and costly to identify and resolve vulnerabilities caused by software design errors. Also, various studies on object-oriented software quality have developed metrics focusing on its different attributes such as understandability and reusability. Despite the fact that security is a very important attribute of quality, the quantification of security for object-oriented design has been given little attention. The work under reference has made some contributions toward addressing security early in the software development life cycle. This may help security experts to find the vulnerable software and take necessary action to mitigate the same in order to prevent serious consequences. The contributions made in the report may be helpful for industry professionals to understand software security within the development life cycle. The work presented in the report may form the basis for other researchers and practitioners to quantify security well in advance during development.

11.9 Conclusions

A vulnerability minimization framework for the software development life cycle is proposed during the research. The framework is exclusively implemented for the design phase of object-oriented software. Implementation of the identification phase is done by the generation of the checklist to identify whether an attribute is vulnerable or not. A set of vulnerability metrics, including AVR, CIVPF, VCC, and VA, were developed during the implementation of the Vulnerability Analysis and Resolution phase. Suggestions are generated from the analysis of the metrics developed in the second phase. Finally, validation of the framework is done by minimizing the vulnerabilities of an object-oriented design. This work explores the development of the security quantification model (SQM^{OOD}) for object-oriented design perspective by using a case study of online shopping and an online purchase management system. Security quantification will be performed successfully after developing quantification models for security attributes, including confidentiality, integrity, and availability models. These models are validated through a t-test to check their effectiveness.

Key Terms

Software Security; Confidentiality, Integrity, Availability, Metrics, Quantification Model.

Points to Remember

- Every software company wants to be certain that its security protocols are up to par. There is no question about that. However, in today's complicated IT environment, with businesses utilizing more software than ever before and cyber-attacks on the rise, ensuring software is truly secure can be difficult.
- Computer security software is widely accessible nowadays, and it assists businesses and end users in ensuring that they are utilizing the appropriate software and tools to stay safe.
- The concept of implementing procedures in the building of security to assist it remain functional (or resistant) against attacks is known as software security. This means that before a piece of software is released, it is subjected to software security testing to see how effectively it can withstand malicious attacks.
- At the push of a button, software security threats will vanish. Employee education is a key aspect of ensuring software security and lowering the amount of security holes.
- One of the most obvious and significant security KPIs is dwell time. It refers to the amount of time a threat actor has access to a network before being detected and removed. This is significant because the longer a corporation waits to contain an assault, the more money it will cost.

Objective-Type Questions

1 What are security controls?
   a)   Controls that are intended to ensure that attacks are unsuccessful
   b)   Controls that are intended to detect and repel attacks
   c)   Controls that are intended to support recovery from problems
   d)   All of the mentioned
2 In which of the following, a person is constantly followed/chased by another person or group of several peoples?
   a)   Phishing
   b)   Bulling
   c)   Stalking
   d)   Identity theft

3 The term 'CHAP' stands for _____
   a) Circuit Hardware Authentication Protocols
   b) Challenge Hardware Authentication Protocols
   c) Challenge Handshake Authentication Protocols
   d) Circuit Handshake Authentication Protocols

4 Which of the following refers to exploring the appropriate, ethical behaviors related to the online environment and digital media platform?
   a) Cyber low
   b) Cyber ethics
   c) Cybersecurity
   d) Cyber safety

5 Which one of the following refers to the technique used for verifying the integrity of the message?
   a) Digital signature
   b) Decryption algorithm
   c) Protocol
   d) Message Digest

Short-Answer Type Questions

1 What is software security quantification?
2 What are the differences between vulnerability and security quantification?
3 What are the attributes of security metrics?
4 Explain CIA triad.
5 Explain the difference between asymmetric and symmetric encryption.

Descriptive Questions

1 What are the differences between VA (Vulnerability Assessment) and PT (Penetration Testing) in details?
2 Define and discuss about security tools and techniques of assessment?
3 How analyzability can impact on security? Put your views on it.
4 Complexity is inversely proportional to security? Provide your opinion to prove this.
5 How security improvements will enhance the quality of software design? Prove it.

References

1. S. Chandra and R. A. Khan, "Availability State Transition Model", *ACM SIGESOFT SEN, ACM*, 36(3), May 2011, DOI: 10.1145/1968587.1968603.
2. Y. Chen, B. Boehm and L. Sheppard, "Value Driven Security Threat Modeling Based on Attack Path Analysis", *Proc. 40th Annual Hawaii International Conference on System Sciences(HICSS'07)*, IEEE, 3–6 January 2007, p. 280a, DOI: 10.1109/HICSS.2007.601.
3. P. Manadhata and J. M. Wing, "An Attack Surface Metric", CMU-CS-05-155, July 2005. Available at: http://www.cs.cmu.edu/%7Ewing/publications/CMU-CS-05-155.pdf
4. S. Chandra and R. A. Khan, "Object Oriented Software Security Life cycle – Design Phase Perspectives", *Journal of Software Engineering* 2(1),39–46,ISSN: 1819-4311.
5. K. Mustafa, R. A. Khan, "Quality Metric Development Framework", *Journal of Computer Science* 1(3), 2005, 437–444, ISSN: 1549-3636
6. M. Dowd and John Mcdonald, *The Art of Software Security Assessment: Identifying and Preventing Software Vulnerabilities*, Addison Wesley Professional, ISBN: 978-0-321-44442-4.
7. S.A. Khan and R.A. Khan, "Securing Object Oriented Design: A Complexity Perspective", *International Journal of Computer Application* 8(13), October 2010, 8–12.
8. G. H. Walton, T. A. Longstaff and R.C. Linder, "Computational Evaluation of Software Security Attributes", *IEEE*, 1997.
9. R. G. Dromey, *Software Product Quality: Theory, Model, and Practice*, Software Quality Institute, Available at: http://www.sqi.gu.edu.au/docs/sqi/misc/SPQ-Theory.pdf
10. S. Chandra and R. A. Khan, "Software Security Metric Identification Framework (SSM)". *International Conference on Advances in Computing, Communication and Control, ICAC3'09*, ACM.
11. S. Chandra and R. A. Khan, "Confidentiality Checking an Object Oriented Class Hierarchy", *Network Security* 2010(3), March 2010, 16–20.
12. L. W. Henry, "Maintenance Metrics for the Object Oriented Paradigm", *Proceeding of the First International Software Metrics Symposium*, May 1993, pp. 52–60.
13. S. Chandra and R.A. Khan, "A Methodology to Check Integrity of a Class Hierarchy", *International Journal of Recent Trends in Engineering* 2(4), November 2009, 83–85.
14. F. Copigneaux and S. Martin, "Software Security Evaluation Based On A Top Down McCall-Like Approach,"*Proc. Fourth Aerospace Computer Security Applications conference*, IEEE Press, 1988, pp. 414–418, DOI: 10.1109/ACSAC.1988.113352.
15. J. Alves-Foss and S. Barbosa, "Assessing Computer Security Vulnerability", *ACM SIGOPS Operating Systems Review* ACM, 29(3), July 1995, pp. 3–13, DOI: 10.1145/206826.206829.
16. S. A. Butler, "Security Attribute Evaluation Method: A Cost-Benefit Approach,"*Proc. International Conference on Software Engineering (ICSE 2002)*, ACM Press, 2002, pp. 232–240, DOI: 10.1145/581339.581370.
17. A. Agrawal and R.A. Khan, "Assessing and Improving Encapsulation for Minimizing Vulnerability of an Object Oriented Design", *International Conference on Computational Intelligence and Information Technology, CIIT-2011* (Proceeding to be published by LNCS, Springer-Verlag).
18. A. Agrawal and R.A. Khan, "Assessing Impact of Cohesion on Security- an Object Oriented Design Perspective", *Journal of Brazilian Computer Society*, (Communicated), 76(2), 2014, 144–155.
19. R. A. Khan and K. Mustafa, "Metric Based Testability Model for Object Oriented Design (MTMOOD)", *SIGSOFT Software Engineering Note*, 34(2), pp: 1–6, March 2009.
20. Software Technologies for Embedded and Ubiquitous Systems, Springer, 1 edition, November 14, 2007, ISBN: 10: 3540756639.
21. W. Li and S. Henry, "Object Oriented Metrics Which Predict Maintainability", Technical Report 93-05.
22. A. Epping and C. M. Lott, "Does Software Design Complexity Affect Maintainability Effort?", *19th Annual Software Engineering Workshop*, 30 November–1 December 1994, citeseerx.ist.psu. edu/viewdoc/download? DOI: 10.1.1.6.5828.

23. B. Lilburne, "Measuring Quality Metrics for Web Application", Technical Report No: CIT/08/2004.

24. M. Perepletechikov, C. Ryan, and Z. Tari, "The Impact of SERVICE Cohesion on the Analyzability of Service Oriented Software", in IEEE Transactions on Services Computing, vol. 3, no. 2, pp. 89–103, April-June 2010, doi: 10.1109/TSC.2010.23.

25. A. L. Wang and E. Arisholm, "The Effect of Task Order on the Maintainability of Object Oriented Software", *Information and Software Technology*, 2008, DOI:10.1016/j.infsof2008.03.005.

26. M. Genero, J. Olivas, M. Piattini, and F. Romero, "A Controlled Experiment for Corroborating the Usefulness of Class Diagram Metrics at the early phases of Object Oriented Developments", *Proceedings of ADIS 2001, Workshop on decision support in Software Engineering*, 2001.

27. S. R. Chidamber and C. F. Kemerer, *Towards A Metrics Suit for Object Oriented Design*, OOPSLA, ACM, 1991, pp. 197–211.

28. J. Bansia, "A Hierarchical Model for Object Oriented Design Quality Assessment", *IEEE Transaction of Software Engineering*, 28(1), January 2002, 4–17.

29. S. A. Khan et al., "An Empirical Validation of Object-Oriented Design Security Quantification Model", *Journal of Information Assurance and Security*, 9, 2015, 9–18, ISSN: 1554-1010.

30. S. A. Khan and R. A. Khan, "Security Quantification Model", *International Journal of Software Engineering IJSE*, 6 (2), 2013, 75–89, ISSN: 2090-1801.

Useful Links

https://www.securitymetrics.com
https://owsap.org
https://securityscorecard.com
https://www.educause.edu

12

Knowledge, Management, and Governance for Higher Security

For success of any mission, it is necessary to have creative leadership. Creative leadership is vital for government, non-governmental organizations as well as for industries.

A. P. J. Abdul Kalam

A famous writer and management guru Peter F Ducker in his book entitled *Management Challenges for the 21st Century* quotes: 'Knowledge is fast becoming the sole factor of productivity, sidelining both capital and labor'. The term 'knowledge' is explained as the facts or the information and skills obtained through experience or learning. Knowledge can be acquired though theoretical or practical understanding of a subject. Knowledge is having capabilities to enlighten decisions and actions with respect to achieve the desired outcome. Tacit and explicit are the two primary forms of knowledge. Tacit is a type of unarticulated knowledge, which is context specific and difficult to formalize. On the other hand, explicit knowledge can be easily formalized and experienced.

Knowledge management is about the proficient management of various information and resources used in commercial or non-commercial organization. Knowledge management is a systematic process for enhancing productivity of information for quicker availability and improved decision making for the achievement of objectives. Various goals are associated with respect to knowledge management that must be addressed as follows:

- To acquire, organize, and sustain knowledge
- To apply, allocate, and renew implicit and explicit knowledge
- To upgrade organizational performance
- To increase business adaptability
- To upgrade values of accessible services and products
- To build novel knowledge exhaustive process

The practice begins with the collection of raw facts and is processed into information with a purpose to reduce uncertainty and then transform into knowledge for better utilization of preferred solutions. It is an idea to freely share more information. Knowledge management system can be customized as information system to facilitate organizational knowledge through further classification, acquisition, integration, and dissemination [1]. The knowledge management phases are mentioned in Figure 12.1.

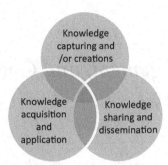

FIGURE 12.1
Phase of Knowledge Management System.

12.1 Objectives

On the successful completion of this chapter the students would be able to accomplish following:

- To understand about knowledge and knowledge management system
- To know the various aspects of knowledge management in general
- To enumerate and realize the generic view of secure knowledge management
- To know about secure knowledge management
- Security issues related to knowledge management system
- To realize the various security issues with respect to knowledge management
- To elaborate the concept of governance and security
- To enumerate and realize the generic view of governance and security
- To describe about effective security governance and management
- To enumerate and realize the generic view of enterprise software security framework
- To finalize the enterprise software security framework
- To realize how security influences project plans and management actions
- To know the purpose of measuring both product and development processes successful software development
- To understand the organization's legal obligation and ethical responsibility to protect personal information
- To formulate the strategies for E-governance framework and rules in India

12.2 Secure Knowledge Management (SKM)

The ultimate use of knowledge management system within the organization for business perspective must be seen as increased manpower utilization and maximum profitability. Security is always one of the major concerns with respect to KMS. This can be protected through proper authentication and authorization of services. With the help of secure languages, secure knowledge system access knowledge resides on multiple sources across the organization serves as gateway to warehouse of intellectual content for collaborative efforts. The knowledge which is transferable through cross-organizational platforms becomes more significant for management of digital-rights. The two more factors are responsible for security knowledge-management system is access control and identity management [1, 2].

It is highly enviable to preserve the principles of knowledge management with respect to security and privacy. Organizations must build such type of strategies to ensure the privacy of e-customers based on cost-effective solutions. It is extremely necessary to deliver important information only to authentic recipients and on the basis of accessing profile need to structure revenue-generating services. Knowledge management system are being protected against various issues including threat, attacks, security policies, and enforcement through various security methods like authentication, intrusion detection, access control and cryptography. The triple C's including communication, collaboration, and content are the foremost elements to describe secure knowledge management (SKM). Some important aspects of secure knowledge management are mentioned in Figure 12.2 are as follows:

- Knowledge conception and acquisition manager
- Knowledge representation manager
- Knowledge manipulation and sustainment manager

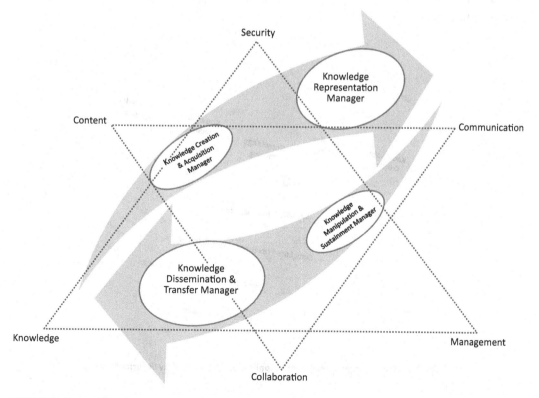

FIGURE 12.2
Architecture of Secure Knowledge Management System.

- Knowledge distribution and transfer manager
- Secure languages for access control and identity
- Digital-rights protection management
- Secure content management

12.2.1 Security Concerns for Knowledge Management System

Knowledge management is a source that allocates organizational expertise and resources for increasing competitiveness by structuring intellectual repository. Enabling security is one of the most challenging tasks for knowledge management. Data mining, multimedia, and collaborative web are various fields of expertise where knowledge management is deeply incorporated. Therefore, incorporation of security mechanism to such domain that is highly associated toward secure knowledge-management enforcement is highly required to bridge the gap. Secure strategies, processes, and metrics are the ultimate requirement toward secure knowledge management. Security policies must frame in accordance with knowledge creation, refining, storing, sharing, and utilization to deal with various security concerns on knowledge management. Cloud-based knowledge management application is taken as case study to understand the security concerns as depicted in Figure 12.3. Various security issues highlighted with respect to the steps involved for knowledge management are mentioned below:

- Data issues
- Confidentiality issues

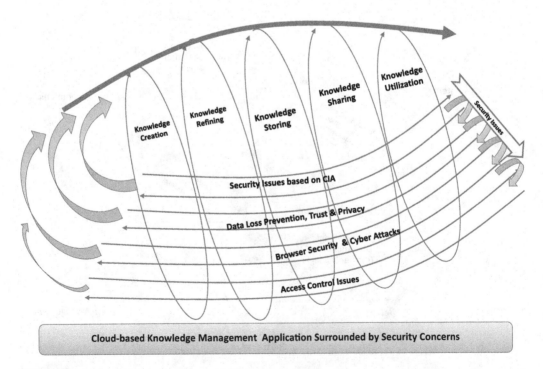

FIGURE 12.3
Cloud-Based Knowledge Management Application to Understand the Security Concerns.

- Access control issues
- Cyber attack issues
- Availability issues
- Reliability issues
- Trust issues
- Privacy issues

From the above discussion, it is required to know the process for the collection of knowledge through raising some sort of questions, including the following:

- How frequently should knowledge be composed?
- How frequently should the institute perform inspection strategy?
- What are the safety procedures that require to be imposed for secure knowledge allocation?

There is ultimate connection between business approach and secure knowledge-management policies. Unsatisfactory enforcement of business strategies may have deeper negative impact for the successful execution of secure knowledge management policies. It demands secure workflow process for smooth functioning for knowledge management. [3–5]

12.2.2 Importance of Security Knowledge and Expertise

The idea of secure knowledge management has a twofold environment keeping in mind the principles of security and secure information in organizations. For the reason of this argument, we circumvent the gap between knowledge, data, information, and wisdom, and in particular seem at an unusual question: Are we acquiring knowledge, supervising security knowledge, or both? The primary part of this environment preserves the correctness and secure usability of knowledge asset. It prevents the functionality of secure operation from the issues raised by confidentiality, integrity, assurance, and no refutability and preserves applicability of the functions through encryption, firewalls, intrusion detection, and myriads of other tools. On the other hand, it is necessary to employ this capability to monitor security knowledge, secure knowledge management, validation and change capability, and to maintain a decent security profile in relation to immediate threat changes. From the above discussion, it is evident that the seven key terms are responsible for the measurement of software security knowledge which is the direct and indirect inclusion of knowledge categories, including historical, perspective, and diagnostic as follows in Figure 12.4. [6–9]

This realization can help secure against potentially unexpected measures and provide a reliable benchmark for identifying and assessing their incidence in context of ambiguous information. The perceived complexity of an organization's information about security is escalating exponentially with security threats. Enhancement in attack quantity, complexity, and probable responses has been increasing. So there are many good reasons to expect that the requirements for both information management and security information management will remain important.

A contextual relationship between knowledge components with relevant SDLC artifacts is examined to strengthen software architects' critical observation on software security as depicted in Figure 12.5. These resources will provide support for architectural risk

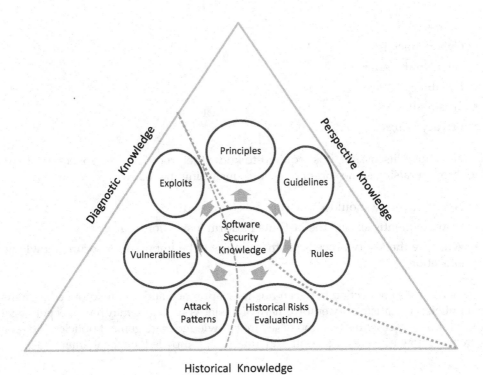

FIGURE 12.4
Components of Software Security Knowledge.

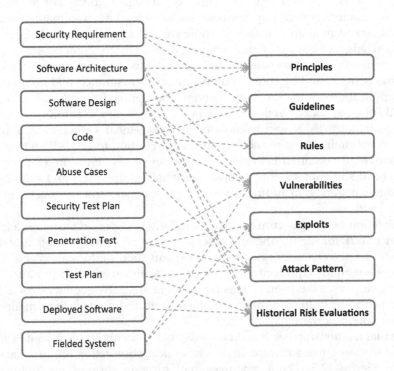

FIGURE 12.5
Relation between Software Security Knowledge Components With Relation SDLC Artifacts.

analysis. It demands for various queries to know the actual status by asking which issues to consider and which mitigation measures to pursue. The actual proposition of demonstrated incidents through potentially dangerous circumstances is identified on the basis of corrected sensitive knowledge that may lead to an accident. It has been evidently acknowledged that if punitive damages are assessed in litigation, prior knowledge of the hazardous situation can have a significant effect. [10]

12.3 Security Governance

The 'Information Security Audit and Control Association (ISACA)', established as the IT Information Auditors Association in the late 1960s and which is now a global organization with more than 70,000 security professionals, states that governance is responsible for:

> *The set of responsibilities and practices exercised by the board and executive management with the goal of providing strategic direction, ensuring that objectives are achieved, ascertaining that risks are managed appropriately, and verifying that the enterprise's resources are used responsibly.*

The organized behavior is the key to success for an effective security governance and management. Governance sets clear expectations for business operations and then follows the organization to meet those expectations. The action of governance runs from higher division to all business units and projects. Governance facilitates the organization's approach to almost any business problem, including security. The wide use of term *'Security'* is incorporated in the field of information, software; application, network, cyber-security and information and software security assurance. There are various factors involved, including action, beliefs, behaviors, and capabilities for establishing and sustaining the building blocks of security in any organization. It should be recommended as non-negotiable prerequisite to strengthen adequate security in business. The NIST model for information security governance aligned to establish and maintaining framework structuring and providing assurance to security strategies. It provides support for business objectives to manage risk at inclusive aspects and align rules and regulations focused on business policies and driven responsibilities. An article published by John Steven from Cigitel entitled 'Adopting an Enterprise Software Security Framework' discusses decision-making process to software-induced risk for enterprise software security. The ability of governance is not only to trace the process for remittances to software risk management but also to be a repo between cost-effectiveness and budget. Consistency in decision making across an enterprise improves self-assurance and reduces risk [11–15].

12.3.1 Effective Security Governance and Management

The recognized definitions of corporate governance, guided by the 'International Federation of Accountants (IFAC)' and the 'Information Auditing and Auditing Association (ISACA)', are as follows:

> *Enterprise governance is the set of responsibilities and practices exercised by the board and executive management with the goal of providing strategic direction, ensuring that objectives are achieved, ascertaining that risks are managed appropriately and verifying that the organization's resources are used responsibly.*

According to the 'Carnegie Mellon University (CMU) Software engineering Institute (SEI)', The 11 essential characteristics for effective security governance are discussed below:

1. **Enterprise-wide problem**: It requires the proper management between all the issues rose at organizational level including horizontal, vertical or cross functional covering the scope of 5P's likewise people, process, product, policies, and procedures involved in business venture.

2. **Accountability of key holders**: Accountability should be framed to protect socio-economical infrastructure and resources for each stake holder.

3. **Business necessity**: Earlier the field of software security was infancy, but the growing business threats have proven as a serious concern with security business requirement align with business objectives, risk management, and business policies.

4. **Risk-exposure analysis**: Risk exposure analysis is responsible to speculate the actual impact responses. It will provide support to build strategies to mitigate compliances, operational interruptions, economic loss, and harm to reputations.

5. **Determining roles and responsibilities**: Segregation of responsibilities for business helps to provide the finest visualized repots for concerned person with more accountability.

6. **Policy enforcement**: It is highly required for structuring and expressing security requirement policies and procedures to provide technical solutions with proper management, training, scrutinizing, and practices.

7. **Sufficient dedicated resources**: Adequate resources are highly required to preserve core competencies in enterprise security, including IT experts and recourses.

8. **Skilled manpower**: Skilled manpower is highly appreciable for appraising a comprehensible, planned guidance for the organization with definite objectives and knowledge to access digital assets and security postures.

9. **Need of development life cycle**: To ensure that solutions are executed as planned through effective management, metrics, and compliance policies driven from development life cycle models covering all phases.

10. **Measured services**: Strategic, capital, and operational planning are considered as integral components for security that are supportive to achieve stated expectations through appropriate direction and control.

11. **Reviewed and audited**: To conduct an appropriate meticulousness and audits of operations and managerial practices.

12.3.2 Effective versus Ineffective Security Governance

A comparison table is being prepared which illustrates set of activities and procedures effective versus ineffective for security governance. [16–17] This information will provide a support for researchers to all do's and don'ts in the area of security governance mentioned in Table 12.1.

TABLE 12.1

A Comparative Table for Effective Versus Ineffective Security Governance

Effective Practices	Ineffective practices
Executive committee is responsible to address security information which is critical for organizations and needs regular updates for performance and security incidents.	Executive committee is not responsible for security incident reports and their mitigation, only focus to deal with governance and profit.
Need permanent committee to address security incidents and their mitigation plan and regulations	Address on ad-hoc basis
Regular review	Only on the major issue occurrence
Annual audits and report generation	No audit plan
Need proper alignment with acceptable risk level, and their strategies goals are reflected in their security policies and procedures	No proper reflection of security plan with captured security requirement of organization and digital assets
Cross-organization meetings with CIO, CFO, CSO, HR with CEO/CTO for effective security strategic plans and recent incidents of breaches	CTO/CIO is responsible for handling all technical issues.
Risk is regularly reviewed and must be documented and included in business unit and business leaders authorize to deny or accept their operation-ability.	All issues related to security must be dealt with technical department.
Key systems and digital assets are documented with explicit owners and detailed security requirements.	Digital systems and assets are not properly documented or analyzed for potential security risks that could affect operations and profits.
Zero tolerance for unauthorized change with known significance	Change management process is not effective.
Accountability must be framed with respect to employees on the basis of security policies and procedures.	With availability of such mechanism, no enforcement is practically applicable or accountability is not framed on routine basis.
Implementation of standard security practices is applicable to provide business support at early stage.	Minimal support granted
Use of appropriate products, tools, services, consultation as per security incident with proper research	An organization is not really safe because it uses products, tools, services, management and consultants.
Continuous improvement	Ad-hoc practices
Suggestive measures are taken timely and reviewed.	Audits and reviews are performed after major security incidents are reported.

12.3.3 Enterprise Software Security Framework

There is no doubt that software security at enterprise level is the novel approach to align appropriate resources, including human resources and knowledge, relevant technologies, and software development activities to build secure software that is structured under Enterprise Software Security Framework (ESSF). [10]

About enterprise software security framework: An organizational approach is highly appreciable to build an effective software security framework under the predefined roles, responsibilities, various associated activities, deliverables, and the criterion for measurement for successful deployment under well-defined communication plan. Enterprise software and data architectures are important pillars of the target state defined by the ESSF. It is therefore part of the framework's task to define and transition to secure enterprise architecture.

Knowledge management, training: Structured set of security information likely includes guidelines, principles, design and attack patterns, threat models, code behavior, and ultimately reference architecture and secure development environment. An added constituent of this competence is the design and delivery of the curriculum. Topics include assisting assurance activities as well as security information. This direction also includes the modernization of the existing curriculum taking into account software security concepts as well as the new curriculum.

Security touch points: Defining responsibilities and actions formally or informally to accessible development processes helps developers to provide security for any custom software development process, as well as on-site outsourcing and commercial-ready validation processes. This capability defines the mechanism for software assurance [10].

Assurance: It is evident from literature review on enterprise security that transformation of security requirements into secure software design has capabilities to provide protection against threats and attacks. To conduct architectural risk assessment of software provides strength and assurance by proper execution of security touch points. Trust building activities depend closely on the knowledge and competence of education to determine what to look for. The implementation of tools can be part of this effort in the short and medium term. This will include purchasing, configuring, and deploying dynamic analysis assistants as well as static analysis tools. For example, your organization may have already implemented a penetration-testing product.

Governance: It is considered with respect to effective software security framework that governance is the ability to quantify software-related risks and support an objective decision-making process for software improvement and release. It will provide space to address the issues related to planning and budget. Governance should also apply to the deployment and development of an organization's ESSF. Infrastructure providers can measure the scope of the project and the depth of assurance activities, the reported risks with their severity analysis, and the development of software security knowledge and skills.

12.4 Secure Project Management

This section describes how security influences project plans and management actions and suggests several approaches for inserting security practices into a defined SDLC. Continuous risk management and periodic risk estimation is the foremost concern that guides project managers in determining which security procedures should be incorporated into each activity in the life cycle and to what extent. Software security requirements involve project planning and monitoring, especially in relation to the following characteristics of the project: [18–21]

- Scope of the project
- Reflection of software security practices on project plan and life cycle
- Required tools, knowledge, and expertise
- To estimate the nature and duration of desired resources
- To know about project and associated product risks

12.4.1 Scope of the Project

The impact of security on the scale of the project has several aspects that should be taken into account when planning and executing a project. These parameters affect all SDLC transactions and must be specifically handled in the final software and system before being approved for release:

- To count various threats and its scope for damages
- To require strong elaborative mechanism to deal with intruders
- To respond an attack with substantial capacity
- To provide assurance for security requirements as per specified standards of active system

12.4.2 Reflection of Project Plan

It is apparent that nature and consequences of security risks affect both project planning and resources. Actions to reduce the impact and the likelihood of low risk can be left to the prudence of the project manager, often with coherent management oversight.

- It demands adroit assistance and exhaustive systematic review process to manage severity impact of risk from higher to medium.
- Performance and intended functionality as per requirement with higher coupling may be responsible for increased complexity with product development.
- Shared services have higher possibilities to get involved in the varieties of risk.
- The higher level of trust and combination of risks mean that risks to shared services must include all integrity, privacy, and usability issues.

12.4.3 Tools, Knowledge, and Expertise

At least, the software development environment should be as secure as the planned security level of the software produced. It is highly observed that appropriate monitoring and configuration is required to include development artifacts for operational and execution purpose. As part of the development of these controls, you may need specialized tools to help you produce or test secure software such as static code analysis. Highly reliable configuration management; audit should support traceability and process compliance requirements. For highly sensitive code segments, security management may always demand amendments to be prepared by two developers to restrict a person's ability to add malicious code.

Security expertise on most projects is limited and may be provided via an internal means or a contracted service. Determining how best to allocate this limited resource is challenging even when security activity involves only networks, authentication, and access control. When security has to be incorporated into application development, this expertise is even more difficult to come by. Also, any increase in the level of assurance can significantly affect the need for security and software engineering expertise. The security expertise required to develop more secure software can be divided into two categories:

- Information about security features and functions, such as access control, authentication, and encryption features and implementation.
- Security professionals need to be responsive of security problems related to project development and management.

- Abilities to identify and fix vulnerabilities that could be exploited. Unfortunately, software development teams infrequently have the required security knowledge to congregate this demand.
- Vulnerabilities may be located in the least affected parts of the system or due to aspects of system interfaces that are unlikely or difficult to predict.
- Software development teams tend to focus on core software and security features, so they can overlook such vulnerabilities.

12.4.4 To Estimate the Nature and Duration of Required Resources

Increasing the level of development of the required program can have a long-term impact on cost and development capabilities. When designing systems with medium to high reliability, traditional cost-effective approaches such as reusing components or common purpose commercial elements may not work. Until a more comprehensive explanation of the software, such as software architecture and detailed design or a more detailed model of aggressive actions and effective responses is available.

- Security knowledge can be extended early in the planning and implementation phase
- Security test planning should begin after the architecture has been defined
- Knowledge required for risk analysis
- Detailed design analysis may require deep analytical techniques
- Analysis relies on detailed knowledge of known exploits

12.4.5 Project and Product Risks

Many times it is very difficult to avoid for the desired functionalities that are operational in nature and inherent from various security risk. Such cases are described as hard to block well-supported denial-of-service attack. Others can be seen in the form of various tradeoffs visible in the project. For example, an organization might permit employees to access information assets using personal laptops or PDAs because the need for such access outweighs its perceived risks. There are numerous security requirements under project management that are identified for secure software system, specifically human resources, communications, risk management, procurement, quality, and integration under the realm of knowledge management. Activities such as architectural risk, threat analysis, and static analysis for source code provide applications for specific development stages.

- There are two essential development tools defined: development controls and change management.
- Software assurance issues that occur during development are dynamic in nature that demands project managers to establish proper linkage between business and technical perspectives.
- It is mandatory for assurance mechanism to build such environment for identification and refinement of threats and responses during development for appropriate mitigation.
- Under the act of project management, software security can be achieved only by integrating software assurance practices into development processes.

12.5 Measuring Software Security

Measuring product performance and development is believed to be a necessary activity for successful software development. Good measurement methods and data allow you to realistically plan your project, track project progress, and status in a timely manner, accurately identify project risks, and improve processes effectively. Software design requirements and source codes are treated as relevant measures, and indicators for structuring software must be analyzed for diagnosis. It may be helpful to reduce implementation errors by identifying problems and their related solutions, including resource cost and cycle times. Unfortunately, useful metrics for software designed to meet security requirements are still in their infancy, and there is no consensus on which measures represent best practices. However, some measures and techniques used in software development can be efficiently extended to meet security requirements. Effective use of the security software development measurement process depends primarily on agreement on desired security features and measurement objectives that can be functional together for product and the development process. These goals are dependent on open system requirements, which mean that security issues must be identified early in the SDLC. To address potential risks, an organization must assess the risk landscape and translate these concerns into specific security requirements, and then design and implement a development process to develop those requirements. [10, 17]

Measurement objectives can be formulated to provide an understanding of the security, health, or safety state of the software. Below are some examples of analytical questions that can lead to measurement goals:

- What vulnerabilities are found in our products?
- Are our current development practices sufficient to prevent the transmission of security vulnerabilities?
- What steps or actions in the process can lead to security threats?
- How many of the defects are related to safety requirements? Do defect classification schemes contain safety categories?
- To what extent do developers stick to security-related processes and practices?
- To what extent are security issues addressed in intermediate business products (e.g. requirements, architectural and design descriptions, test plans)? Are security requirements and their implementation measures defined and planned?
- What are the most vulnerable software components? Have security vulnerabilities been identified and fixed?

12.5.1 Process Measures for Secure Development

A process framework that implements safety measures for the development process should address the following issues:

- Availability of security policies applicable to SDLC
- Policy compliance
- Policy effectiveness and efficiency over time

12.5.2 Product Measures for Secure Development

Depending on the scope of the product, safety issues motivated by the measurement goal can take any of the following forms:

- Security requirements that can be determined in terms of scope and completeness, based on privacy policies, legal consequences, risks identified from threat assessments, and other sources
- Security architecture reflecting specified security requirements
- Safe design criteria where safety requirements can be followed
- A secure coding application where integrity can be evaluated and measured

12.6 Maturity of Practice

The emergence of security as a governance and management problem generally occurs in the departments of the institutes that provide and employ it. Currently, very little attention has been paid to such issues in the early stages of the software and systems development life cycle, but more and more focus is paid to this issue during detailed design, coding, and testing. If we consider security as governance and management issue, a risk management issue, and a project management issue in the early stages of the life cycle, it is likely that more reliable and less vulnerable software will result in a reduction in jet, firefighters, and in the most IT and system operations and maintenance organizations [17]. Maturity of practices includes the proper handling of the following:

- It is essential to offer consistent leadership and management action across the organization.
- Requires privileged consideration and involvement of business experts, human resources, lawyers, audit, risk and financial management, and IT, software, and systems development teams in this respect.
- Provides organizational views on security as an enterprise-level governance and management issue.

12.7 Protecting Information

The primary objective is to integrate security, especially for managers in terms of cost–benefit analysis with respect to information as a key participant among all stakeholders. The organizations' reputations are directly connected with authenticity and violations for disseminated information. Few points are observed as follows:

- Customers expect organizations to carefully protect their privacy and information.
- They are increasingly aware of the risks of identity theft associated with accidental disclosures.

12.7.1 Audit's Role

As part of a major US infrastructure project, the 'Internal Audit Institute (IIA)' hosted six summits in 2000 to better understand its leadership role in managing and maintaining information security. The 'Information Systems Audit and Control Association (ISACA)' and its partner organization, the 'IT Governance Institute (ITGI)', have published a comprehensive guide to information technology and information security management [17]. The reports titled 'Governance of Information Security: Board of Directors and Senior Management Guide [ITGI 2006]' address the following issues:

- Issues regarding information security management
- Issues regarding its importance
- Issues regarding responsibility

The same report also explains how to evaluate the maturity point of an organization in terms of information security management.

12.7.2 Operational Resilience and Convergence

Working with the 'Financial Services Technology Consortium (FSTC)', CERT explores the convergence of security, business continuity, and IT operations management in terms of their critical role in operational risk management. The aim is 'to improve the operational resilience of an organization – the ability to adapt to the changing operational risk environment as needed'. Many organizations describe their efforts to achieve organizational resilience while ensuring business sustainability, risk management, operations and technology, compliance and information security, and monitoring support. This combination acquires products and business lines and includes people, business processes, infrastructure, applications, information, and objects. Success pointer includes the following results:

- Less risk of downtime
- Shorter recovery time when cut
- Improved ability to maintain unlimited trust and concentration of customer expectations
- Improved probability of compliance with regulatory and internal service phase requirements

12.7.3 A Legal View

. The foreword for the roadmap is explained as follows: Multidisciplinary team members are involved in highlighting various concerns related to the industry, government policies, technical aspects, and academicals proficiency in their article. They present a roadmap which is capable to bridge the gap of cyber-security puzzle to update procedures that are directly linked with standard best practices under the regulatory requirements for public and private domain and other law enforcement agencies. Roadmap is nothing but a standard framework capable to strike a repo between highly dependable associations of components, including governance, security operations, implementation, evaluation, and its regulation and control [17]. The following steps are involved for the management:

- To establish structural layouts for policies development, governance, and audits
- To establish repository for digital assets including network, information, and applications
- To build a structure for the safety of digital assets and frame responsibility for ownership values
- To describe requirements for compliance with laws, regulations, guidelines, standards, and agreements in terms of privacy, security, and cyber crime
- To conduct review plan for assessing risk and various security plans, and it must be accredited
- To apply risk management plan and categorize and prioritize digital assets and their respected risk level

12.7.4 A Software Engineering View

New knowledge defines the different aspects of how to relate leadership and management principles for designing and development of secure software. It describes a series of secure software development activities and practices that must be performed during the software development life cycle. [10, 17] Describes the components of an enterprise software security program that addresses the following issues:

- Work environment
- About change management by adding four common mistakes:
  - Relying on testing
  - Control without measuring
  - Learning without evaluating
  - Lack of high-level dedication
- To establish an improvement program
- To establish an indicator plan, together with a three-step implementation in the business:
  - Points and plan
  - Assembly and piloting
  - Publish and develop
- Continuous improvement
- Inclusion of enterprise information architecture with COTS
- To adopt a safe development life cycle

12.8 E-governance Framework in India: e-Kranti: National e-Governance Plan (NeGP) 2.0

In 2006, the 'National Electronic Government Plan (NeGP)' was developed and approved for accomplishment as depicted in Figure 12.6. Before this, a number of efforts were made to implement e-government projects in various departments and institutions of both central

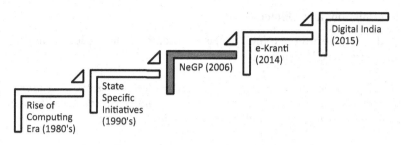

FIGURE 12.6
E-governance Plan in India.

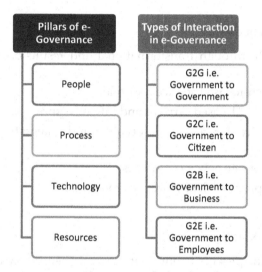

FIGURE 12.7
Pillars and Types of Interactions for E-governance.

and state governments. NeGP aimed to construct a comprehensive structure in India and to give significant momentum to e-government. NeGP has made significant progress in its implementation in the last 8 years. To date, 24 of the 31 MMP projects are available to citizens, businesses, and other stakeholders as depicted in Figure 12.8. 222 of the 252 services provided by these projects are already underway [22].

The NeGP analysis raises a few implementation questions that need immediate attention. From this analysis it is clear that there is an urgent requirement for significant improvements in the existing NeGP structure. It is obvious that shortcomings and threats inherent in nature can unfavorably influence the realization of various MMPs and lead to unsatisfactory results. Opportunities exemplify realizing the complete prospective of e-government in improving the delivery of public services to their citizens and other stakeholders. The NeGP 2.0 concept called 'E-Kranti' was developed in the above context. The structure of e-Kranti is based on the understanding achieved more than the past 08 years with the execution of the NeGP. Nevertheless, it recommends latest and largely amends delivery and service models based on the strengths, weaknesses, capabilities, and threats of the analyzed current NeGP. The important pillars and types of interactions for e-governance are mentioned in Figure 12.7.

12.8.1 Vision, Mission, and Objectives

The main goal of e-government (NeGP 2.0) is to accelerate the implementation of e-government to achieve the NeGP vision:

> *Providing all public facilities from the point of provision of general services to an average person in the region and ensuring the effectiveness, transparency and trustworthiness of these services at reasonable cost. Have the fundamental requirements of the average person met.*

E-Kranti's vision is to '*Transforming e-governance for transforming governance*'.

E-Kranti's mission is to '*Provide citizens with all public services electronically through integrated and interoperable systems in multiple modes, ensuring the efficiency, transparency and reliability of these services at affordable prices*'.

12.8.2 The Objectives of e-Kranti

- Rethinking NeGP through transformational and results-oriented e-government program
- Expand the citizen-focused service portfolio
- To optimize basic ICT-based services and infrastructure
- To provide facility for acute prototyping and integration of e-government applications
- To access and promote new technologies
- To develop and promote flexible application models

12.8.3 Principles of e-Kranti

There are various principles ofe-Kranti that are described below and the details of task mode (MMP) projects under NeGP are depicted in Figure 12.8.

- Transformation, not translation

Changes can take many forms, such as major changes in the update process to a distribution point with new features, predefined service levels, adoption of innovative technologies, self-financing withdrawals. Promoting innovative business models and services for service models is the essential property to ensure financial sustainability.

- Integrated services, not independent services

Most of the e-Government projects, both inside and outside of NeGP, are implemented to provide specific services to citizens, automating the business operations of specific departments only from the perspective of the implementing departments/institutions. In the existing model, in order to obtain special electronic services, a citizen or business is required to afford a supporting documentation, usually accompanied by an application for services. Some of these attachments are provided by organizations outside the department that provides the electronic services. The solution lies in the concept of developing and implementing a comprehensive and integrated set of services. GPR will be required in the process of

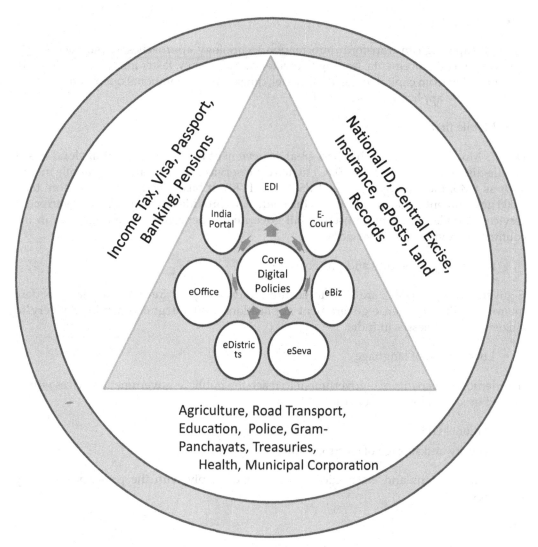

FIGURE 12.8
Details of Task Mode (MMP) Projects Under NeGP.

micro-reform (MPR) to be reorganized as the first step of all new MMPs, and without this project this project would not have been approved.

- Infrastructure on demand

In addition to supply government-to-business (G2B) and government-to-government (G2G) support, DeitY has built essential infrastructure such as government data centers, state-wide inclusive networks, shared facility centers and government access ports to bring government services closer to its citizens. Ongoing initiatives such as fiber network, National Data Center Network (NDC), National Information Infrastructure (NII) and National Knowledge Network (NKN) are also anticipated to an important responsibility in the countries electronic and ICT environment.

- Default cloud

Cloud computing can transform information technology approaches, deployments, and management advancements, leading to greater cost efficiency, faster innovation, adoption, and transition from capital to business model, quicker representational operations, and the ability to scale applications as needed.

- Mobile first

DeitY's Mobile Seva project has had great achievement in building a central cloud-based mobile distribution gateway (MSDG) to deliver e-services over a variety of mobile modes such as SMS, mobile applications, USSD, and IVRS. It has already attracted more than 1,000 government departments across the country to provide a wide range of government services. Mobile Seva will be used by all government departments and agencies in the country to provide mobile services.

- Mandatory principles and protocols

E-government principles are vital to ensure the exchange of information, flawless data interoperability between e-government applications, and integrated service delivery to citizens and businesses in India.

- Localization of language

In order for the benefits of e-government to reach the public, e-government services will be offered in several local languages.

- National GIS
- Security and storage of electronic data

Online applications and electronic services must comply with the prescribed security measures.

Strengths

- There is a general understanding of the importance of e-governance, both within and outside the government.
- There are 24 out of 31 MMPs in live mode and are producing over 11Cr transactions per month.
- Increased number of experts in subsequent areas, including private and government sectors producing a significant figure of the development.
- Development of IT infrastructure to all states is a good sign of electronic development.
- There are various sources of funding, including GOI to states and by states to promote eGov sector.
- Need to provide political support for eGov program.
- Covers the strong legislations on the citizen's right for the delivery of public services in timely manner.
- To expand the portfolio of online services, many eGov projects have been created under NeGP environment.

Weaknesses

- NeGP did not successfully produce the expected impact, especially in the rural areas.
- Considerable timeout.
- Poor highlighting on principles and interoperability.
- Lower extent of process-engineering.
- Lack of criticality on mission approach.
- Adaptation of outdated procedures which are responsible for hampered pace and stifled enthusiasm.
- Lack of dedicated human resources toward e-Gov.
- Inadequate adoption of PPP model.
- Weak monitoring and evaluation process.
- Need to set accountability for timely execution and producing qualitative responses.
- Poor connectivity issues in rural areas.

Opportunities

- Significant advances in the technology environment over the last seven years have facilitated the more efficient, cost-effective, and agile solutions that are being developed today.
- The initiation of the cloud encourages agencies to adopt the concept of shared software, platform, and infrastructure as services.
- Adoption of new business models based on OpEx.
- Dominance in the quality of service is now achievable through a radical restructuring, shifting away from the conservation enhancement mechanism that has been widely practiced to date.
- To recognize the acute requirements of many e-Gov professionals to keep track of ongoing applications.
- It is highly required to establish an international institution for capacity building in the field of electronic governance.

Threats

- Allowing the NeGP to move in the current direction and to move forward at its current pace could lead to group resentment, leading to e-governance losing the need for public sector change.
- Accessible e-Gov projects become obsolete or unproductive without any rejuvenation or involvement of fresh energy.
- Need to bridge the gap of IT connectivity.
- Indian software development professionals are capable to take lead in software development globally by developing such in-house e-Gov project as a benchmark for quality development and deployment of services.
- Indians should take lead for using latest technologies for development purpose because technology rejuvenation is the essential requirement for NeGP. [23]

TABLE 12.2

Details of Services under MMP Projects under NeGP

S. No.	Proposed MMPS	Category	Owner Department	Key Components
1	e-Sansad	Central	Parliament of India, Lok-Sabha Secretariat	Bills, Gazette notifications. Budget, Parliamentary Questions database, Parliamentary proceedings, Publications
2	e-Vidhaan	State	Parliament of India, Lok-Sabha Secretariat	As above for State Legislatures
3	Financial Inclusion	Integrated	Financial Services	Strengthening Banking & Insurance services in the rural areas through strategic use of ICT
4	Roads and Highways Information System (RAHI)	Integrated	M/o Road Transport & Highways	Integrated citizen centric services related to roads and highways
5	Agriculture 2.0	State	D/o Agriculture	Sector specific services for horticulture and fisheries, governance & citizen-centric services for co-operatives and fertilizer testing labs
6	NGIS	Integrated	D/o Science & Technology	Integrated GIS platform
7	Rural Development	State	D/o Rural Development	A portfolio of rural development services including NREGA
8	Social Benefits	Integrated	M/o Social Justice and Empowerment as the leader and other welfare departments as co-owners	Online benefit schemes, Integrated e-services for NGOs
9	Women and Child Development	State	M/o Women and Child Development	Integrated Child Development Scheme, Integration with Health MMP
10	Common IT Roadmap for Para Military Forces	Central	MHA	
11	e-Bhasha Takniki	Integrated	DeitY	Language localization

12.9 Digital India Initiatives

Digital India is a program started by the Indian government to guarantee that the government's services are made available to residents electronically through enhanced online infrastructure and increased internet connectivity or to make the country digitally enabled in technology. Plans are in progress to connect rural communities to high-speed internet networks as part of the effort. It is made up of three main components: the creation of safe and resilient digital infrastructure, the delivery of government services online, and universal digital literacy. Indian Prime Minister Mr. Narendra Modi established it on July 1, 2015. It acts as both a facilitator and a beneficiary of other key Government of India programs such as BharatNet, Make in India, Startup India, Standup India, industrial corridors, Bharatmala, and Sagarmala. Experts address nine key pillars to take digital India initiatives to a new high as depicted in Figure 12.9. [24]

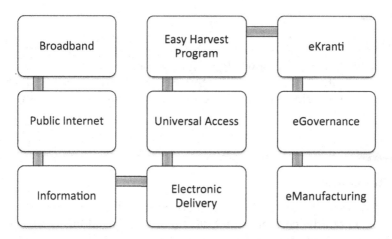

FIGURE 12.9
Pillars of Digital India Initiatives.

12.10 Conclusion

Regardless of the scope of security applications included in the SDLC, software security and system security cannot be achieved without knowledgeable, knowledgeable, dedicated leaders – business leaders, project managers, and technical leaders. This section provides guidelines and best practices to help software project managers meet the management challenges of more secure software development, and steps they can take to bring business leaders and top management to management level. The main recommendations and practices are as follows:

- Recognize that security awareness and understanding of the importance of solving security problems during software development should be a cultural norm.
- Include managers in a better understanding of security issues such as leadership and management issues, and the features and actions required to address the consequences of non-compliance.
- Develop a framework and roadmap to address software security issues in the enterprise and remove some traps and barriers immediately.
- Determine how to determine what constitutes an adequate security practice based on risk management, established risk resilience levels, and risk assessment.
- Implement a continuous business-oriented risk management framework and assess acceptable and unacceptable risk levels within the SDLC.
- Follow guidelines for incorporating security into the SDLC as part of traditional project management activities, including the use of specific security touch-points at each stage of the life cycle.
- Include security as part of the software development measurement process, including the implementation of the proposed process and product measures.

Key Terms

Knowledge and Security, Knowledge Management System, Secure Knowledge Management, Security Governance, Effective Security Governance and Management, Enterprise Software Security Framework, Secure Project Management, Maturity of Practice

Points to Remember

- •. Identifying security risks and interdependencies between business functions and processes within the enterprise and developing managed business process solutions to address these risks and interdependencies.
- •. The described five imperatives convergence demonstrates the value of addressing security issues as part of a broader convergence effort and supporting organizational readiness.

Objective-Type Questions

1. _____ is about the efficient handling of various information and resources used in commercial or non-commercial organization.
   a) Secure System
   b) Knowledge Management
   c) Security Framework
   d) Security Management

2. Knowledge management is a systematic process for enhancing productivity of information for quicker availability and improved _____ for the achievement of objectives.
   a) Security Requirement Specification
   b) Security Requirement Analysis
   c) Secure System
   d) Decision Making

3. _____ is always one of the major concerns with respect to KMS.
   a) Knowledge
   b) Security
   c) Decision Making
   d) Risk

4. The knowledge which is transferable through cross-organizational platforms becomes more significant for management of _____.
   a) Intellectual rights
   b) Security best practices
   c) Digital rights
   d) Risk preventive guidelines

5. The two more factors responsible for security knowledge-management system are_____ and _____.
   a) Access control & Identity Management
   b) Authorization & Authentication
   c) Security & Privacy
   d) Integrity & Availability

6. Which security issues are not highlighted with respect to the steps involved for knowledge management?
   a) Confidentiality issues
   b) Reliability issues
   c) Access control issues
   d) Project management issues

7. Which one is not the type of interaction in e-Governance?
   a) G2G i.e. Government to Government
   b) G2B i.e. Government to Business
   c) B2C i.e. Business to customer
   d) G2E i.e. Government to Employees

8. To date, what are the total number of Task Mode (MMP) projects under NeGP serve citizens, businesses, and other stakeholders out of 31 MMPs?
   a) 24
   b) 22
   c) 21
   d) 26

9. Which one of them is not the working MMP project under integrated category?
   a) e-Bhasha Takniki
   b) NGIS
   c) Roads and Highways Information System (RAHI)
   d) e-Vidhaan

10. Which one is the ineffective practice for security governance?
    a) Regular review
    b) Address on ad-hoc basis
    c) Continuous improvement
    d) Zero tolerance

Short-Answer Type Questions

1. What do you understand by secure knowledge management?
2. Discuss the various important aspects of secure knowledge management?
3. What are the security issues highlighted with respect to knowledge management?
4. Describe the importance of security knowledge and expertise.
5. What do you mean by security governance?
6. Define secure project management and its components.
7. Define the vision and objectives of e-kranti?

8. What are the strengths and weaknesses for e-kranti?

9. What are the opportunities and threats for e-kranti?

10. What are the pillars of e-governance?

Descriptive Questions

1. Explain the security concerns for secure knowledge management system and discuss the framework based on cloud knowledge management system.

2. Define the architecture of secure knowledge management system.

3. Explain the established relation between software security knowledge components and SDLC artifacts.

4. Explain effective security governance and management in brief.

5. Provide a comparative study based on effective and ineffective practices for security governance.

6. Explain enterprise software security framework in detail.

7. Discuss e-governance framework and concept of e-kranti for India in detail.

8. What are the principles of e-kranti? Discuss.

9. Define the software engineering views with respect to enterprise software security in detail.

10. Discuss national e-governance plan with all related components and their brief description.

References

1. Yogesh Kumar Mittal, Santanu Roy and Manu Saxena, "Role of Knowledge Management in Enhancing Information Security", *IJCSI International Journal of Computer Science Issues*, 7(6), pp: 320–324, November 2010.

2. Eliot Rich, Finn Olav Sveen and Matthew Jager, "Overcoming Organizational Challenges to Secure Knowledge Management", *Proceedings of the Second Secure Knowledge Management Workshop, 2006*, Brooklyn, NY 2006.

3. Thanyatida Gunadham and Pramote Kuacharoen, "Security Concerns in Cloud Computing for Knowledge Management Systems", *International Conference on Information Technology and Statistics*, 2016.

4. B. K. Samanthula, Y. Elmehdwi, G. Howser and S. Madria, "A Secure Data Sharing and Query Processing Framework via Federation of Cloud Computing", *IS*, 48, 2015, pp. 196–212.

5. I.M. Khalil, A. Khreishah and M. Azeem, "Cloud Computing Security: A Survey", *Computers*, 3, 2014, pp. 1–35.

6. International Federation of Accountants. "Enterprise Governance: Getting the Balance Right," *International Federation of Accountants, Professional Accountants in Business Committee*", 2004. http://www.ifac.org/Members/DownLoads/EnterpriseGovernance.pdf (pdf). Last Access: 30/09/2020.

7. T. Rajpathak and A. Narsingpurkar, Knowledge from big data analytics in product development. TCS white paper, 2013.

8. B. Thuraisingham and P. Parikh, "Trustworthy Semantic Web Technologies for Secure Knowledge Management. In *2008 IEEE/IFIP International Conference on Embedded and Ubiquitous Computing*, IEEE, 2008, pp. 186–193.

9. S. Upadhyaya, H.R. Rao and G. Padmanabhan, Secure Knowledge Management. Idea Group Inc, 2006.

10. J. Viega and G. McGraw, *Building Secure Software*, Addition Wesley, 2005.

11. R. Khan Latifur and Ravi Sandhu, "Secure Knowledge Management: Confidentiality, Trust, and Privacy", *IEEE Transactions on Systems, Man, and Cybernetics—Part A: Systems and Humans*, 36(3), May 2006.

12. Shambhu J. Upadhyaya et al. "Secure Knowledge Management." *Encyclopedia of Knowledge Management*, pp: 795–801, IGI Global, 2011, DOI: 10.4018/978-1-59140-573-3.ch104, 2011.

13. T. Rajpathak and A. Narsingpurkar, Managing Knowledge from Big Data Analytics in Product Development. TCS white paper, 2013.

14. B. Thuraisingham and P. Parikh, "Trustworthy Semantic Web Technologies for Secure Knowledge Management", In *2008 IEEE/IFIP International Conference on Embedded and Ubiquitous Computing*, IEEE, 2008, pp 186–193.

15. Petros Belsis and Spyros Kokolakis, "Information Systems Security from a Knowledge Management Perspective", *Information Management & Computer Security*, 13(3), 2005, pp. 189-202.

16. https://www.kannan-subbiah.com/2012/12/effective-vs-ineffective-security.html#. Y0wWVHZBxPY. Last Access: 10 July 2022.

17. Julia H. Allen, Sean Barnum, Robert J. Ellison, Gary McGraw and Nancy R. Mead, *Software Security Engineering: A Guide for Project Managers*, Addison Wesley Professional, 2008.

18. http://csrc.nist.gov/publications/history/dod85.pdf. Last Access: 17 February 2010. http://www.ssi.gouv.fr/site_documents/ITSEC/ITSEC-uk.pdf. Last Access: 17 February 2010.

19. The Common Criteria for Information Security Technology, http://www.commoncriteriaportal.org/files/ccfiles/CCPART1V3.1R3.pdf. Last Access: 15 December 2009.

20. The Common Criteria, http://www.commoncriteriaportal.org/files/ccfiles/CCPART3V3.1R3.pdf. Last Access: 17 March 2010.

21. http://www.pcisecuritystandards.org/security_standards/pci_dss.shtml. Last Access: 17 February 2010.

22. https://www.meity.gov.in/divisions/national-e-governance-plan. Last Access: 30 August 2022.

23. https://negd.gov.in/mission-mode-projects. Last Access: 10 July 2021.

24. https://www.digitalindia.gov.in/. Last Access: 25 June 2021.

Useful Links

http://blog.trendmicro.com/vmware-bug-provides-escape-hatch/[accessed February 17, 2010].

http://www.wired.com/threatlevel/2008/04/nsa-releases-se/[accessed February 17, 2010].

http://www.informationweek.com/news/security/cybercrime/showArticle.jhtml? articleID¼188702216 [accessed February 17, 2010].

http://www.wired.com/dangerroom/2008/11/army-bans-usb-d/[accessed February 17, 2010].

http://www.army.mil/-news/2007/04/19/2758-army-releases-new-opsec-regulation/[accessed February 17, 2010].

NIST Assessment of Access Control Systems. NIST IR 7316,Applying the Take-Grant Protection Model,http://csrc.nist.gov/publications/nistir/7316/NISTIR-7316.pdf[accessed March 27, 2010].

http://ntrs.nasa.gov/archive/nasa/casi.ntrs.nasa.gov/19920018318_1992018318.pdf[accessed March 27, 2010].

www.cs.nmt.edu/_doshin/t/s06/cs589/pub/2.GD-Protection-PP.pdf[accessed February 17, 2010].

http://www.cs.unibo.it/babaoglu/courses/security/resources/documents/harrison-ruzzoullman.pdf [accessed February 17, 2010].

https://www.nic.in/servicecontents/remote-sensing-gis/ [Last Accessed: 10 August 2022].

13

Research Trends in Software Security Estimation

As a rule, software systems do not work well until they have been used, and have failed repeatedly, in real applications.

Dave Parnas

Software and web applications are presently assuming a significant function in each part of human lives, including exchanges, data stockpiling, and its recovery. Software security estimations are used in every sector including government, military, aerospace, banking, defense, agriculture, communication, etc. In such a situation, it is attractive to keep all delicate information, data, and exchange safe from security penetrates. In this chapter, we will review the goals of software security estimation, and we will be introduced to the software security estimation, which will be the foundation for learning the concepts of research trends in software security estimation. By the end of this chapter, readers will be able to:

- Identify the research trends in software security estimation.
- Describe the different software security issues.
- Explain the different software security strategies – with the help of security attributes, model, and metrics.

13.1 Objectives

Software security estimation has a great demand of having such a system in order to perform task accurately and timely [1–5]. The secure system prevents any type of data loss, misuse, and theft. The main objectives of the software system are:

- To make the software and web application defect-free software, higher-quality, continue perform task correctly under attack and robust.
- To make software remains dependable despite intentional efforts to compromise that dependability.
- To make software and web applications as vulnerability and defect-free as possible.
- To ensure that the effects of any attack are not propagated and limit the damage resulting from any failures caused by attack-triggered faults, and it recovers from those failures as quickly as possible.

DOI: 10.1201/9781003330516-13

13.2 A Multidimensional Approach

In a software development life cycle, software security is considered to be the primary asset of an organization. It is also at constant risk, at more risk than ever before. Software and web applications are the backbone of any organization. Software enhances the business operation, facilitate management decision making, and deploy business strategies [6–9]. The security of software becomes very important; this leads to a corresponding increase in the demand of software security estimation. The different security estimation approaches are as follows:

- *Use Case Point* gives an assessment technique dependent on use case charts to measure the cost, size and exertion of article arranged programming to be finished [1]. Use case point assessment approach depends on the product measuring. The pre-owned case point approach is a very much characterized methodology to change over the utilization case chart components into a bunch of measurements that mirrors the work exertion expected to achieve a safe programming venture.

- *Non-Algorithmic Estimation* is the comparison method of previous develop project. It can be classified, expert judgment, analogy technique, price to win, bottom up and bottom down, and wideband Delphi [2].

- *Algorithmic estimation* is the mathematical calculation of the equations. These include source line of code, objects point, function point, constructive cost model-I (COCOMO-I), and COCOMO-II [2].

- *Bayesian Belief Network* is including an organization of probabilities that catches the probabilistic connection between factors in authentic information. The benefit of this strategy is not being subject to knowing precise recorded information. Then again, it requires information on related boundaries of past task to be utilized in assessment [3].

- *Neural network method* is the more appropriate quantitative approach of security estimation. The neural organization strategy is prepared with a progression of contributions from past tasks to foresee the exertion of the current undertaking. Neural organization gave a more precise gauge contrasted with different strategies, yet it relies upon information from past ventures [4].

- *Agile security estimation method* has presented many challenges and opportunities. The primary challenge of estimation is the effort of development of software. Deft improvement approach is a famous advancement technique as it underlines on joint effort with client, correspondence among engineers, fast conveyance of programming, and change of prerequisites on request. Agile techniques are extreme programming, scrum, precious stone, feature-driven turn of events, and learn improvement [5]. The difficulties of assessing agile approaches are work assigned to a group rather than an individual, the emphasis is on aggregate exertion, and work is measured regarding exertion instead of time and changing prerequisites on request.

- *Planning Poker* is an assessment strategy that depends on cooperation and agreement among colleagues. It was proposed by Greening and Cohn for dexterous programming improvement, for example, scrum [2]. Toward the start of the Planning poker meeting, it is done at first of an emphasis of light-footed advancement, including a group of engineers from various controls. Every group member is given a deck of arranged poker cards with values, ideally a Fibonacci arrangement, which speaks to various security credits. It contains direct and non-straight successions. The nonlinear arrangements reflect less vulnerability with more modest units and more prominent vulnerability when managing more noteworthy units. A lithe improvement is a concise depiction of usefulness as seen by the client or item proprietor.

13.3 Research Trends in Security Estimation

In this part of the chapter, we have discussed here information security estimation by different methods/approach.

- *Analytic Hierarchy Process and Fuzzy Comprehensive Method*: It is the multi-criteria decision-making approach; this approach gives weight of the estimation factor of software. Further, after getting the weight of factor, we estimate the security of software [6]. It contains the following steps as shown in Figure 13.1.
- *Bayesian prioritization procedure*: It permits treatment of missing information or fragmented data utilizing information increase methods. The incorporation of multi-dimensional capacities has been the significant restriction toward the wide utilization of Bayesian investigation [7]. To figure the back appropriations of decisions and assess the vector of needs. This methodology depends on the earlier presumption of the presence of agreement among the chiefs. This methodology gives the connection between chiefs which are conversely relative to the leaders'. The irregularity is more proficient when contrasted with them. This technique additionally can be reached out to the instance of deficient pairwise examination networks, which is a typical issue in complex dynamic issues.
- *Fuzzy ANP-TOPSIS* – Fuzzy Analytic Network Process (F.ANP) used for prioritizes the weights and fuzzy-symmetrical technique for Order of Preference by Similarity to Ideal Solution (TOPSIS) is used for the ranking of the factors [8].

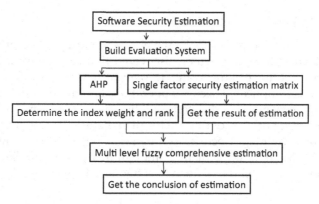

FIGURE 13.1
Software Security Estimation Model.

- *Fuzzy AHP-TOPSIS* – Fuzzy Analytic Hierarchy Process (F.AHP) and fuzzy technique for Order of Preference by Similarity to Ideal Solution (TOPSIS) integrated approach used to determine the effect of security criteria's. Fuzzy-AHP applied to evaluate the weights of the criteria and their interdependence on each other in the AHP network [9]. TOPSIS techniques are being applied to evaluate the ranking of given criteria.

13.4 List of Security Research Problem

13.4.1 Trend No. 1: Cyber-Security Mesh

A contemporary conceptual framework for security architecture called the cyber-security mesh enables scattered enterprises to extend and deliver security where it is most needed. With the acceleration of digital business brought about by COVID-19, many digital assets—and people—are now more frequently found outside of the conventional company infrastructure. Additionally, cyber-security professionals are expected to secure a vast array of new technologies and digital transformations. The organization must be able to move into the future while maintaining security. This calls for security alternatives that are adaptable, agile, scalable, and composable.

13.4.2 Trend No. 2: Cyber-Savvy Boards

Boards are paying more attention to cyber-security as a result of an increase in extremely public security breaches and an increase in the frequency of business disruptions caused by ransomware. They see it as a significant risk to businesses and are creating special committees to address cyber-security issues. These committees are frequently run by board members with security expertise (such as a former chief information security officer [CISO]) or outside consultants. This implies that CISOs can anticipate greater scrutiny, higher standards, and more resources. Be ready for your board to pose more challenging questions as a result of your need to enhance how you communicate with one another.

13.4.3 Trend No. 3: Vendor Consolidation

Security executives have too many tools, which is the current state of security. In their 2020 CISO Effectiveness Survey, Gartner discovered that 78 percent of CISOs had 16 or more cyber-security vendor products, and 12 percent have 46 or more. Too many security providers lead to complicated security operations and more staff needed for security. Most organizations recognize vendor consolidation as a way to improve security, with 80% either implementing or considering such a plan. Better-integrated products are being produced in response by major security companies. Consolidation, however, is difficult and frequently takes years to implement. Although many people believe that decreased costs are the driving force behind this trend, it is frequently simpler to attain more risk-free operations.

13.4.4 Trend No. 4: Identity-First Security

The transition to cloud apps and hybrid work has consolidated the identity as the perimeter trend. Even though identity-first security is nothing new, it has recently become more crucial as attackers start to focus on identity and access management systems in an effort to obtain silent persistence. The most common method used in breaches today is the misuse of credentials. Active Directory and the identity infrastructure are being successfully attacked by nation-state-level adversaries. Identity is a crucial air-gapped network lateral movement strategy. Although more people are using multifactor authentication, it is not a cure-all. Identity infrastructure needs to be properly set up, kept up, and closely supervised.

13.4.5 Trend No. 5: Managing Machine Identities Becoming a Critical Security Capability

The number of nonhuman entities that make up modern apps has grown dramatically as the digital transformation process moves forward. Consequently, managing machine IDs has emerged as a crucial component of security operations. All contemporary applications are built from services connected by APIs. Since your suppliers' API access to vital data can be exploited by attackers, each of these services needs to be verified and closely watched. Tools and methods for enterprise-wide machine identity management are still being developed. But your company's digital transformation will be safer if it comes up with an enterprise-wide plan for managing machine identities, certificates, and secrets.

13.4.6 Trend No. 6: 'Remote Work' Is Now Just 'Work'

Sixty-four percent of employees can now work from home, and two-fifths do so in reality, according to the 2021 Gartner CIO Survey. What was formerly only accessible to top workers, executives, and sales is now widely used. Over 75% of knowledge workers anticipate future hybrid work conditions, making the shift to hybrid (or remote) work) a long-lasting trend. This calls for a full rethinking of policies and tools from a security perspective in order to better manage risks.

13.4.7 Trend No. 7: Breach and Attack Simulation

To assist organizations in assessing their security posture, a new market is starting to emerge. Breach and attack simulation (BAS), which evaluates the organization's defenses against external threats, allows ongoing testing and validation of security procedures. Additionally, it provides specialized evaluations and emphasizes the hazards to valuable assets like sensitive data. To help security organizations develop, BAS offers training.

13.4.8 Trend No. 8: Privacy-Enhancing Computation Techniques

Secure data processing, sharing, cross-border transfers, and analytics are made possible even in un-trusted situations by privacy-enhancing compute approaches that protect data while it is being used, as opposed to when it is at rest or in motion. This technology is quickly moving from academic research to real-world applications that create real value. This is because it makes it possible for new kinds of computing and sharing with less risk of data breaches.

13.5 Future Prospects in Security Estimation

Based on the existing study in the above section, further research may be covering the following areas:

- Future prospects of software security estimation may include designing procedure of software development, which covers security incidents, regulatory issues, customer's & investor's concerns with definition of training, target audience identification, delivery frequency & support from management.

- Future exploration may incorporate building up a security mindfulness crusade which tends to issues like absence of public data on assaults, trouble in clarifying wanted representative conduct, and forestalling over immersion/cover of data security messages, enormous, generally conveyed worker base, and decentralized appropriation of messages.

- The future exploration might be done on planning a viable preparing program for senior leaders with center around calculated level, designing administration with center around programming security rehearses and programming engineer with center around specialized side.

- The future work may incorporate coordination of test outcomes acquired with other framework produced information with its expansion to different grounds or associations for similar examination purposes.

- Few future suggestions may remember the work for mindfulness where the understudies can spread security mindfulness by methods of occasions, ventures, screensavers, banners, test, informal communication, and so forth.

- In the future may be done the research on identifying core area of effective cybercrime remedies like periodic penetration testing of the systems, designing and implementing periodic security education and awareness program for the employees, and receiving and delivering of regular communication from the senior management.

- The work to address security issues related to an insider with respect to Software Development Life Cycle like to periodic security awareness training, timely enterprise-wise security estimation, and secure system administration may be taken as future work.

- Designing awareness, training and declaration programs like Certified Secure Software Lifecycle Professional accreditation program with center around building security in SDLC might be a portion of the novel work in the concerned territory.

- Future work may incorporate planning programming security mindfulness preparing remembering inclusion of staff and occupation functions over the improvement association like chief level, the board level, and advancement and security level, thought of starting, middle and progressed classes for various necessities.

- Further study might be directed to explore the part of mindfulness in advancing self-coordination. In addition, text based errand rather than code based assignment ought to be contemplated to defeat the issue of changes in specialized fitness.

- Validating the pattern toward selection of more 'proactive' the board techniques at higher development levels prompting the foundation of prerequisites instability the executive structure on the measurements 'nature of the board approach' and 'venture qualities' might be a portion of the serious regions for research.

- Future research objectives might be to discover a component to channel warning messages with the end goal that they arrive at just beneficiaries that should know about the notice, in this manner decreasing message volume and forestalling mindfulness over-burden.

- Future examination might be embraced to consider the different states by which the mindfulness can be made among the various partners in the SDLC. A positioning of these approaches to spread mindfulness might be done to improve the nature of the equivalent.

Some recognized fields are discussed by the above research directions which are as following:

- *To get awareness from Questionnaire and Interview*
- *To get awareness from Survey*
- *To get awareness from Education & Training*
- *To get awareness from Campaign*
- *To get awareness from Academia & Industry tools*
- *To get awareness from Experiments& Test*
- *To get awareness from Simulation& Games*
- *To get awareness from Online Community*
- *To get awareness from Academia & Industry interaction*

13.6 Conclusion

In the era of Information Technology (IT), the software and web based application are in always on the fear and attack by the attackers. The exploration discoveries have referenced that the security assessment draws near. The hugeness of security concerns increments when a SDLC have a few escape clauses that can jeopardize the whole system. Subsequently, some model structure is developed and implemented that could create a sense of understanding among the members (insiders) of an organization with regard to the security of the model and its implementation. This chapter begins with an introductory survey and then examines various strategies for actualizing awareness as the evaluation approaches. At the same time, assorted critical examination zones are also distinguished for extra evaluations in the uptight territory. This book chapter would be helpful for the students and researchers who want their examination in security concern by providing a concise however entire audit on the current writing alongside the momentum research points. This chapter can be used as a base paper for security estimation analysts who take the exploration themes through our chapter. The advancement of a solid framework for making and advancing consciousness can be incorporated into future work with valid preparation of inward and outward parts with SDLC stages and different open awareness techniques. Measurements may also be made at that stage and added to the schedule for the assessment of the characteristics. This would thus lead to building up the accuracy level precision of the devising. This work would certainly assist the organization from the earliest starting point in the SDLC in carrying out awareness among the representative right.

Key Terms

Software security estimation, fuzzy AHP, fuzzy ANP, fuzzy TOPSIS, SDLC.

Point to Remember

- Software security estimation has a great demand of having such a system in order to perform task accurately and timely.
- Software security is considered to be the primary asset of an organization.
- Use Case Point offers an estimation approach based on use case diagrams to estimate the size, cost and effort to be accomplished by object-oriented software.
- Analytic Hierarchy Process and Fuzzy Comprehensive Method it is the multi-criteria decision-making approach; this approach gives weight of the estimation factor of software.
- Bayesian prioritization procedure enables the treatment missing data or incomplete information by using data enlargement dc techniques.
- F–ANP is used for evaluate the weights of criteria and fuzzy-Symmetrical TOPSIS is used to determine impact of security factors.
- F–AHP is used for evaluate the weights of criteria and fuzzy-Symmetrical TOPSIS is used to determine impact of security factors.

Objective-Type Questions

1. COCOMO II is an example of a suite of modern empirical estimation model that requires sizing information expressed as:
   a. Function points
   b. Lines of code
   c. Object points
   d. Any of the above
2. In the agile software development estimation techniques focus on the time required to complete each
   a. Increment
   b. Scenario
   c. Task
   d. Use-case

3. Which of following is not one of the elements of a security model?
   a.　Criminal background
   b.　External interface requirements
   c.　Rules of operation
   d.　Security policy objectives

4. Security correctness checks should be included which of the following activities?
   a.　Audits
   b.　Deployments
   c.　Inspections
   d.　Testing

5. Which is not one of the elements of a security case?
   a.　Arguments
   b.　Bug reports
   c.　Claims
   d.　Evidence

6. Research trends in security estimation techniques are
   a.　AHP
   b.　Fuzzy-AHP-TOPSIS
   c.　Fuzzy-ANP-TOPSIS
   d.　All of these

7. What is meant by the term cybercrime?
   a.　Any crime that uses computers to jeopardize or attempt to jeopardize national security
   b.　The use of computer networks to commit financial or identity fraud
   c.　The theft of digital information
   d.　Any crime that involves computers and networks

8. Which security estimation technique is the best?
   a.　Bayesian prioritization
   b.　Neural network
   c.　Fuzzy ANP-TOPSIS
   d.　Fuzzy AHP-TOPSIS

9. Security estimation techniques are effective in security assessment
   a.　Yes
   b.　No

10. Which types of awareness building the software secure during the SDLC phase
   a.　Designing awareness
   b.　Training
   c.　declaration program
   d.　All of these

Short-Answer Type Questions

1. What is security estimation? Explain with example.
2. What is software security? How to secure the software explain?

3. Write the steps which are used in secure software development.

4. Discussed the Analytic Hierarchy process (AHP) technique.

5. Discussed the software security estimation model with diagram.

Descriptive Questions

1. Discussed the COCOMO-I and COCOMO-II estimation model with diagram.

2. What is software estimation technique? Explain any one technique in details.

3. Discussed the Neural network (NN) estimation approach and explain how to estimate security with the help of NN.

References

1 S. Bagheri and A. Shameli-Sendi, "Software Project Estimation Using Improved Use Case Point,"*2018 IEEE 16th International Conference on Software Engineering Research, Management and Applications (SERA)*, Kunming, 2018, pp. 143–150, doi: 10.1109/SERA.2018.8477225.

2 M. Cohn, *Agile Estimating and Planning*, Pearson Education, 2006

3 M. Mehrtash, M. Raoofat, M. Mohammadi, and H. Zareipour, "Fast Stochastic Security-Constrained Unit Commitment Using Point Estimation Method," *International Transactions on Electrical Energy Systems*, 26(3), 2016, 671–688.

4 T. L. Saaty, *Multicriteria Decision Making: The Analytic Hierarchy Process*, 2nd Edition, RSW Pub., Pittsburgh, 1990.

5 H. J. Hwang and H. S. Hwang, "Computer-aided Fuzzy-AHP Decision Model and Its Application to School Food Service Problem," *International Journal of Innovative Computing, Information and Control*, 2(1), 2006, 125–137.

6 I. Nakaoka, M. Matsumura, J. I. Kushida and K. Kamei, "A Proposal of Group Decision Support System for Kansei Commodity Purchase Using SOM and its Applications," *International Journal of Innovative Computing, Information and Control*, 5, 12(B), 2009, 4915–4926.

7 I. Syamsuddin and J. Hwang, The use of AHP in Security Policy Decision Making: An Open Office Calc Application, *Journal of Software*, 5(10), 2010, 1162–1169.

8 M. Y. Huang, "Research on Information Security Evaluation of Internet of Things Electronic Commerce Based on AHP," *Advanced Materials Research*, 217–218, 2011, 1355–1360.

9 X. Zhang, Z. Huang, G. Wei, and X. Zhang, Information Security Risk Assessment Methodology Research: Group Decision Making and Analytic Hierarchy Process," *Proc. of IEEE the 2nd World Congress on Software Engineering*, 2, 2010, 157–160.

Useful Links

https://www.informit.com/articles/article.aspx

Index

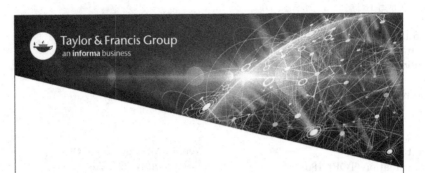

Printed in the United States
by Baker & Taylor Publisher Services